The Little Library Cookbook

Kate Young is a London-based food writer and cook. After a sunny Australian childhood (spent indoors, reading books), she moved to London in 2009. Through her time working as a teacher, and then as a young people's theatre producer, she found comfort, inspiration and distraction in food – a passion that has gradually taken over her life. She now works as a private cook, hosts regular supper clubs, caters weddings, and writes about food and books for various publications, including a regular column in the *Guardian*. *The Little Library Cookbook* is her first book.

Lean Timms is a freelance travel, food and lifestyle photographer. Although born in Australia, Lean has been lucky enough to photograph for editorials and publications throughout the world. She is based in Canberra, Australia.

My Life in France — JULIA CHILD

STELLA GIBBONS — Cold Comfort Farm

DONNA TARTT

DODIE SMITH   I CAPTURE THE CASTLE   VINTAGE

THE BOOK THIEF   Markus Zusak

A Little Princess   FRANCES HODGSON BURNETT

Northern Lights   Philip Pullman

THE GREAT GATSBY

A Christmas Carol and Other Christmas Writings   Charles Dickens

Emma   Jane Austen

Alice's Adventures in Wonderland and Through the Looking-Glass   Lewis Carroll

THE ADVENTURE OF THE CHRISTMAS PUDDING

A. A. MILNE   WINNIE-THE-POOH

EXCELLENT WOMEN   BARBARA PYM

The Secret Garden   FRANCES HODGSON BURNETT   lauren child

BEATRIX POTTER   THE COMPLETE TALES

Goblet of Fire   J.K. ROWLING   BLOOMSBURY

Philosopher's Stone   J.K. ROWLING   BLOOMSBURY

Green Eggs and Ham

Roald Dahl   Quentin Blake

DANNY   The Champion of the World

NANCY MITFORD · The Complete Novels

A Thousand Splendid Suns   KHALED HOSSEINI

ELENA FERRANTE · My Brilliant Friend

WHITE TEETH   ZADIE SMITH

KATE ATKINSON   BEHIND THE SCENES AT THE MUSEUM

Virginia Woolf · A Room of One's Own

Tove Jansson   Comet in Moominland

The Little Library Cookbook

100 recipes from your favourite stories

KATE YOUNG

Photographs by Lean Timms

an imprint of Head of Zeus

First published in 2017 by Head of Zeus Ltd

1 3 5 7 9 10 8 6 4 2

A catalogue record for this book is available from the
British Library.

ISBN
9781784977672 { HB }
9781784977665 { E }

Design by Jessie Price
Photography by Lean Timms

Printed in China by 1010 Printing International Ltd

Head of Zeus Ltd
5–8 Hardwick Street
London EC1R 4RG

For all writers who send their stories out into the world

One cannot think well, love well, sleep well,
if one has not dined well.
Virginia Woolf

Eating and reading are two pleasures
that combine admirably.
C. S. Lewis

contents

before noon

around noon

after noon (tea)

the dinner table

midnight feasts

Introduction

I have always been a highly suggestible, hungry reader. When discovering a new book, or revisiting an old favourite, my mind wanders, imagining what the food the characters are enjoying would taste like. A passing mention of a ripe summer strawberry, a fragrant roast chicken, or a warming mug of hot chocolate sends me straight to the kitchen, book still in hand.

I can't remember not being able to cook; I have been doing so since I was old enough to reach the kitchen bench. I grew up in a home where food was much more than sustenance; it was intrinsic to our social lives, what we played and experimented with, and an enduring passion for all of us. From an early age, I read cookbooks for their stories and for their recipes, marking up things I wanted to try, and committing beloved phrases to memory.

The food I cook now is inspired by many things: the English seasons, my childhood in Australia, meals I have eaten with family, trips I have taken, techniques I've learnt from friends. As I left home, and began to cook for myself, I also drew inspiration from my favourite books, which hold in their pages some of the most tangible food memories I possess.

When I wasn't in the kitchen, my childhood was spent in books. I'd read anything I could get my hands on: instruction manuals, road directories, the backs of cereal boxes. I was hungry for words and for stories in whatever form I could get them. On weekends, my dad would push me out of our front door towards the park, encouraging me to run around in the fresh air until dusk. Little did he know that I always had a book tucked into my bike shorts, and would instead hide under a tree somewhere, losing myself in Jane Austen's Regency England, Enid Blyton's seaside Devon or Harper Lee's Depression-era Alabama. My childhood was idyllic: sunny, surrounded by green space, and with a brilliant little sister by my side, but I spent much of it in parallel fictional worlds.

As I grew up and then moved away from Australia, my love for reading didn't dim. Instead, the books I had read as a child became imbued with a strong sense of nostalgia and found places on my shelves alongside new favourites. I found that I could often remember exactly where I was when I had read each book for the first time. Far away from home, these memories provided real comfort. I re-read books when I was missing my folks, or my friends, or the beach. Doing this, I discovered that the passages utmost in my memory were often food-related. And so, as well as reading them, I started cooking from them too.

The food I created was like a portal to my past. One bite of a treacle tart took me straight back to my bottom bunk at my dad's, where I first read *Harry Potter and the Philosopher's Stone*. I toasted a batch of muffins, slathered them in butter, and could picture my mum reading *A Little Princess* to my sister and me from the floor of our bedroom. The scent of a honey cake transported me to the back seat of our old car, listening to Alan Bennett read *Winnie-the-Pooh* on audiotape as we drove to Canberra.

As I started writing about these literary/culinary links, friends and family (and, later, strangers) began to get in touch, telling me of their favourite fictional food memories. So many of us seemed to have a shared childhood: time spent dreaming of eating sardines and drinking ginger beer on Kirrin Island with the Famous Five; feeling jealous of Bruce and his infamous chocolate cake; and wondering what on earth Green Eggs and Ham might taste like. It is not something we grow out of either. We imagine the dripping crumpets at Manderley in *Rebecca*, and find our mouths watering at the thought of the perfect steak in *The End of the Affair*.

I wanted to write this book to share some of my favourite representations of food in fiction. I sincerely hope that these pages will take you back to places you discovered as a child, reveal new books you're yet to discover, send you to parts of the world you have wanted to visit, and seat you at the kitchen table with characters you would like to spend time with. Happy reading, and happy eating.

On the recipes

This book is a bringing together of recipes that made my mouth water when I first read of them. I love to spend a Saturday in the kitchen, so there are extravagant baking projects to be found that will take a good few hours to finish. I am also, most often, impatient to sit down to a plate of something delicious, so there are also simple suppers and quick breakfasts (many appropriate to eat at any time of day), which can be on the table in less than 30 minutes.

While I have experimented with Georgian, Regency and Victorian recipes, especially when cooking from books like *Anna Karenina* or *A Christmas Carol*, I want the recipes to work well for your oven, using ingredients available from your local supermarket. So, for the most part, I have updated the recipes rather than adhering religiously to the original techniques.

Where appropriate, I have spoken with friends, acquaintances and sometimes strangers about the dishes that were initially less familiar to me. What has become abundantly clear is that there is no 'right way' of making anything – much like my mum and her curried sausages, families and individuals will have their own variations. What I have included here are the versions I find most delicious.

On ingredients and equipment

The cookbooks I love most are the ones that feel like a helpful grandmother standing with you at the stove, offering advice, helpful hints and suggestions. I want this book to fill that place in your kitchen.

There are very few recipes in this book that you will need to buy equipment for. I am really keen that these recipes are accessible and achievable in any kitchen and so, where possible, I have included alternatives to mixers, ice-cream machines and any equipment that serves only one use. There are always alternatives. In testing recipes for this book, I have rolled out pastry with an empty wine bottle, made my own cream horn molds from scrap cardboard and aluminium foil and used drinking glasses in place of biscuit cutters. The equipment listed is, therefore, only a guide. It is not there to put you off, rather to let you know before you reach Step 8 that a fine-mesh sieve might be useful.

That said, when it comes to baking, I have included specific dimensions for cake tins. If you want to use something you already have in your cupboard (which I regularly do), be aware you may need to slightly adjust baking temperatures or cooking times. If you're not a confident baker, I would recommend sticking with the tin size and temperature if possible.

In terms of baking ingredients, unless otherwise stated I have tested these recipes using large eggs, whole milk and unsalted butter. Again, I often end up using what I have in my fridge/cupboard when I cook, but if you are new to cake baking, I would suggest you try, where possible, to use the ingredients without substitutions – different sugar, flour or butter will often make a difference to the outcome.

Most of the ingredients included in this book are ones I can find at my local supermarket, but I am lucky to have easy access to places stocking ingredients from Asia and the Middle East. If you're finding it tricky to source an ingredient, and really want to give a recipe a try, there are lots of online shops that deliver, or feel free to run a quick Google search for an alternative.

xvii

On reading

I am a hoarder of books. No matter how tatty they become, I find it difficult to let them go. I have copies that have swelled and distorted because I've dropped them in the bath; a couple that I rescued after finding them abandoned on a footpath; and two or three that seem always to have sand trapped in their spines, because I once read them on the beach. Quite apart from the stories they contain, the books themselves are stories; they've been with me on holidays, we've survived long commutes together, and they have sat happily on my bookshelves until the precise moment I needed them.

I have been collecting books for as long as I can remember. Battered paperbacks and beautiful clothbound editions, bought with vouchers and pocket money, lined the shelves in my childhood bedroom. Most of them now inhabit the spare room at my mum's house, including the very special hardcover set of Harry Potter novels that my family bought for me when I turned twenty-one – the last books I read before I left home.

My local libraries were a haven during my years at school. On their shelves I discovered exciting worlds and characters I wanted to meet. I wasn't an unhappy child, but I was plump and a little awkward and certainly shyer than I pretended to be, and so school wasn't always easy. I excelled in lessons, but my weekends were spent with my parents, my sister and our extended family. At school I never had a solid group of friends and so, like so many other people I know, books became a refuge for me through those tricky teenage years.

At university, I finally found my crowd; people around whom I could properly be myself. I immersed myself in theatre, reading plays in their dozens, alongside books on producing and teaching. I got to know the university library and its extensive fiction section. In my final summer in Australia – after graduation, but still in possession of my student card – I would borrow six novels at a time, and race through them, as if the move to England would somehow mean I'd have fewer books in my life. Nothing could have been further from the truth.

When I moved, I only knew three people: Reilly, Alex and Tim, all friends from university, trying their hand at life in London too. This circle grew over the months that followed, but in those early days, when I spent much of each day on long tube journeys, I read voraciously. I particularly sought out books set in England, delighting in moments where I would happen upon a street or a building referred to in something I was reading. I arrived in the UK with three books, but soon had hundreds, arranged in piles in every room of my flat.

I have lived a somewhat transient life for the past couple of years, and so most of my books are now in storage. When I visit friends, I spend time in front of their bookshelves, scanning the spines of familiar titles, searching for an old friend, or a new one. This practice has introduced me to new titles – well-read copies pressed into my hands by people I love.

Whenever I've neglected them, books have sat, waiting patiently, always ready for me to come back. They are the true constant in my life, the grounding force, the comfort when I am homesick, anxious or lonely, a true joy when I am not. With them, I can travel in space and time, around the world and to places that don't exist, except on the page.

All the books I have featured here in this book are ones that I have read, and that are part of my story. Please consider this book a little library of personal recommendations; books I, as the librarian, would press into your hands with a glowing endorsement.

before noon

before noon

I can always think of a hundred things I'd rather do than get out of bed in the morning. It's been this way for as long as I can remember; those first minutes of waking up are my least favourite of the day. My stepfather, sick of Mum yelling upstairs to rouse me and my little sister, installed an intercom between our bedrooms and the kitchen when he moved in. Each morning, he would lean on the buzzer until we finally appeared downstairs. I wouldn't recommend it – it is a terribly unpleasant way of being woken up – but it is hard to deny its effectiveness.

Once downstairs, our bare feet on the cold tiles, we'd all have breakfast together. Mum would stand in front of the stove, stirring or grilling or flipping, as we hunted down clean school shirts and finished homework. My sister and I grew up confident in the kitchen and often had a hand in the evening meal, but our morning meal remained my mother's domain through to the end of school and, despite my initial reluctance to rise, it was always my favourite of the day.

As an adult, breakfast is still the meal I look forward to the most. I luxuriate in long mornings spent over food and despair on those rushed days when I have to dash out of the house with only a banana in my bag.

I could happily eat breakfast at any point of the day. The recipes that follow here, though eaten by characters to break their fast, might seem more suitable for lunch or dinner in your house. I wholeheartedly support this flexibility. I often make the green eggs and ham for lunch, the apple pie for dessert (with a scoop of ice cream) and the rice, miso and pickles have appeared on my dinner table on more than one occasion. I also regularly make a bowl of porridge when writing late at night; it could just as easily have made its way into the chapter on Midnight Feasts.

The Secret Garden, Frances Hodgson Burnett

Porridge

Porridge has always been a part of my life. In winter, wrapped in a dressing gown, my mum would stir a large pot of oats, spooning it up for us to top with dark brown sugar or honey. For years I'd roll my eyes, grumbling about it being a 'boring' breakfast option. I longed for mushrooms on toast, roasted tomatoes or her scrambled eggs instead.

And then I moved to England. My first teaching job was in Bushey, a long daily commute from my flat in Whitechapel. Rising before the sun each morning, cold and hungry, I needed something simple and warming to see me through my morning classes. My mum, of course, suggested porridge. And just like Mary Lennox, I was surprised to discover that porridge, suddenly, tasted nice.

I am now never far from a jar of oats and have played around with countless variations, searching for something that offers exactly what I need at 6 a.m. (or mid-afternoon, or late at night). This is my perfect porridge.

Porridge

Serves 1

1. Warm a frying pan over a low heat, and tip in the oats. Toast until golden, then allow to cool for a moment off the heat. Pour the oats and water into a saucepan and leave to soak while you have a shower or check your emails or snooze against the doorframe – 10 minutes will do.

2. Add the salt. Place a saucepan over a low heat and, with the handle of a wooden spoon (or a spurtle if you have one), stir the oats enthusiastically in little circles for 5 minutes. I find this intensely calming and a lovely way to start the day. Most of the water will evaporate and the oats will gradually thicken. Stop once they are cooked to your liking.

3. Spoon the oats into a bowl and pour the cream and treacle on top. Eat immediately.

VARIATIONS: Martha suggests a spoonful of treacle or sugar for Mary's porridge, both of which go down a treat. Alternatively, give some of these a try:
~ A spoonful of marmalade (see p. 6) and, if you fancy (I really can't encourage this enough), a glug of whisky
~ A couple of tablespoons of milk, a handful of blueberries and some chopped hazelnuts
~ A tablespoon of Greek yoghurt, a drizzle of honey and a teaspoon of toasted sesame seeds
~ A couple of drops of rosewater, a handful of chopped pistachio nuts and a squeeze of orange juice
~ A spoonful of crunchy peanut butter, a dribble of golden syrup and a splash of milk
~ A tablespoon of tahini, a squeeze of honey and a handful of toasted flaked almonds

INGREDIENTS
30g/1oz/⅓ cup oats, a mixture of rolled and steel cut*
250ml/8½floz/generous 1 cup cold water
Pinch of salt
TO SERVE
1tbsp single/light cream
2tsp black treacle/molasses

EQUIPMENT
Spurtle** (or a wooden spoon)

*The rule here is three times the volume of water as oats. If you don't have cups for the measurements, use a small teacup per serving, or a 250ml/8½floz mug for three portions (one mug of oats, three of water). I measure out ⅓ cup rolled oats, then take out 2tbsp and replace them with 2tbsp steel-cut oats. This is optional – you can also use all rolled oats if you prefer.

**A spurtle is a Scottish utensil that is designed for stirring porridge. It is a narrow wooden rod; if you don't have one, the handle of a wooden spoon is an ideal substitute.

Marmalade

Bending down, the bear unlocked the suitcase with a small key, which it also had around its neck, and brought out an almost empty glass jar. 'I ate marmalade,' he said, rather proudly. 'Bears like marmalade.'
A Bear Called Paddington, Michael Bond

With cheese, meat, cake or toast, marmalade is just fantastic. I make jars of it every Christmas, handing them out to family and friends, and snaffling a few away for the New Year. I have yet to find a citrus fruit that doesn't work, but I will say that pink grapefruit is particularly special, and I try not to miss the brief Seville or blood orange seasons early each year. These bright little jars keep me going all year.

Like Paddington, I arrived in this country with a jar of something to eat on toast – mine was Vegemite. On 12 March 2009, I walked off a plane and into Heathrow Airport, before tackling the long journey to Mile End and a friend's spare room. I felt lost, alone and overwhelmed by the decision I'd made to move halfway across the world. In my fragile state Paddington Bear started to mean even more to me as an adult than he did when I was a child.

Though a big batch makes sense when cooking for gifts, I'm just as happy to make just one jar at a time. If you don't fancy having a huge amount, or you only find a handful of oranges, you can reduce the quantities; judge the amount of sugar you need based on the weight of your fruit.

Marmalade

Makes around a litre/quart – enough to fill three gift jars (with some left over for personal use)

1. Juice your oranges through a sieve. Seville oranges have a large number of seeds, so this is the best way to keep them out. Scoop the pulp out of each orange and add it to the seeds in the sieve.

2. Measure the juice into a large bowl, and add water to make it up to 1.25 litres liquid. Slice the skins as finely as you can into long strips. Add them to the juice and water. Wrap the seeds and pulp in the cloth, tie it up tightly, and push this beneath the surface of the juice. Cover the bowl, and store in the fridge overnight.

3. The next day, place a couple of small plates in your freezer. Tip the contents of the bowl (including the seed-filled muslin) into a large saucepan and bring to a slow simmer. Cover and cook for 1.5–2 hours, until the rind is soft. Stir occasionally to ensure that the pieces of rind don't stick. Leave to cool.

4. Remove the pieces of rind and set aside for later. Strain the liquid through the sieve, squeezing the cloth full of pulp and seeds until it stops releasing juice. Much of the pectin (which will help the marmalade set) is in here, so do squeeze it well. Measure the liquid, and add water to make it up to 750ml.

5. Place the orange juice back into the saucepan, and add the lemon juice. Tip in the sugar and stir over a medium heat until dissolved. Add the strips of rind and bring to the boil.

6. Simmer for 20–25 minutes without a lid, stirring occasionally until setting point is reached. Skim the top every now and then to remove any scum that floats to the surface. To test whether the marmalade is at setting point, turn off the stove and take the plate out of the freezer.

INGREDIENTS
800g/1¾lb Seville oranges
Juice of 2 lemons
1kg/2¼lb preserving sugar*

EQUIPMENT
Piece of muslin/clean cotton
Sterilized jars

*Preserving sugar is a large crystal sugar with no added pectin. Oranges are naturally high in pectin, so you don't need to use specialized jam sugar for this recipe. Using preserving sugar will mean that the sugar melts evenly and slowly, resulting in a clearer marmalade. If you can't find preserving sugar, or you decide to make marmalade at midnight when the shops are closed (I've been there), granulated will do fine. Just skim the top more frequently as your marmalade boils.

Drop a teaspoon of the marmalade onto it, wait for 20 seconds and then push one edge. If it wrinkles rather than remaining liquid, then the marmalade is ready. If it's not there yet, turn the heat back on under the saucepan and continue to boil.

7. Leave the marmalade to cool for 10 minutes, which will ensure that the rind is evenly distributed.

8. Once the marmalade is ready, transfer it into the jars. Seal the jars while the marmalade is still hot and leave to cool. The jars will keep in a cool, dry place for at least 6 months. Once opened, store in the fridge and eat within a few weeks.

Tunna Pannkakor

'Eat,' she cried. 'Eat, before it gets cold!'
So Tommy and Annika ate, and they thought it was a very good
pancake.
Pippi Longstocking, Astrid Lindgren

I'm always thrilled when Shrove Tuesday rolls around. When I was younger we lined up for plates of pikelets and jam at our after-school religion classes – a final treat before the long chocolate-free weeks of Lent. Nowadays, though I no longer give anything up, I often find myself making at least four different types of pancake when the big day arrives. Big, fluffy American ones with maple syrup, buckwheat ones with cheese and ham, paper-thin French crêpes with a squeeze of lemon juice and these Swedish pancakes, best served with jam. I love them all.

In Sweden, where Pippi hails from, pancakes are traditionally eaten on Thursdays for dessert. Personally, I prefer them for breakfast – these ones aren't too sweet or heavy, and the first in a batch can be on the table in less than five minutes. They're also foolproof, and were my secret weapon for getting my nannying charges out of bed and downstairs for breakfast.

Swedish Pancakes
Makes around 16

1. Beat the eggs with a couple of tablespoons of the flour (there's no need to be precise with the amount – just 'some') until they form a smooth mixture. Add the rest of the flour and milk, beating continuously. The batter should have the consistency of single/light cream. Flavour with the salt and sugar and then add the melted butter (just before cooking).

2. Heat the frying pan over a low heat with a little bit of butter. As there's butter in the batter, you won't need to re-grease the pan between each pancake, but this initial greasing helps prevent the tricky first one from sticking. Pour about 2tbsp of the batter into the centre and swirl the pan around until the mixture covers the base evenly. Cook until the pancake is light brown in small patches underneath, then turn over using a spatula – or jerk your wrist and toss it in the air if you're very good at flipping pancakes (I am not).

3. Once the pancake is cooked through, place in a low oven on an ovenproof plate/baking tray to keep warm until you've used up all the batter. Make sure you continue to whisk the batter in between each pancake so that the flour doesn't settle in the bottom of the jug.

4. Serve with jam, sugar and lemon, chocolate spread or honey – the options are endless.

INGREDIENTS

2 eggs
240g/8½oz/1¾ cups plain/all-purpose flour
600ml/1 pint/2½ cups milk
½tsp salt
1tsp sugar
30g/1oz/2tbsp melted butter

TO SERVE

Jam
Lemon and sugar
Chocolate spread
Honey

EQUIPMENT

Measuring jug (large enough to hold at least 1.5L/quarts)

(Cold) Apple Pie

That was a wonderful breakfast. It is unusual to begin the day
with cold apple pie, but the children all said they would rather
have it than meat.
The Railway Children, E. Nesbit

I must have been about ten when I read *The Railway Children* for
the first time. I read it desperate for adventure, and for a house full
of siblings to have one with. My sister is terrific and was a devoted
partner-in-crime, but we lived in parent-heavy households, so
rarely experienced the kind of freedom we read about in books
like *The Famous Five*, *Swallows and Amazons* and, of course, *The
Railway Children*. We longed to become grown-ups so we could
explore new lands, stay up all night and eat apple pie for breakfast.

When I started blogging about food, I spent a lot of time and
energy trying to take my photographs in natural light. This became
a daily challenge, especially in winter, when I'd leave for work in
the first light of the morning and come home in darkness. I would
frequently cook in the evenings after work, then wake up first
thing and take the photographs before rushing out of the door
the next day.

And so, when I first made this apple pie, I really did eat it for
breakfast. It more than fulfilled my childhood desire to try it. With
a spoonful of yoghurt, a slice of this is a great start to the day. Of
course, it also works as a dessert, but I'd encourage you to live like
the railway children and give it a try in the morning.

Apple Pie
Serves 8

1. To make the pastry, combine the flour, icing sugar and salt in a bowl. Rub in the cold butter until the mixture resembles breadcrumbs. Add the egg yolk and 1–2tbsp of very cold water. Combine with your hands in the bowl until the mixture comes together. Turn onto a lightly floured surface and bring into a ball. Don't work the mixture too much, or knead it, as the pastry should be short and crumbly.

2. Wrap the pastry in plastic wrap and pop in the fridge for 30 minutes. Don't be tempted to skip the chilling, as you risk the pastry shrinking in the oven.

3. For the filling, squeeze the lemon into a bowl filled with water. Peel and core the apples, then cut as thinly as you can. Drop the slices straight into the bowl of water as you go, to prevent them turning brown. Once all the apples are chopped, drain and pat dry with kitchen paper. Mix together the sugar, cinnamon, nutmeg and cornflour and then toss this through the apple pieces.

4. Cut the pastry in two and put one half back in the fridge. Roll the pastry out on a lightly floured surface (if the pastry is sticking – as it is wont to do in a warm kitchen – roll it between two pieces of greaseproof paper rather than straight onto the work surface). Stop rolling when you have a large circle that is around the thickness of a coin.

5. Drape your pastry over your rolling pin and lay it in the pie dish. Press the pastry into the corners using a small ball of spare dough. If there are any tears in the pastry, patch them up with extra dough. Place in the fridge. Preheat your oven to 200°C/400°F/Gas 6 and put the baking sheet in the middle of the oven to heat up.

6. Roll the second half of the pastry out to the same thickness as the base. Aim for a rectangle that is as wide as

INGREDIENTS

PASTRY
250g/8¾oz/2 cups plain/ all-purpose flour

2tbsp icing/ confectioners' sugar

Pinch of salt

175g/6oz/1½ sticks butter, chilled and cubed

1 egg yolk

FILLING
1 lemon

1kg/2¼lb crisp eating apples

70g/2½oz/scant 6tbsp caster/superfine sugar

2tsp ground cinnamon

1tsp grated nutmeg

1tbsp cornflour/ cornstarch

1 egg

EQUIPMENT
Large pie dish (mine is 25cm/10in diameter along the base)

your pie dish, and as long as possible. Slice into 1.5cm/⅝in-wide strips, then arrange these in a lattice on a piece of greaseproof paper. Make a cross with two pieces, laying the vertical underneath the horizontal. Add another vertical piece, on top of the horizontal piece this time, a couple of millimetres to the right of the first vertical one. Take the bottom half of the first vertical piece and fold it up and over the horizontal piece for a moment. Place a fourth piece horizontally, a couple of millimetres below the first horizontal piece, and then fold that first vertical piece down again. You should see a lattice start to form now. Continue to lay the pieces, weaving them in and out by folding pieces up and out of the way, and then over the new piece again. Stop when it's large enough to cover the top of your pie. If this is the first time you have latticed pastry, practise with some strips of paper first; you don't want to be wrestling with sticky pastry while you're working it out.

7. Whisk the egg with a teaspoon of water and paint a little of this around the edge of the pastry in the pie dish. Tip the apples into the dish and carefully slide the lattice off the greaseproof paper and over the top. Press the edges to seal and trim the pastry. If you don't fancy making a lattice top, or it's a hot day and your pastry isn't co-operating, then just roll the other half of the pastry into a circle, the same thickness as the base, and seal it on top as above, making a few slashes in the pastry lid for the steam to escape.

8. If you like, use the off-cuts of pastry to shape a couple of decorative leaves (I use the leaves that came on my apples as a template). Paint the top of the pie with the rest of the beaten egg, then arrange the leaves on top and paint them too. Place it in the oven on the preheated baking tray.

9. After 10 minutes, turn the temperature down to 180°C/350°F/Gas 4. Bake for a further 35 minutes, keeping an eye on the top to ensure it doesn't burn.

10. Serve immediately, if you like, but it's lovely the next morning too. The pastry will be short and crisp so should slice cleanly, but the first slice (as with most pies) may be a bit of a mess to lift out.

Fruity Nutbread

*Matthias seated himself to an early breakfast in Cavern Hole:
nutbread, apples and a bowl of fresh goatsmilk.*
Redwall, Brian Jacques

During my first year of writing about food in books, I spent a lot
of time apologizing for not having read *Redwall*. Thankfully, this
situation has now been rectified. Though I had been warned, I
couldn't quite believe how much food the first book contained;
every second page of my copy is dog-eared, each fold pointing me
towards mentions of feasts hosted in the Abbey enjoyed by a group
of anthropomorphic mice.

Though one of those feasts nearly made it into the book, I decided
to offer this bread instead: breakfast fodder eaten by various
characters throughout. Served sometimes with goat's curd and
sometimes with fruit, it needed to be dense, sweet and suitable for
toasting. It also needed to be built for eating on the go, should you
be running late for work, or should Cluny the Scourge (that most
villainous of rats) mount a surprise attack.

This is bread in the way that banana bread is bread. It's not really.
It's cake.

Fruity nutbread

Makes 10 slices

1. Heat the oven to 190°C/375°F/Gas 5. Grease the loaf tin and line with greaseproof paper.

2. Combine the grated apple, eggs, melted butter, cinnamon, vanilla, honey and chopped walnuts in a mixing bowl.

3. Fold in the ground almonds, flour and baking powder. Don't over mix the batter – stop stirring as soon as the flour and almonds are incorporated.

4. Pour the batter into the lined tin and level off the top. Place in the centre of the preheated oven for an hour. Insert a skewer into the nutbread to check that it is done; it should come out clean.

5. Cool the loaf in the tin for 10 minutes, then turn out onto a wire rack. Eat warm or toasted, with butter, goat's curd/cheese or ricotta and honey.

INGREDIENTS
500g/3¾ cups grated red apples (about 5 – use sweet, crisp ones)
3 eggs
60g/2oz/½ stick butter, melted
1tsp ground cinnamon
1tsp vanilla extract
3tbsp honey
100g/3½oz/1 cup chopped walnuts
200g/7oz/2 cups ground almonds
80g/scant 3oz/heaping ¾ cup spelt flour
2tsp baking powder

EQUIPMENT
Grater
Loaf tin (2lb/9x4in)

Redwall, Brian Jacques

Cinnamon Rolls

I hadn't even known I was hungry until I'd stepped into the hallway, but at that moment, standing there with a rough stomach and a bad taste in my mouth and the prospect of what would be my last freely chosen meal, it seemed to me that I'd never smelled anything quite so delicious as that sugary warmth: coffee and cinnamon, plain buttered rolls from the Continental breakfast.

The Goldfinch, Donna Tartt

There are few better smells to wake up to than cinnamon rolls and coffee. The butter, the cinnamon, the sweet, enriched dough all work together in some sort of holy trinity of breakfast scents. It is this smell that greets Theo as he stands on the stairs of his Amsterdam hotel, certain that the morning will be his last.

When I read *The Goldfinch* on a rooftop in Marrakech, I could not have been further from Christmastime in Holland. Nonetheless, I started to crave cinnamon rolls for breakfast, and couldn't wait to get back to England and give these a try. I became so obsessed with finding the ideal cinnamon buns – the ones worth the kneading and proving in those first sluggish hours of the day – that I tried more recipes than I can count. This one is an amalgam of the best.

Most pleasingly, you can start this recipe the night before, if you like. I often do – anything that allows me to get the first steps out of the way before bed and have a slightly easier start to the morning is a win in my book.

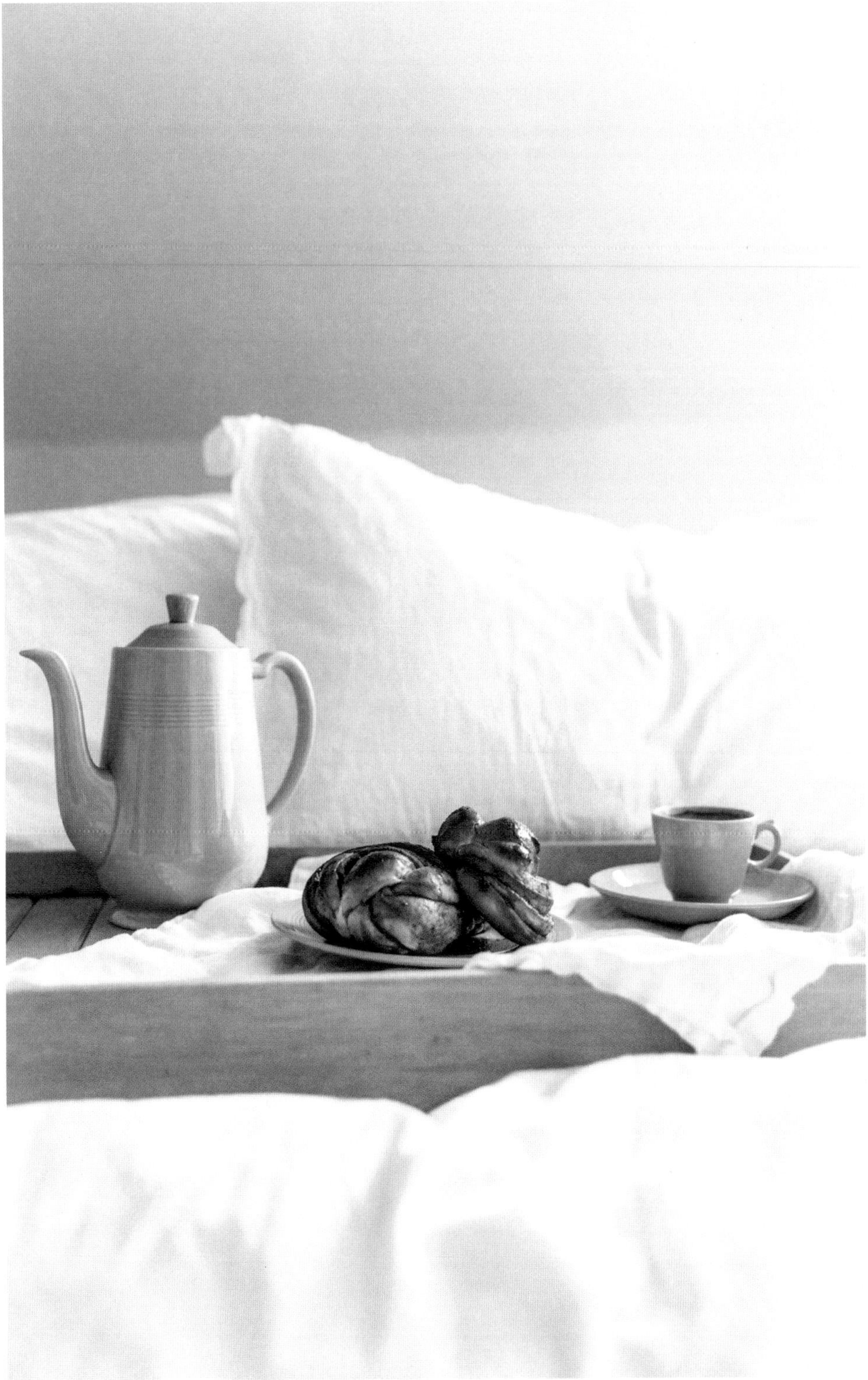

INGREDIENTS

20g/heaping 1tbsp fresh yeast (or 7g/1tsp fast action yeast)

250ml/9floz/generous 1 cup whole milk, at room temperature

½tsp ground cardamom (or 10 cardamom pods)

200g/7oz/1½ cups plain flour

200g/7oz/scant 1½ cups strong white bread flour

70g/2½oz/⅓ cup light brown sugar

Pinch of salt

70g/2½oz/5tbsp unsalted butter

FILLING

75g/2½oz/5tbsp unsalted butter, softened

75g/6tbsp dark brown sugar

2tsp ground cinnamon

GLAZE

3 cardamom pods, crushed

70ml/scant 5tbsp water

50g/4tbsp dark brown sugar

1tsp ground cinnamon

EQUIPMENT

Pastry brush

A mixer is helpful (you can do this by hand if you don't have one, but it will take quite a lot of kneading).

Cinnamon rolls
Makes 14

1. In a bowl, crumble the yeast into the lukewarm milk. Stir until dissolved and allow to stand for 10 minutes.

2. If you're using cardamom pods rather than ground cardamom, crack open the green casings and bash the seeds inside to a powder. Put the flours, light brown sugar, salt and cardamom into the bowl of a mixer. Tip in the milk and yeast and mix for 5 minutes until the dough is smooth and elastic. Keep the mixer running and drop in the butter, bit by bit, continuing to mix until it is fully incorporated.

3. Clean the bowl and grease it well. Place the ball of dough inside and cover with plastic wrap. Leave to rise for 90 minutes or so, until doubled in size (or for 30 minutes start the rise, then transfer to the fridge to prove overnight).

4. While the dough is proving, make the filling by beating the butter, sugar and cinnamon together until creamy.

5. Once the dough has risen, tip it out onto a floured surface and roll into a large rectangle about ½cm/¼in thick, 30cm/12in wide and 60cm/24in long. Keep the short side of the rectangle parallel to the edge of your surface. Spread the spiced butter over the dough, right to the edges, and fold it into thirds, folding up the edge closest to you, and then folding the top third down over it. Slice the dough into 14 pieces, cutting perpendicular to the folds and the edge of your surface.

6. Stretch a piece of the dough to lengthen it, then wind it round your 2 forefingers until you have 4cm/1½in length left. Tuck the end around the rest of the dough and through the hole created by your fingers. Repeat until you have 14 round buns, or little spirals. Place each on a lined baking tray (with the little end poking through the middle hidden underneath), ensuring you give them space to rise again during a second prove.

7. Cover the buns and allow them to rise for an hour. Preheat the oven to 230°C/450°F/Gas 8. Bake the buns for about 8 minutes, until golden brown.

8. While the buns are in the oven, put the glaze ingredients into a small saucepan, bring to a gentle simmer and cook until the sugar has melted. When you pull the buns out of the oven, brush them with the glaze immediately and then allow them to cool on a wire rack for a few minutes before eating them warm.

An Egg Boiled Very Soft

'Mrs. Bates, let me propose your venturing on one of these eggs. An egg boiled very soft is not unwholesome. Serle understands boiling an egg better than any body. I would not recommend an egg boiled by any body else; but you need not be afraid, they are very small, you see – one of our small eggs will not hurt you.'

Emma, Jane Austen

When I started thinking about writing this book, deciding on the list of recipes that would make the cut gave me the most pause. Would they be varied enough? How many sandwiches could I really justify including? (Just the one, it turns out.) Were they accessible enough?

When I moved to England and started properly cooking for myself, it was my mum's instinctive knowledge of all the basics that I missed most. In those first years, the thing I googled more than anything else was 'how do I boil an egg?' You see, for years, I was too nervous to do it. I like really soft eggs with very runny yolks, so I preferred making poached eggs, where I could at least see what state the yolk was in during the cooking. Boiled eggs are hidden away inside the shell. Anything could be happening in there.

There are so many methods: starting in cold water; adding the egg once the water is simmering; turning the heat off and allowing the egg to cook in the residual heat of the water. I have tried them all.

Here is my favourite method for a very soft-boiled egg that Emma's father would approve of. You can serve it with just a pinch of salt and pepper (Mr Woodhouse probably wouldn't have even gone that far), but my favourite thing to do is create a mini hollandaise of sorts, by adding some vinegar, salt and butter. This is one to eat with soldiers, scooped out of the shell. If you want a soft-boiled egg you can peel, you can find timings on p. 27.

Boiled Egg with Soldiers

Serves 1

1. Bring a small pan of water to the boil. Lower the eggs into the water using a spoon, to prevent their shells cracking as they hit the bottom. Set a timer for 3 minutes.

2. When your timer pings, take the pan over to the sink and run lots of cold water into it. When the eggs feel cold to the touch, place them in egg cups, pointy end up. Slice through the top of the egg, about 2cm/¾in below the point. Shake some cider vinegar over each yolk and add half the butter to each egg. Add salt to taste. Stir with a soldier of toast or a spear of asparagus, and eat.

INGREDIENTS

2 large eggs, at room temperature
Dash of cider vinegar
A knob of butter
Pinch of salt

TO SERVE

Hot buttered toast, cut into soldiers
Asparagus spears – raw, if they're really fresh and tender, or steamed for 2 minutes if they're not

AN EGG BOILED VERY SOFT

Emma, Jane Austen

Green Eggs & Ham*

Weekend breakfasts were special occasions in our house – at my mum's and my dad's. Both my parents are confident that they make the best scrambled eggs, and we'd have them regularly: with mushrooms, beside bacon or sausages, on top of avocado, on toast. They do both make outstanding scrambled eggs, just on the boundary of 'undercooked', with cream (Dad) or milk (Mum) and a bit of butter at the end.

When I moved to the UK, I couldn't decide which version I missed more. I used whatever was closest to hand in the fridge, actively trying not to take a side. That is, until I read *Mastering the Art of French Cooking* cover to cover. Julia Child directs us to add nothing more to the egg than the butter you have in the pan. Her scrambled eggs are the best I've ever had – silky, rich and worthy of the freshest, most beautiful eggs you can get your hands on. Sorry, Mum and Dad. Julia wins this round.

When I was young, green eggs and ham sounded truly awful. Green was what happened to ham if you forgot about it at the bottom of the fridge. And so I sympathized with Dr Seuss's unnamed protagonist, who didn't want green eggs and ham anywhere (in a house or with a mouse, in boxes or with foxes). But scrambled eggs become something gloriously different with the addition of vivid green pesto. Suddenly, green eggs and ham is a rather appealing prospect.

*This one is what it is. No quote necessary.

INGREDIENTS

PESTO EGGS

50g/5tbsp almonds
1 clove garlic
Large bunch of parsley
30g/1oz/¼ cup hard goat's cheese, grated
1tsp coarse sea salt
50ml/3½tbsp olive oil
15g/½oz/1tbsp butter
4 large eggs

TO SERVE

2 thick slices sourdough toast
2 large slices ham (thick or thin cut, whichever you prefer)
Butter, for spreading
Salt and pepper

EQUIPMENT

Food processor
or
Pestle and mortar
or
Knife and chopping board (and a little bit of patience)
Jar for storing pesto

Green (Pesto) Eggs and Ham
Serves 2

1. First, make the pesto. This makes more than you'll need, but it keeps for weeks in the fridge and is brilliant on pasta, in salad dressings and, of course, with eggs. In a dry pan, toast the almonds for a few minutes, ensuring they don't catch and burn. Allow them to cool for a couple of minutes.

2. Blitz/bash/chop the almonds, along with the garlic. Then add the herbs and blitz/bash/chop again. If you're working with a knife, put the ingredients into a mixing bowl at this stage. Add the cheese and salt and then dribble in the oil, stirring/blitzing all the time. You may not need it all; just go until you have a loose, droppable texture. Spoon the pesto into the jar for storage.

3. When you're ready to eat your green eggs and ham, pop your bread in the toaster or on a hot griddle: the cardinal sin with scrambled eggs is to not have the toast ready in time (your eggs will overcook as they sit waiting in the pan). When the toast is ready and buttered and the ham is in position you can cook your eggs.

4. Crack the eggs into a bowl and break the yolks with a fork. Whisk them a little, but don't go over the top; you'll be moving them about in the pan. Heat the butter over a medium heat until foaming, then reduce the heat to the lowest possible level. Tip in the eggs and start to move them around with a spatula. Keep them moving until you have some solid clumps of eggs still surrounded by uncooked liquid. Turn the heat off. Spoon in 2tbsp of pesto and continue to stir until the eggs are just cooked.

5. Spoon the eggs over the ham and toast. Season with salt and pepper. Eat immediately.

Kedgeree

'… Any kedgeree?'
'I ate it.' Polly got up from the table.
'All of it?' Calypso whispered.
The Camomile Lawn, Mary Wesley

On an otherwise uneventful September morning in 1978, Ingela sat down beside Deb outside St Anne's hospital in Tottenham and introduced herself. They had both arrived for their first day – they were (and still are) physiotherapists. Deb is my mum, and she and Ingela became fast friends. Eleven years later, my mum and dad left the UK with me and my little sister Lucy in tow, but they stayed in touch across the ten-thousand mile divide.

When I moved back to England, Ingela and her husband Chris became my surrogate parents. They are the ones who offer me advice on tax, insurance and driving licences, who have a hot meal and a bed for me whenever I want to visit, and who I am always desperate to share good news with. Their son and daughter – Tom and Anna – are my surrogate siblings and best friends.

Though I have been to their home countless times, Ingela and Chris didn't see my Hackney flat until a couple of years after I had moved in. It was very much lived in by that stage. Books lined the shelves and were piled on surfaces, and the kitchen was overflowing with jars and utensils. I had spent hours cleaning, desperate for them to approve of my little flat. To sweeten the fact that they were sitting at a folding table in the same room as my bed, I made kedgeree, one of Chris's favourite dishes.

I first came across kedgeree in Wesley's *The Camomile Lawn*. When I asked my mum to explain what it was I turned my nose up, but I'm now a convert. Mild spicing, flaked fish, a soft-boiled egg: it's everything I am looking for in the morning. I think Polly is quite right to have gobbled the whole dish – it's not only Chris's favourite, but mine too.

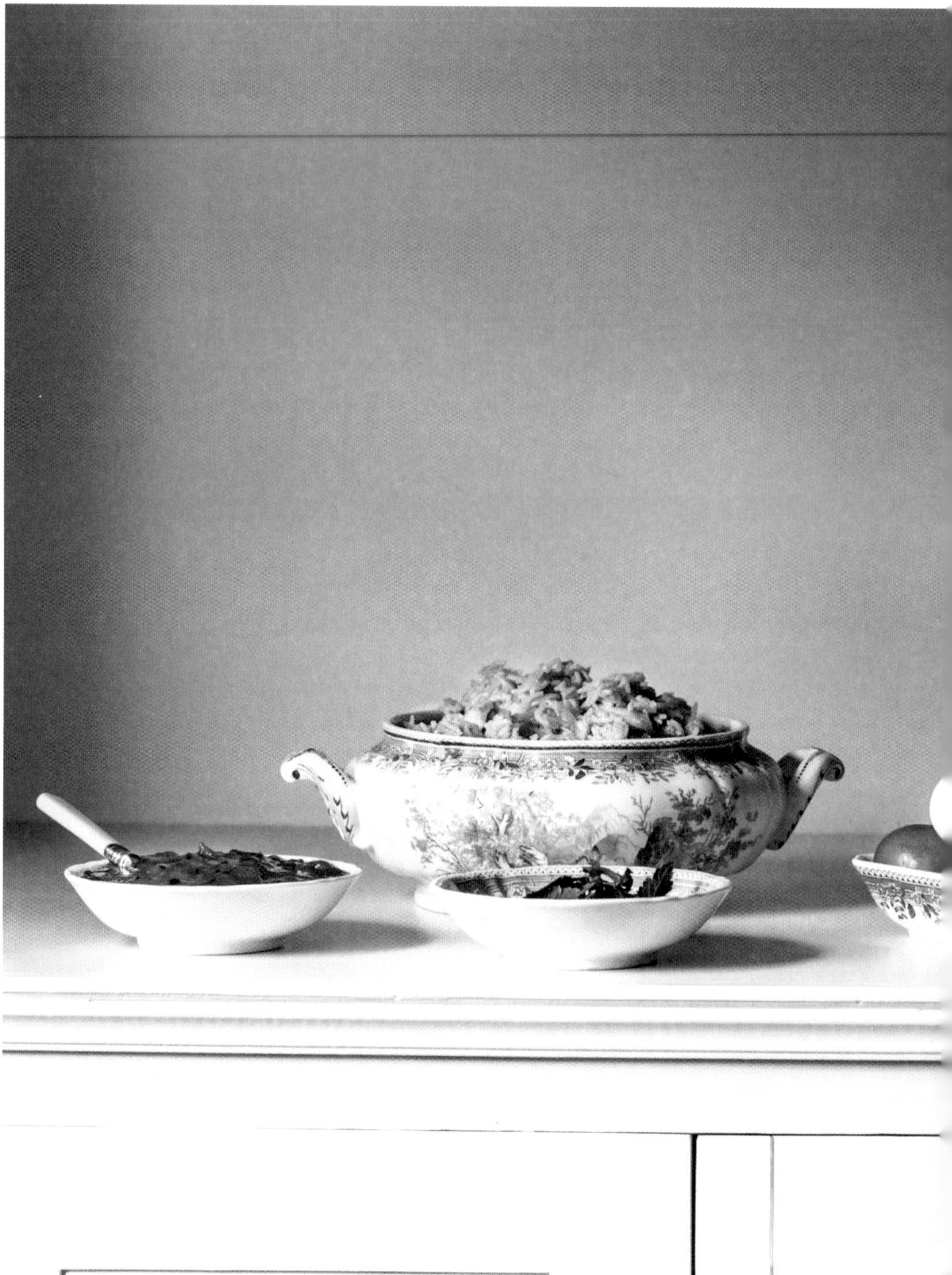

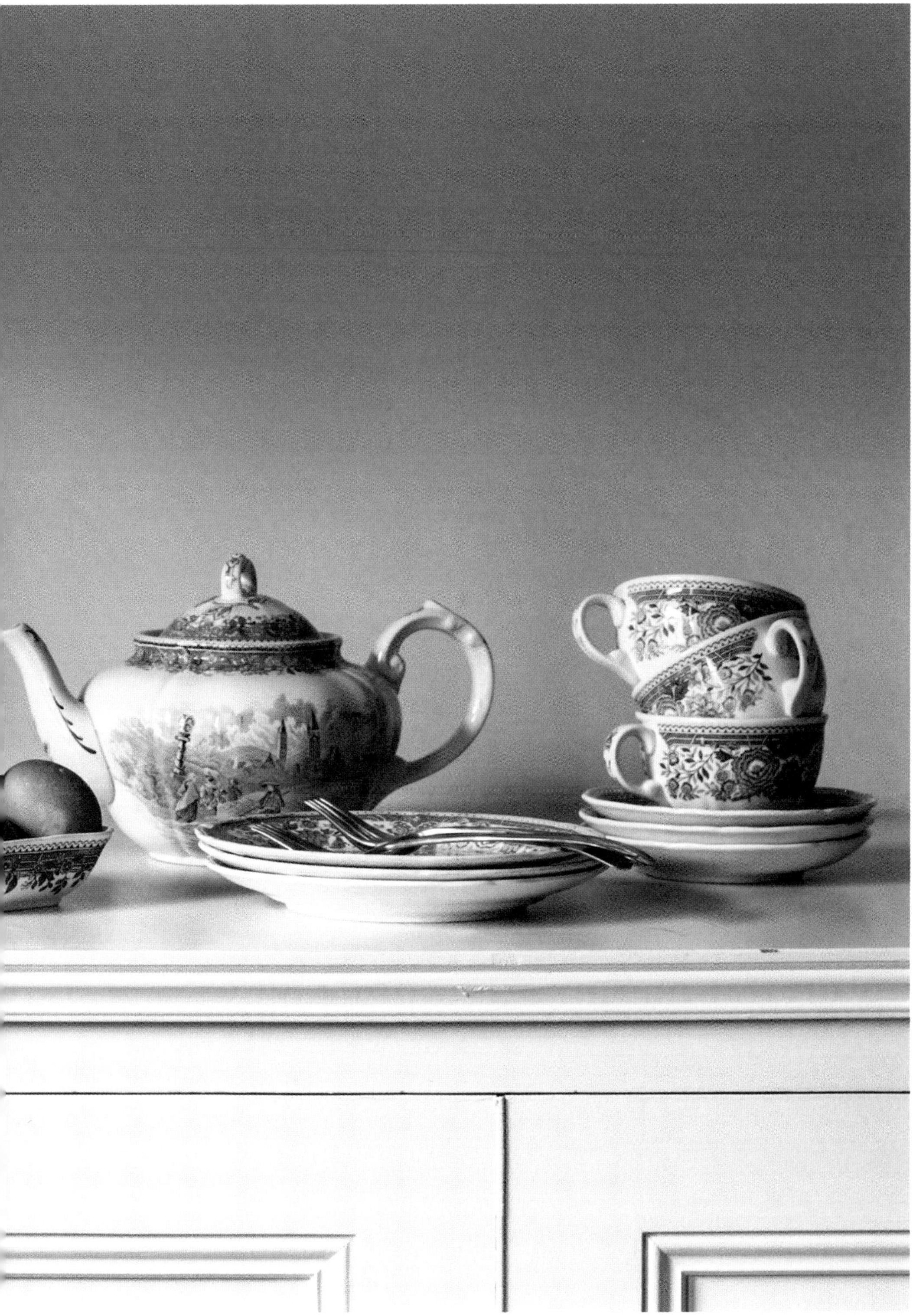

INGREDIENTS

1 onion, roughly chopped

1 small carrot, roughly chopped

1 stick celery, roughly chopped

5 black peppercorns

1 bay leaf

300g/10½oz smoked haddock (undyed)

500ml/17floz/generous 2 cups water

250g/9oz/scant 1½ cups basmati rice

30g/1oz/2tbsp butter

3 small brown onions, finely sliced

2 cloves garlic, finely chopped

1tsp ground turmeric

1tsp ground cumin

1tsp ground coriander

1tsp fennel seeds

3 crushed cardamom pods

180ml/6floz/¾ cup double/heavy cream

4 eggs, at room temperature

TO SERVE

Mango chutney

Parsley

Kedgeree

Serves 4

1. Put the chopped vegetables, peppercorns and bay leaf in a wide-bottomed pan with the haddock. Cover with the water and bring to the boil over a medium heat. As soon as it comes to the boil, turn the heat off and set it aside to cool – the fish will finish cooking as it does so.

2. Pour the rice into a medium saucepan. Rinse and drain three times in cold water. Add fresh water to the pan until it sits one knuckle higher than the top of the rice. Cover, bring to the boil and then turn down to a low simmer and cook until the water is at the level of the rice. This should take around 8–10 minutes. Turn the heat off and leave the lid on, covering the pan with a tea towel if it isn't a snug fit. Leave to steam for 15 minutes.

3. Heat the butter in a frying pan until foaming and fry the onions and garlic until soft and translucent. Add the spices and fry for another 2 minutes. Add 300ml/½ pint/1¼ cups of the fish cooking water and reduce the liquid by half. Finally, add the cream and reduce until thick.

4. Meanwhile, bring a small saucepan of water to the boil. Lower the eggs in carefully, with a spoon, and set a timer to 6 minutes. As soon as the timer pings, run them under cold water. To peel them, tap all over to crack the shell, then pull the shell away at the non-pointy end. Break the membrane. Slip a teaspoon between the membrane and the egg, and run it around the whole egg. Pull the shell off.

5. Tip the rice into the sauce and stir through so that each grain is coated. Flake the fish in and stir this through too. Serve with mango chutney, chopped parsley and a peeled, sliced egg.

Baked Beans

Ma was busy all day long, cooking things for Christmas. She baked salt-rising bread and rye'n'Injun bread, and Swedish crackers, and a huge pan of baked beans with salt pork and molasses.
Little House in the Big Woods, Laura Ingalls Wilder

I have eaten baked beans a thousand and one ways, on a thousand and one occasions. As a child, there were countless tins, eaten with cheerios (cheap cocktail sausages), sealed into toasted sandwiches or served on toast with grated cheese for breakfast. Ever since I read Nigel Slater (in one of his *Kitchen Diaries*, I think) admit a love for the tinned variety, I have felt validated in cherishing them. I don't think I've ever been without a tin, or the wherewithal (sharp cheddar, grainy mustard, Worcestershire sauce, a dash of Tabasco) to make them into something special. I am not proud of admitting this, but I have spent evenings in the theatre watching three-hour plays unfold onstage, with half my mind on what I'll be adding to the tin of baked beans at the back of the cupboard when I get home.

The beans in Ingalls Wilder's autobiographical account of homestead life in America are very different from the tinned ones we're used to. With molasses and some cured pork (if you fancy it), they are thick, rich and full of flavour. You can use dried beans and fresh tomatoes if you like, but the tinned varieties of both provide a speedy alternative, so you can have this on the table in less than thirty minutes.

I have not, as yet, gone so far as to eat baked beans for breakfast on Christmas morning. But this could be the year. Inspired by Ma's homestead kitchen, I might stir up a batch the night before. On the day itself, a heavy pan placed on the stove while everyone explores their stockings would provide a very welcome start to a cold December morning.

Baked Beans

Serves at least 4 for breakfast

1. If you're using the pancetta, tip it into the pan and cook until crisp, then set aside, leaving the fat in the pan. If you're not using the pancetta, add a tablespoon of oil to the pan and heat through.

2. Add the finely diced onion and cook over a medium heat until soft, ensuring that it doesn't brown. Add the finely chopped garlic and cook for another couple of minutes.

3. Add the tins of tomatoes, leaves from the sprigs of thyme, the chopped chilli, mustard and treacle. Simmer over a low heat for 20 minutes.

4. Strain the tins of cannellini beans and stir these through. If you are using the pancetta, add it back into the pan now. Cook for a further 10 minutes, then taste and season with salt and pepper. Serve on toast.

INGREDIENTS

150g/5½oz diced pancetta (optional)

1tbsp vegetable oil (if not using pancetta)

1 onion, finely diced

2 cloves garlic, finely chopped

2 x 400g/14oz tins chopped tomatoes

3 sprigs fresh thyme

1 long red chilli, deseeded and chopped finely

1tbsp mustard (I like hot English mustard here)

2tbsp black treacle/molasses

2 x 400g/14oz tins cannellini beans

Salt and pepper

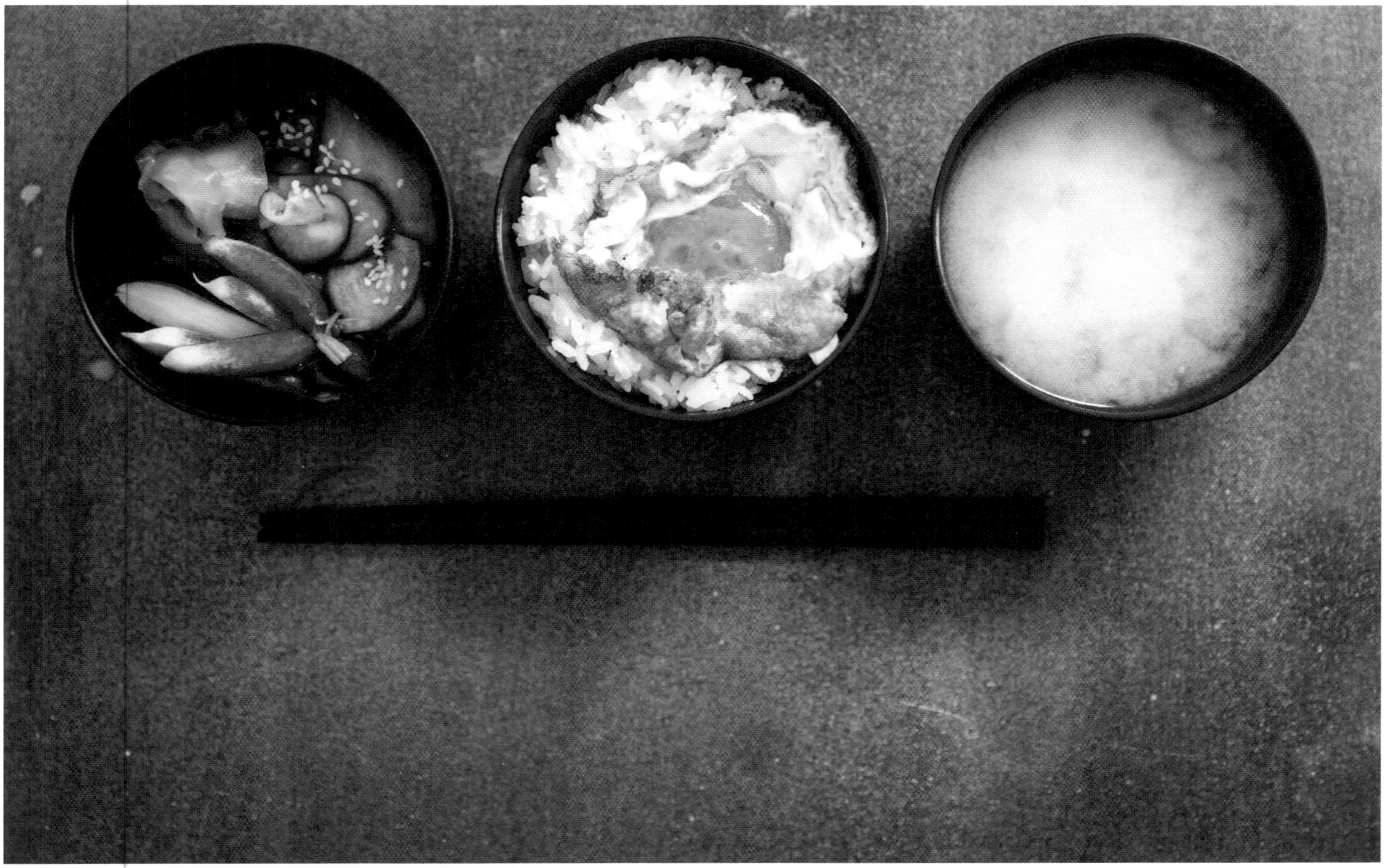

RICE, MISO, PICKLES, EGG { 34 } *Norwegian Wood*, Haruki Murakami

Rice, Miso, Pickles, Egg

On the way I found an open café and ate a breakfast of rice and miso soup, pickled vegetables and fried eggs.
Norwegian Wood, Haruki Murakami

I am confident in my belief that the presence of pickles improves almost anything you can put on a plate, so the idea of this breakfast immediately appealed. Pickles never survive long in my fridge; as soon as I open a jar of gherkins, I find myself frequently drawn back to the fridge for a munch until it's time to open another.

In the past couple of years, I have taken to making my own – turning a glut of cucumbers, radishes or beetroot into candy-coloured jars of pickles that brighten up my fridge or store cupboard no end. I have also taken to collecting vinegars – each one lending something different to the contents of the jar.

Many pickles take preparation and time: boiling vegetables, sterilizing jars, leaving them to develop for a couple of weeks. It's a ritual I relish, but sometimes what I crave is not the slow pleasure of preserving, but the sweet sharpness that a pickle brings to the plate. And so, more often than not, I find myself making a quick pickle: vegetables you would be happy to bite into raw, left to soak up some salt, sugar and vinegar while you get on with the rest of the dish.

This breakfast is a lovely one to wake up to. Bright, sharp and salty, it gives me a boost on days when I have lots to achieve.

Miso Soup
Enough for 4

INGREDIENTS

2 pieces of kombu seaweed

750ml/1¼ pints/3¼ cups water

2tbsp white miso paste

Pinch of salt

100g/3½oz silken tofu

1. Put the seaweed and water in a saucepan, and place over a very low heat, stirring occasionally. As the water boils, pull out the seaweed.*

2. Allow the stock to boil for a couple of minutes, then turn off the heat. Spoon in the miso and stir until it has dissolved. Taste and season with a little salt.

3. Slice the tofu into small cubes and add to the hot stock. Serve immediately.

* This is an incredibly simple stock. If you want to play around with the taste, you can swap the seaweed stock for mushroom, chicken or whatever you have in your cupboard. You could also add a couple of pinches of bonito flakes before you add the miso, which I often do when I'm not cooking for vegetarians.

Rice, Pickles, Egg
Enough for 4

INGREDIENTS

RICE

100g/3½oz/generous ½ cup sushi rice

125ml/4¼floz cold water

2tbsp rice vinegar

1tsp mirin

1tsp caster/superfine sugar

PICKLES

1 cucumber

10 radishes

1tbsp flaky sea salt/ Kosher salt

1tbsp caster/superfine sugar

White pepper

150ml/5floz/⅔ cup rice vinegar

FRIED EGG

2tbsp sesame oil

4 eggs

EQUIPMENT

Mandoline or vegetable peeler

1. Wash the rice 4 times in cold water. Drain well, then pour the water over the rice. Leave the rice to sit for half an hour while you make the pickle.

2. To make the pickle, slice the vegetables into any thickness you fancy: the thinner they are, the more they will pickle. I like to slice the cucumber with a mandoline, so they pick up the pickle, and the radishes into quarters, so they retain most of their crunch.

3. Put the sea salt, caster sugar, white pepper and vinegar into a small bowl and stir until the sugar and salt have dissolved. Split the vinegar between two bowls, adding the cucumber to one and the radish to the other. Set aside while you finish the rice.

4. Bring the rice to the boil and then immediately turn it down to a slow simmer. Boil for 10 minutes, with the lid on, until the water has dipped below the level of the rice.

Lift the lid as little as possible when checking the level, to prevent too much steam from escaping.

5. Remove the rice from the heat and allow to steam for 10 minutes with the lid on.

6. In the meantime, bring the vinegar, mirin and sugar to a simmer and keep warm over a very low heat. Don't allow the mixture to boil down or reduce.

7. Spread the rice out in a thin layer. Pour the vinegar mixture over the top and fold it through, being careful not to squash the rice too much. Spoon into a bowl.

8. For the fried eggs, heat the sesame oil to smoking point in a small frying pan. It will be extraordinarily hot, so do be careful. Crack each egg into a glass, then pour them into the oil and stand back. As soon as the white begins to crisp nicely round the edge, turn the heat off and slide the eggs out of the pan and onto the rice. Serve with the pickles.

Curried Chicken

'Mrs. Hudson has risen to the occasion,' said Holmes, uncovering a dish of curried chicken. 'Her cuisine is a little limited, but she has as good an idea of breakfast as a Scotch-woman. What have you here, Watson?'
'The Adventure of the Naval Treaty', *The Adventures of Sherlock Holmes*, Sir Arthur Conan Doyle

My favourite teacher at primary school was Mr Moynihan. My apologies to my other teachers (many of whom were wonderful), but he was outstanding. Alongside logic problems and algebra far beyond the Queensland state requirements, he read Sherlock Holmes stories to us in class, encouraging us to try to work out the case before the famous detective. Only once did we manage it – with 'The Adventure of the Speckled Band' – and I have a feeling he gave us some pretty big clues as we muddled our way through. We were rewarded with the Holy Grail of primary school prizes: a pizza party. We were chuffed.

In the years that followed, as I worked my way through Conan Doyle's canon, I never forgot this first introduction, or how wonderful it was to have a teacher who loved great stories as much as I did. I continue to return to Conan Doyle, despite knowing the outcome to all the stories. They're wonderfully comforting, not least in their consistency. I love the scenes at the breakfast table, with the paper and a few dishes prepared by Mrs Hudson.

This curry is based on a Mrs Beeton one, and can be made in little more than thirty minutes. The spicing is slightly different to the other curries in the book; a little sweeter and more suited to the morning. If you decide to prepare it the night before you'd like to eat it, it's also lovely cold, straight from the fridge.

Curried Chicken

Serves 4

1. Cut the chicken thighs in half through the bone, with a sharp, heavy knife. Roughly chop 2 of the onions and arrange in the base of a saucepan with the chicken thighs nestled on top.

2. Pour over the stock, then bring to a simmer over a medium heat. Season with a little pepper and salt and simmer for 30 minutes.

3. When the chicken has been cooking for around 10 minutes, bash the coriander seeds to a powder in a pestle and mortar. Peel the ginger, slice it into chunks, then add to the coriander and pound it into a paste. Add the cinnamon, cloves, cardamom and chilli powder.

4. Thinly slice the third onion. Warm a teaspoon of the ghee in a large frying pan and, once it has melted, add the onion. Fry it until it is soft and translucent, stirring frequently to prevent it from browning. Add the spice paste and cook for a couple of minutes. Rinse the chickpeas and add them to the onion mix.

5. Warm the rest of the ghee in a second frying pan. Remove the chicken from the stock and fry it, skin-side down, in the ghee over a medium heat. Sieve the chicken stock into the spiced onion mix and bring to the boil, reducing the liquid by half.

6. To serve, spoon the onions and chickpeas into a dish, and top with the chicken. Serve with some yoghurt and rice, or some griddled toast.

INGREDIENTS

4 chicken thighs
3 large brown onions
300ml/10floz/1¼ cups chicken stock
Finely cracked black pepper and pinch of salt
1tbsp coriander seeds
2.5cm/1in piece ginger
¼tsp ground cinnamon
¼tsp cloves
¼tsp ground cardamom
¼tsp chilli powder
25g/1oz/2tbsp ghee
200g/7oz tinned chickpeas

EQUIPMENT

Pestle and mortar

around noon

around noon

My mum is famous for her packed lunches. I couldn't have got through school without them; the thought of her well-made sandwiches, slices of quiche and boxes of salad would sustain me through long morning classes. At my sister Lucy's hen night, a school friend of hers told us that Lucy used to regularly swap mum's homemade lunch for a pie from the tuck shop. This revelation completely floored me. I can't imagine a better lunch than one of my mum's salad sandwiches (beetroot and tomato packed separately, of course, to prevent the bread going soggy).

When I moved to London and started working in theatre, a packed lunch became essential. I was paid a pittance, and spending four pounds on an uninspiring sandwich was completely out of the question. I would batch cook on Sunday nights, making a soup, chilli, kedgeree, curry or frittata that would see me through busy weeks. On good days, I'd take a break when my colleagues did, find a patch of sun in the park or on the roof, and try to stretch lunch out for as long as possible. In reality, though – much more often than I'd like – I would end up dropping crumbs into my keyboard, trying to snatch ten minutes to eat while I caught up on emails or worked to a deadline. It is not my favourite way to have a meal.

As a freelancer, I've rediscovered the joy of taking time over lunch – testing a recipe for this book or a column, or enjoying another variation on eggs and avocado on toast. It's a luxury, I know, but I find a moment to put the laptop away, pull out a book and enjoy some time to myself.

A Loaf of Bread, Pepper, Vinegar & Oysters

'A loaf of bread,' the Walrus said,
'Is chiefly what we need:
Pepper and vinegar besides
Are very good indeed –
Now, if you're ready, Oysters dear,
We can begin to feed.'
Through the Looking-Glass, and What Alice Found There,
Lewis Carroll

I long assumed I would hate oysters because my mum does. I tried them for the first time when I was twenty-one, and quickly realized I had no idea what I was supposed to do. Should I bite them? Swallow them? How on earth would I get them off the shell? Given how confident I normally feel around food, it threw me. Friends have since confided that they felt (or still feel) much the same. Oysters can be intimidating but, my goodness, they are delicious.

In the years since those awkward first attempts, I have become an enthusiastic oyster-eater. I have enjoyed hundreds: at Happy Hour (£1/oyster) at the bar near where I used to live; standing on the wet floor in Billingsgate fish market at 4 a.m.; from a styrofoam tray at a Sunday market in Normandy; in my kitchen, shucked with the handle of a teaspoon. Most memorably, my friend Nic and I ate dozens, with the help of a couple of bottles of wine, in a Parisian bar one November evening. They came freshly shucked, with wedges of lemon pierced on a couple of forks, a basket of chewy brown bread and a dish of salty butter.

It's this way that I like them best: just a squeeze of lemon, a few drops of good vinegar (or this vinaigrette) and some bread and butter. Slice the oyster away from its shell, tip it back into your mouth, chew, swallow: bliss.

Oysters, Brown Bread and Vinaigrette

Serves 4 as a starter, 2 for lunch, 1 for a feast

1. First, make the bread. Crumble the yeast into the water and stir to dissolve. Add the golden syrup. Leave for 10 minutes until you can see bubbles on top.

2. Put the flours and salt into a mixing bowl. Add the water and yeast, and mix through with your hands. Once it is incorporated, cover with a damp tea towel and leave to rise for an hour.

3. After an hour, tip the dough out and knead for a couple of minutes. You should feel it getting smoother, but it won't ever be as smooth or springy as dough made with white flour. Return it to the bowl, cover with the tea towel and leave for another hour.

4. Grease the base and sides of the tin with oil, and lightly oil your work surface. Tip the dough out and knock some of the air out of it, then shape into a small rectangle: pull the corners into the centre, seal them together, then flip the dough over and smooth the sides. Transfer to the tin, seam-side down. Cover again, and allow to rise until it bounces back when pressed – on a warm day, this could take 30 minutes, but do budget for an hour.

5. Preheat the oven to 200°C/400°F/Gas 6. Before it goes in the oven, score the top of the loaf, straight down the centre. Bake for 45 minutes, turning it out of the tin after 30 minutes and returning to the oven to brown the sides and base.

6. To prepare the vinaigrette, cover the diced shallot with the cider vinegar and a grinding of pepper. Leave in the fridge for 30 minutes, then tip into a jar, add the oil and shake vigorously.

7. Spoon some vinaigrette over each oyster, and serve with slices of bread and butter.

INGREDIENTS

BREAD

20g/¾oz/heaping 1tbsp fresh yeast

400ml/14floz/1¾ cups body-temperature water

1tbsp golden syrup

260g/9¼oz strong white bread flour

260g/9¼oz strong wholemeal/whole wheat flour

1tsp salt

Flavourless oil for greasing the tin

VINAIGRETTE

1 small shallot, finely diced

2tbsp cider vinegar

1tbsp rapeseed/canola oil

Black pepper

AND

12 oysters, shucked*

Butter, for the bread

EQUIPMENT

900g/2lb loaf tin

Jar with a lid

Strong knife – ideally an oyster knife

* To shuck the oysters: use your knife to find the hinge, or the connecting point between the two shells, and twist it in until they open. Ensure that the deeper shell is on the bottom, so that the oyster is left with most of its liquor once opened. Slide a knife or fork under the oyster, cutting through the muscle that joins it to the shell.

Wild Garlic & Potato Salad

Piper could smell wild garlic and onions in a meadow and she came home with armfuls of the stuff, which we shredded up to make potatoes with wild onions and garlic for a change from potatoes without wild onions and garlic. There were days I would happily have traded the entire future of England for a single jar of mayonnaise but unfortunately the opportunity never arose.
How I Live Now, Meg Rosoff

Every April I hunt out wild garlic. The intoxicating smell wafting down country lanes and across fields is well worth following. In the dappled light, at the foot of so many trees in Europe, wild garlic grows – prolifically. Pulling up big handfuls to blitz into a pesto or add to soup or salads has become as much a marker of spring for me as the blooming daffodils or changing birdsong.

The first time I ate wild garlic was with a group of friends in Stroud, Gloucestershire. It grows along the canal there, next to horseradish and onions, and we collected all three in a backpack while on a walk one Saturday in May. Back home, on the deck in the sun, we stirred the vibrant green leaves through boiled new potatoes, still warm from the water. And, unlike the girls in *How I Live Now*, left to fend for themselves as a war rages around them, we had the luxury of adding a generous spoonful of mayonnaise.

Wild Garlic and Potato Salad

Serves 4 – as an accompaniment

1. To make the mayonnaise, put the egg yolk in the bowl. Whisk it for a minute or so until a few bubbles appear. Add 1tsp of the vinegar and whisk again until combined.

2. Dribble the oil in, one drop at a time, whisking continuously. Keep your eye on the oil, not on the bowl. The moment you take your eye off it, you'll accidentally pour a great big glug in – trust me.

3. Keep whisking until the mix resembles thick cream. Once it does, you can start being a little more generous with the oil, adding up to a teaspoon at a time. When you have about 2tbsp of oil left, add the remaining vinegar. Whisk well. The consistency should be thick and spreadable. If it is not quite there, add some of the extra oil.

4. Taste the mayonnaise and add mustard, pepper and salt to taste and set it aside.

5. Scrub the potatoes. If they're unevenly sized, cut some in half to even them out, otherwise leave them all whole. Tip into the saucepan, cover with water and bring to the boil. Cook until tender.

6. While the potatoes are boiling, finely slice the wild garlic leaves. Place in the serving bowl along with 2tbsp each of mayonnaise and crème fraîche. Drain the potatoes and, while they are still warm, toss them through the dressing. Season to taste with salt and a generous amount of pepper.

INGREDIENTS

MAYONNAISE
1 egg yolk
2tsp cider vinegar
150ml/5floz/⅔ cup good rapeseed/canola oil
¼tsp hot English mustard
Salt and pepper

SALAD
400g/14oz small new potatoes
50g/scant 2oz freshly picked wild garlic/ ramps*
2tbsp crème fraîche/sour cream
Salt and pepper

*Out of season, these are nearly impossible to lay your hands on. Instead, smash 3 garlic cloves and place them in the oil. Heat in a saucepan for 5 minutes, then allow to cool, strain the garlic out and make the mayonnaise with the garlicky oil. Add some diced spring onion/ scallion tops to the salad.

Crab & Avocado Salad

Arrayed on the Ladies' Day banquet table were yellow-green avocado
pear halves stuffed with crabmeat and mayonnaise…
The Bell Jar, Sylvia Plath

I grew up in the era of Nineties girl power: my family, my girls'
school and the Spice Girls ensured that I dreamed big. It never
really occurred to me that things were once different for women –
or still were in so many parts of the world. And so my first reading
of *The Bell Jar* as a teenager was eye-opening. I was suddenly
overwhelmed by the support of those around me, who had always
made me feel unstoppable.

My dad's neighbour, Rodger, was one of these people. My sister and
I spent countless evenings and holidays with him, sitting on the
floor of his living room with take-away pizza and Coke (things we
rarely had at home), watching *Crocodile Dundee* and mapping out
our futures. He passed away when I was at university, and so didn't
see us reach the milestones we had always talked about.

I think of Rodger often, and how much I wish he could see where
Lucy and I arc now. I think of all of us on my dad's back deck, Roger
with a beer in a cooler, telling the terrible joke he used to tell
about sand crabs and mud crabs. I won't go into it here – it's long
and without a worthy pay-off – but suffice it to say that our state,
Queensland, is home to both aforementioned types of crab. We had
family and friends who dedicated long hours (and innumerable
pots) to putting them on the table. I have spent memorable summer
afternoons working meticulously to extricate the sweet meat from
its scarlet casing. The experience has ensured that I am forever
grateful for every skerrick of crabmeat that arrives on my plate. I
like it with lemon or plain white bread, but the this rich salad is
something special too.

INGREDIENTS

MAYONNAISE

1 egg yolk

1tsp lemon juice

½tsp hot English mustard

Salt and pepper

150ml/5floz/⅔ cup olive oil

SALAD

1 large brown crab (about 1.5kg/3¼lb) or 200g/7oz white crabmeat, pre-cooked

1 spring onion/scallion, finely chopped

1tbsp flat-leaf parsley, finely chopped

1tbsp dill, finely chopped

2tbsp natural/plain yoghurt

Salt and pepper

AND

1 avocado

Generous squeeze of lemon

EQUIPMENT

Hammer or crab crackers

Crab and Avocado Salad

Serves 2 – as a generous starter

1. To make the mayonnaise, whisk the egg yolk until thick and creamy. Whisk in the lemon juice and mustard, along with a pinch of salt and pepper. Very slowly add the oil to the yolk, whisking continuously. Keep your eye on the oil, rather than the mayonnaise and don't let it pour out too quickly. You just want a couple of drops every few seconds. Once the mayonnaise has started to thicken, you can pour a little faster. Continue whisking until you have used most of the oil and the mayonnaise is very thick.

2. Place your crab upside down on a work surface. To get at the white meat, twist the legs and claws off the body. Crack their shells with a hammer and pull the meat out. The claws have a significant amount of meat in them, so make sure you crack each part – use a skewer to get into the crevices.

3. Combine the crabmeat with the finely chopped spring onion, parsley and dill, 1tbsp of the mayonnaise and the yoghurt. Taste for seasoning.

4. Cut the avocado in half and remove the stone/pit and the skin. Take a small slice off the curved side, so it will sit on the serving plate with a bit of stability. Spoon a generous amount of the crab mixture into the hole left by the stone. Squeeze some lemon over the top and serve (with a Martini).

A FINAL SUGGESTION: You don't need the brown meat for this recipe but, to access it, place the body of the crab belly-up. Place your thumbs under the base of the centre piece of the shell and push up. The body will come out. Discard the white gills and scoop out the brown meat. If you have any of the crab salad left, mix the brown meat in too, and add a little more mayonnaise. Serve it on toast with avocado. It was one of my favourite things we cobbled together from leftovers during the photo shoot.

Potato & Leek Soup
with Rye Bread

Strangely, one of Liesel's favourite distractions was Frau Holtzapfel.
The reading sessions included Wednesday now as well, and they'd
finished the water-abridged version of The Whistler *and were onto*
The Dream Carrier. *The old woman sometimes made tea or gave*
Liesel some soup that was infinitely better than Mama's. Less watery.
The Book Thief, Markus Zusak

I didn't read Zusak's wonderful book until adulthood. I have a
vivid memory of being reduced to tears by the ending, trapped
in a window seat on a flight to Italy. Perhaps inevitably for a story
narrated by Death and set in Germany during the Second World
War, it's devastating. When I closed the book, all I wanted was
comfort. And there's nothing more comforting than bread dipped
into hot soup.

When I'm short on time, money or motivation, I make soup, and I
make bread. This particular combination is one for cold days, when
you have bed socks on and a blanket wrapped around your knees.
This bread is lovely: chewy and full-flavoured, with a dark crust.
Liesel eats her mother's pea soup countless times in the book, and
rarely enjoys it. Here I wanted to make something simple from
vegetables that could be grown in the back garden.

The resulting soup couldn't be easier; the ingredients are cheap
and unfussy and can be added in flexible proportions. It's all
a matter of taste – a blender or liquidizer can yield a smooth,
consistent texture, while the masher or fork I've suggested will
leave you with identifiable pieces of both vegetables. Play around
with the other ingredients too; if you have caraway seeds and bay
leaves, that's great, but if you don't, try cumin or fennel seeds.
It's pretty forgiving.

INGREDIENTS

~~1tsp rapeseed/canola oil~~

2 medium brown onions, finely chopped

1 large leek, finely chopped

800g/28oz/1¾lb waxy potatoes, in 2cm/¾in dice

1tsp caraway seeds

2 bay leaves

Salt and pepper

1L/1¾ pints vegetable stock

Potato and Leek Soup

Serves 4

1. To make the soup, warm the oil over a medium heat and then fry the chopped onions and leek until soft and translucent. Add the diced potatoes, caraway seeds, bay leaves and seasoning. Pour in the stock.

2. Simmer the soup for 20 minutes before removing the bay leaves and attacking it with a potato masher. You could also blitz it in a blender, but I doubt even the Holtzapfels would have had one, and I like the not-quite-smooth texture.

3. Continue to simmer until it reaches the texture you want (it will thicken as the water evaporates), then serve with the bread.

Rye Bread

Makes 1 large loaf

1. Tip the flours and salt into a mixing bowl and combine with your hand. Put the fresh yeast in a measuring jug and pour in the water. Mix with a fork. Leave the yeast until it is foaming slightly on top.

2. Tip the yeast into the flours and combine with your hands. Add the caraway seeds, then knead for 10 minutes until smooth and elastic. Try not to add any more flour to the dough while you're kneading, but if it is unmanageably sticky, lightly flour your work surface and hands, then continue to knead. Return the dough to the mixing bowl, cover with a tea towel and leave in a warm, draught-free place to rise until doubled in size.

3. After an hour or so, tip the dough back out and flatten it. Reshape into a round loaf by stretching each edge out and then folding it back into the middle. Flip the loaf over, so that the seam is underneath. Keep pulling the sides underneath the ball with your palms to form a tight ball. Place the loaf on the lined baking tray. Sprinkle liberally with flour and place the tea towel back on top. Leave to prove until doubled in size. When the bread has risen most of the way, preheat the oven to 245°C/475°F/Gas 9.

4. When the dough is ready, transfer the tray to the oven. After 10 minutes, reduce the temperature to 200°C/400°F/Gas 6 and bake for a further 35 minutes. The loaf should be brown on top and should sound hollow when tapped on the bottom. Leave to cool for 10 minutes before slicing.

INGREDIENTS

400g/14oz/4 cups rye flour

400g/14oz/3 cups strong white bread flour

1tsp salt

20g/¾oz/heaping 1tbsp fresh yeast

560ml/19floz body-temperature water

1tbsp caraway seeds

Stuffed Eggplant

At eleven o'clock in the morning, Fermina Daza was in the kitchen preparing stuffed eggplant when she heard the shouts of the peons, the neighing of the horses, the shooting of guns into the air, then the resolute steps in the courtyard and the man's voice: 'It is better to arrive in time than to be invited.'

Love in the Time of Cholera, Gabriel García Márquez

Before I catered my first wedding, a couple of vegetarian friends sat me down and asked me to promise never to serve mushroom risotto as the vegetarian option. I love mushroom risotto, but I could see their point; I can imagine growing tired of eating it at every catered event. Stuffed vegetables (fruit, really, if you're as pedantic as I am) – tomatoes, peppers, aubergines – came up in that conversation too, but I was adamant that these aubergines were something special.

They'd have to be, to earn a place on Fermina Daza's table. She enters into marriage with one proviso: that her husband will never make her eat eggplant. This stuffed aubergine dish would, I hope, pleasantly surprise her. I learnt the technique on a cooking course in Istanbul; it started life as İmam bayıldı and, although the flavours are Turkish, they are endlessly adaptable – you can add herbs local to you, chilli if you like it, and spices that please you. This dish should be made in summer, when the smell of the tomatoes will be heady and the aubergine will be firm and plentiful. If you want to eat it in winter, tinned tomatoes provide a very worthy alternative.

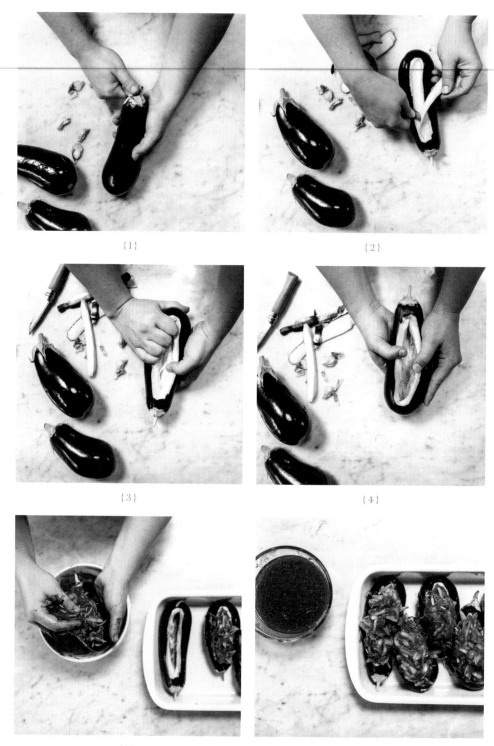

{1}

{2}

{3}

{4}

{5}

{6}

Stuffed Aubergine

Serves 6 – very generously

1. Place an aubergine on your work surface and see which way it naturally rests without rocking. Use a sharp knife to peel a strip, around 1cm/⅜in wide, down the length of the aubergine. Repeat this with two other strips at evenly distributed points around the aubergine; as they cook, this will allow the sauce to soak through the flesh. Return to the first strip and, holding the tip of your knife at a 45-degree angle, slice about 1cm/⅜in into the flesh of the aubergine. Turn the aubergine around and repeat this cut from the other edge of the peeled strip. You should end up with a long triangular piece of flesh to remove. Set this aside, then use your fingers to compact the central flesh of the aubergine against the walls. You will have created a sizeable cavity for stuffing. Repeat with the other aubergines.

2. Preheat the oven to 160°C/325°F/Gas 3. Sprinkle the salt over the sliced onions and squelch them together with your hands until they soften. Place the tomatoes into a sieve over a bowl to drain off any excess liquid. Reserve the juice.

3. Add the tomato flesh to the onions, along with the garlic, tomato purée, chopped herbs and pepper.

4. Push the stuffing into each aubergine, piling it up high. Squash them into an oven dish, arranging any leftover stuffing on top. Mix the tomato juice with the olive oil and tip this over the aubergines.

5. Cover with foil and bake for 80 minutes, until the aubergines are tender. Remove from the oven and allow to cool. Serve lukewarm, rather than piping hot.

INGREDIENTS

6 medium aubergines/ eggplants

1tbsp flaky sea salt/ Kosher salt

5 brown onions, finely sliced

1.5kg/3¼lb tomatoes, skinned, deseeded and chopped (alternatively, use 3x400g/14oz tins chopped tomatoes)

8 cloves garlic, finely crushed

5tbsp tomato purée/paste

5tbsp chopped parsley

8tbsp/½ cup chopped coriander/cilantro

2tbsp chopped chives

2tbsp dried guasca (optional)*

Generous grinding of black pepper

300ml/½ pint/1¼ cups olive oil

*Guasca is a herb that grows in Colombia, where Fermina Daza lives. You can order it online; it has a unique flavour that will really contribute to the dish. If you can't get your hands on it, don't worry too much. There are plenty of other herbs lending their flavour.

Love in the Time of Cholera, Gabriel García Márquez

Roasted Pheasant

*'When we have our roasted pheasant supper with our new oven,
do you think we could invite Doctor Spencer and Mrs Spencer to
eat it with us?'*
Danny, the Champion of the World, Roald Dahl

In terms of fictional dads, I don't think that William can be bettered.
Danny's marvellous father is a proper dream – a rule breaker, a
good cook, a storyteller.

William and Danny's late-night poaching adventures always thrilled
me. I had images of game shooting from the English films we would
watch on Sunday afternoons, but this was something different. This
wasn't men in tweed with guns hooked over their arm, this was
a father-and-son team with some well-soaked raisins and a box of
sleeping tablets. Their ingenuity and sheer nerve are rewarded in
the end – as they often are in Dahl's stories. Most of the birds they
poach escape, but they do end up with a couple of greedy pheasants
for the oven.

There is a sense of ceremony to roasting a bird; it is one of my
favourite things to do in the kitchen. The smell, the presentation
and the joy of everyone having exactly the piece they want (except
in my house, where legs are gold dust). Pheasants have a tendency
to be a bit dry, so roasting them in a covered dish allows them to
retain as much moisture as possible. Serve this pheasant with some
roasted new potatoes or mash. I can't conjure up a more perfect
Sunday lunch. It's worth buying an oven for.

Pot-Roasted Pheasant

Serves 4

1. Preheat your oven to 200ºC/400ºF/Gas 6. Melt the butter in the pot over a medium heat, season the pheasants with pepper and brown them well in the butter. Remove from the pan and set aside.

2. Add the bacon to the butter in the pan and fry it for a minute before adding the onion and quince. Stir occasionally, cooking until they are coloured, but not crisp. Add the sage and allspice berries, and then the wine. Stir it through, then pour in the stock. Depending on how salty your stock is, season with salt.

3. Place the pheasants back into the pot, side by side. Cover the pot with a lid and transfer to the oven for 20 minutes. Remove the lid and give the birds a final 10 minutes uncovered to get some colour.

4. Take the birds out of the pot and cover them with foil. While they rest, strain the rest of the contents of the pot. Retain the quince, bacon and onion for serving, and put the liquid back over a medium-high heat. Boil, stirring occasionally, until the liquid has reduced by at least half.

5. Serve the rested bird with the sauce, on top of the onion, quince and bacon.

INGREDIENTS

30g/1oz/¼ stick unsalted butter

2 oven-ready pheasants

Generous grinding of pepper

4 rashers/slices bacon, cut into thin strips

1 large brown onion, peeled and quartered

1 large quince (or 2 medium eating apples), peeled and cut into wedges

2tbsp chopped sage

5 allspice berries

300ml/½ pint/1¼ cups red wine

200ml/7floz chicken stock

Salt, to taste

EQUIPMENT

Ovenproof pot, with a lid, that will fit both pheasants

Sole Meunière

I closed my eyes and inhaled the rising perfume. Then I lifted a forkful of fish to my mouth, took a bite, and chewed slowly. The flesh of the sole was delicate, with a light but distinct taste of the ocean that blended marvellously with the browned butter. I chewed slowly and swallowed. It was a morsel of perfection.
My Life in France, Julia Child and Alex Prud'homme

I holidayed alone for the first time when I was twenty-six. I picked Paris; I had been before, loved the food and knew that I would find plenty to do. I booked a tiny studio in Montmartre and headed off early one Saturday in December. Travelling solo was a joy – I could do exactly what I wanted, eat when and where I fancied and explore the city on foot with music in my ears. On my final evening there, I picked up a copy of Julia Child's autobiography, *My Life in France*, and took it back to the apartment with the ingredients for her potage parmentier.

Unlike the other books featured in these pages, *My Life in France* is not a work of fiction. Julia Child didn't cook until she was in her mid-thirties, but she was a voracious and enthusiastic eater. She fell in love with France, its people and its cuisine when she moved there with her husband Paul in the 1950s. This meal is the first she had there, fresh off the boat.

I'm not sure if it's possible for one meal to change someone's life, but if there was such a meal, it sounds as if this was it. A whole sole, perfectly cooked, served with the simplest of sauces. It is food I love to eat; the type that honours the ingredients and lets them shine. After a lifetime of overcooked meat, soggy vegetables and food from tins, I understand completely why it had such an impact. This recipe is, of course, based on hers.

Sole Meunière
Serves 1

1. First, prepare the fish. Place it dark-side up and make a cut through the skin, perpendicular to the spine, very close to the tail. Peel the skin slowly towards the head, using the point of a knife to help you start. Once you have a piece of skin large enough to grip, rub some coarse salt between your fingers and hold the skin firmly with one hand. Place the heel of your other hand on the tail, and then pull back the skin, being particularly careful once you reach the head.

2. Flip the fish over, and repeat with the pale skin on the other side. Pat dry and set aside while you prepare the butter.

3. To clarify the butter, melt 45g/1½oz/3tbsp over a low heat. Skim off the white foam that floats to the top with a spoon. Pour the remaining butter into a bowl, stopping before you pour the white milk solids that will have collected at the bottom.

4. Put the flour into a shallow bowl, and coat both sides of the fish. Shake off any excess. Spoon the clarified butter into your widest frying pan and warm over a medium heat until very hot.

5. Place the fish in the pan. Cook for around 3 minutes, until golden brown, then carefully flip over using a fish slice. Cook for a further 3 minutes. When it is ready, the fish should spring back when you press it rather than flaking under your finger. Remove the fish to a plate and season with salt and pepper.

6. Wipe the pan out and add the remaining unclarified butter. Cook the butter until it starts to brown, keeping a careful eye on it. Once the butter is an almond colour, pour it over the fish. Sprinkle with parsley and serve immediately with a slice of lemon.

INGREDIENTS

1 small Dover sole, gutted (if you don't have access to Dover sole, substitute other types of sole or flounder)

55g/2oz/½ stick unsalted butter

30g/1oz/3⅔tbsp flour

Salt and pepper

A handful of parsley leaves, finely chopped

A wedge of lemon

EQUIPMENT

Fish slice/fish spatula

61

My Life in France, Julia Child and Alex Prud'homme

Thin Pastry with Spiced Beef

... the women begin to meet up for lunch in Kilburn Park, often with the Niece-of-Shame, the three of them squeezed on to a generous bench where Alsana presses a thermos of P. G. Tips into Clara's hand, without milk, with lemon. Unwraps several layers of cling-film to reveal today's particular delight: savoury dough-like balls, crumbly Indian sweets shot through with the colours of the kaleidoscope, thin pastry with spiced beef inside, salad with onion...
White Teeth, Zadie Smith

I had formed a detailed image of London long before I moved here. My parents' stories about their time in the city, discovering the parks, theatres and the restaurants, helped, then the books I loved – full of scenes at Paddington Station, Kensington Gardens and on the streets of Bermondsey – filled in the rest of the picture.

For years after I arrived, I would suddenly realize that I was standing somewhere that one of my favourite characters had been: that I was walking through central London with Mrs Dalloway, or sitting in the park where Peter and the Lost Boys find themselves before their journey to Neverland. I had an excited jolt re-reading *White Teeth* earlier this year, when I discovered that these beef pastries (samosas in my imagining) are eaten exactly where I used to have lunch with my colleagues in Kilburn every day. I have always loved the book, but I felt, all of a sudden, as if I really recognized these characters.

When I first moved to London, I lived above an Indian restaurant. I have vivid memories of their samosas – nothing like the ones wrapped in robust pastry that I used to serve in my waitressing job, but tiny ones, wrapped in crisp, wafer-thin pastry. It's the type of pastry that is better to buy than to make, thinner than I could ever roll by hand. I use completely inauthentic filo pastry here, but I think it works a treat.

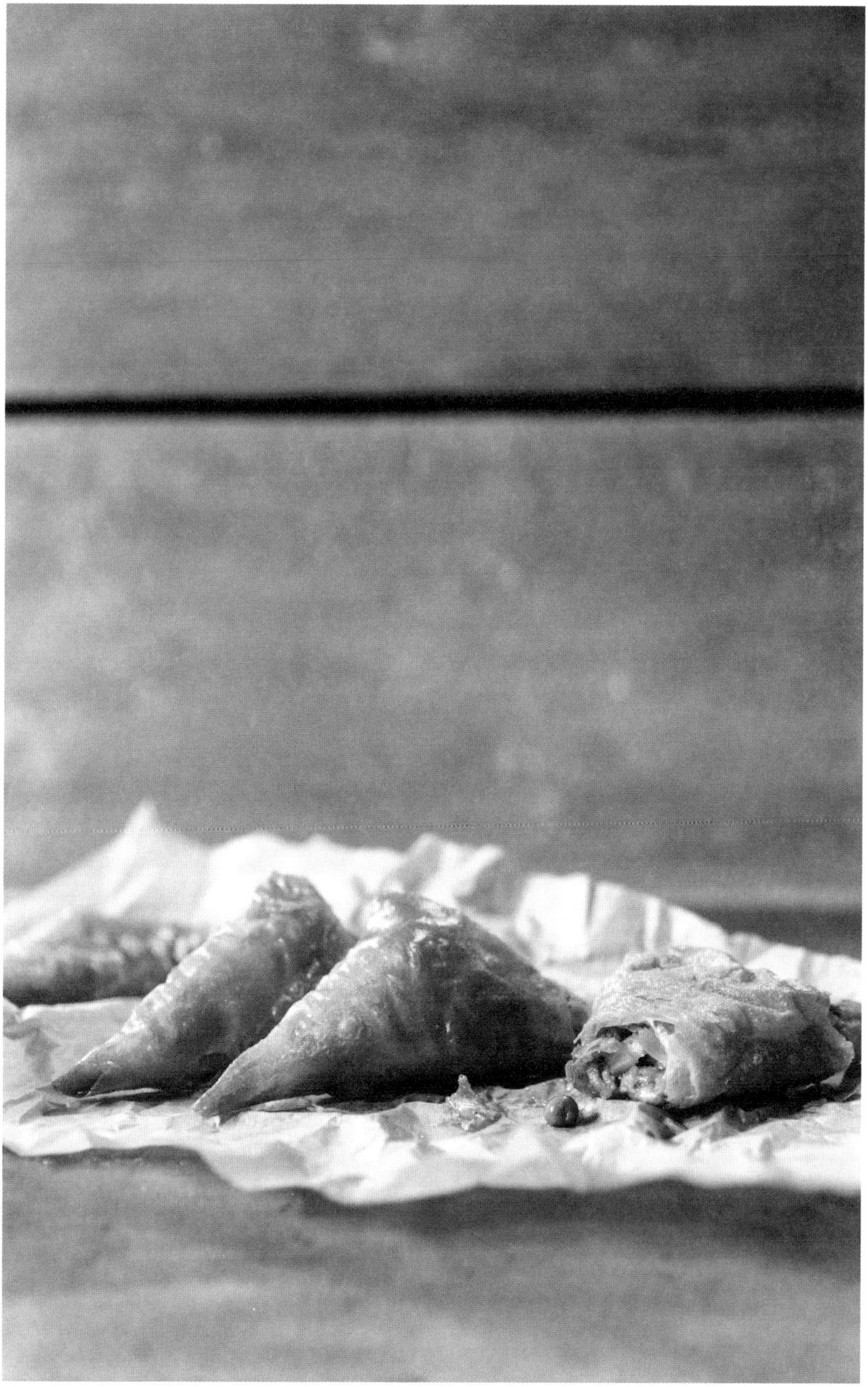

Beef Samosas
Makes around 30

INGREDIENTS

1tbsp ghee, or vegetable oil

2 brown onions, finely chopped

2 cloves garlic, finely chopped

2tsp ground cumin

1tsp ground coriander

1tsp ground turmeric

400g/14oz beef mince/ground beef

2 medium sized potatoes, peeled, finely diced

60g/2oz/scant ½ cup frozen peas

1tsp flaky sea salt/Kosher salt

10 sheets filo/phyllo pastry

2L/3½ pints/8½ cups vegetable oil

1. Warm the ghee in a frying pan over a medium heat until bubbling. Add the chopped onions and cook until soft and translucent. Add the chopped garlic, then fry for another minute or so, stirring constantly. Add the spices and stir well to coat the onions.

2. Add the mince and cook until just browned; it will cook through as the rest of the filling cooks. Add the diced potato and cook until tender. Finally, add the peas and warm through for another minute. Taste the filling, and season with a little salt. Set the samosa filling aside to cool completely.

3. Slice each piece of filo lengthways into thirds. Place 1tbsp filling at the base of each strip and fold the bottom edge over it diagonally to make a small triangle. Continue folding up, over and over, until you reach the end of the length of pastry. Dampen the edge of the filo with a bit of water to seal it.

4. Heat the oil to 180°C/350°F in a deep-sided pan. Fry the samosas a handful at a time, moving them around occasionally to ensure they don't stick to each other.

5. Once the samosas are golden brown, remove them with a slotted spoon and drain on some kitchen paper. Serve with yoghurt or mint chutney.

Gin Martini &
Chicken Sandwich

Sickler's Table for 2
1 x chicken sandwich
1 x glass of milk
1 x snails
1 x frogs' legs
1 x green salad
4 x gin martini
Franny and Zooey, J. D. Salinger*

My sister and I would have to be on the edge of death before Mum would let us stay home from school. But once we really were sick, Mum was the best nurse imaginable. The sofa would be lined with brushed flannelette sheets and pillows, a stack of books would appear and *The Princess Bride* would be put into the VHS player. We'd even be given a small bell to ring in case of emergencies. At lunchtime, we would have white bread chicken sandwiches.

I remember these sandwiches so well. They're the plainest of plain; the white of the chicken breast matching the white of the supermarket bread. They're the sandwiches I will one day make for my children, when they are curled up on the couch feeling poorly.

I wish that Franny was eating her sandwich on the sofa at home, instead of enduring an awkward lunch with her boring boyfriend and crying in the bathroom. But she pushes on, through the martinis, and the stilted conversation and the not feeling at all like herself. The chicken sandwich is inspired ordering, even if she does end up leaving it untouched. It's what I'd want on my plate after two martinis and an anxiety attack; it's certainly much better on the stomach (and the mind) than Lane's snails and frogs' legs.

*This is not a direct quote from the book. To find out why, please refer to *My Salinger Year* by Joanna Rakoff

INGREDIENTS

~~Ice cubes~~

10ml/2tsp dry vermouth

50ml/scant 2floz/scant ¼ cup gin (I particularly love Sipsmith, Yorkshire and Hendricks, but have never been known to turn my nose up at a martini made from other gins)

Single green olive

EQUIPMENT

Martini glass

Mixing glass (a pint glass works well) or cocktail shaker

Gin Martini

Serves 1

1. Chill your martini glass by filling it with lots of ice and a little water. Set aside.

2. Tip a large handful of ice cubes into your mixing glass or cocktail shaker. Add the vermouth and stir until the ice is coated.

3. Add the gin and stir again for about 10 seconds, being careful not to chip the ice (or you'll end up with a watered-down martini).

4. Empty the martini glass and give it a very quick wipe to dry it. Strain the martini into it. Add an olive and serve immediately.

A NOTE: Franny tells us that she is glad her martini is not 20:1; that she hates it 'when they're absolutely all gin'. I respectfully disagree. I love it when a martini has barely a whisper of vermouth in it – my ideal is when the vermouth just touches the ice and is then poured away. If this is how you like it too, then do tip the excess vermouth away after the second step.

INGREDIENTS

CHICKEN

1 whole chicken (around 2kg/4.5lb)

2 carrots, unpeeled

2 brown onions, peeled

2 sticks celery

5 cloves garlic, peeled

Thumb-sized piece of ginger

Stalks of a bunch of parsley

5 black peppercorns

2L/3½ pints/8½ cups water

SANDWICH

Good white bread

Butter for spreading

Chicken Sandwich

Makes 1 sandwich – and enough leftover chicken and soup to last you through a cold

1. Put the chicken into a large saucepan. Roughly chop the vegetables, garlic and ginger and add to the pan. Add the parsley stalks and peppercorns, then pour over the water.

2. Place over a medium heat and bring to the boil. Reduce to a slow simmer and cook without a lid for an hour and a half, topping the water up slightly if it dips below the top of the chicken. The smell in your kitchen at this point may be enough to cure your cold there and then.

3. Turn off the heat. Once cool enough to handle, remove the chicken to a dish or bowl and set it aside for a moment.

4. Peel the chicken flesh from the bones and shred. Discard the skin, which will be flabby.

5. Make your sandwich with good white bread, a scrape of butter and some of the shredded white meat. If you want to go for proper sick-day fare, slice the crusts off too, and cut into quarters. Serve with a cup of strong, milky tea. Or the martini, if it will help.

ANOTHER NOTE: Strain the broth into a container you can store in the fridge or freezer. When you fancy some restorative chicken soup, bring it back to boiling point and then ladle over fresh vegetables and pieces of chicken.

Toad-in-the-Hole

Nigel got thrown out of school dinners today for swearing at the toad-in-the-hole, he said it was 'all bleeding hole and no toad'.
The Secret Diary of Adrian Mole, Aged 13¾, Sue Townsend

Like many other teenagers, my exposure to Adrian Mole at the impressionable age of twelve turned me into a prolific diary writer. At least for a couple of weeks at a time. My teenage attempts all run in the same sorry way: starting every six months or so with long rambling entries, and then ending mere weeks later with an admission that my life isn't actually interesting enough to warrant a diary.

That's nonsense, of course, but my teenage self didn't know it. All my thoughts about the boy from the Saturday-night dance, or the girl who unpegged my tent during school camp, or how much I loathed getting changed in front of everyone after PE, now read as the perfect teenage diary. The brilliance of Adrian Mole is in the pettiness, the mundane, the everyday. It's the toad-in-the-hole and the Sunday roast, the things we all share.

I do hope, however, that you don't share Nigel's frustration with this dish. I promise that this one has plenty of toad, just the right amount of hole, and red onion gravy to boot. Do feel free to leave the herbs out if you're making it for little ones – my nannying charges requested this weekly 'without the green stuff'. It's best served as soon as it comes out of the oven, as it starts to deflate after it has sat around for a little while. That said, any leftovers are pretty great for breakfast the next day, with a drizzle of maple syrup.

Toad-in-the-Hole with Onion Gravy

Serves 4

1. Preheat the oven to 200°C/400°F/Gas 6. Tip the flour into a bowl, make a well in the centre, crack in the eggs and whisk. Add the salt and then whisk in the milk until you have a smooth, runny batter. Set aside for 15 minutes, while you cook the sausages.

2. Add the fats to a pan, heat until bubbling and fry the sausages over a medium heat until they are cooked. Allow them to blacken and blister in places.

3. Scatter the herbs over the sausages, stalks and all. Pour the batter into the smoking hot pan, around the cooked sausages. It may spit a bit, so protect your arms with a tea towel. Put the tin straight into the hot oven. Bake for 25–30 minutes, pulling it out when the batter is risen, crisp and browned it patches.

4. While the toad-in-the-hole is in the oven, make the gravy. Melt the butter in the saucepan and, once it is bubbling, add the onions. Cook for 10 minutes over a medium heat until softened.

5. Add the sugar, stirring until it has dissolved into the butter. Pour in the Worcestershire sauce, and stir through. Sprinkle in the flour and stir to coat the onion. Pour in about 100ml/3⅓floz of the stock and whisk until the sauce surrounding the onions is smooth. Add the rest of the liquid and bring to the boil, stirring with the wooden spoon until thick. Remove from the heat and warm again when you're ready to serve.

6. Remove the toad-in-the-hole from the oven and serve immediately. Make sure that everyone has plenty of crispy bits from the sides of the dish and a generous slug of the gravy.

INGREDIENTS

HOLE

120g/4¼oz/scant 1 cup plain/all-purpose flour

3 eggs

Pinch of salt

300ml/½ pint/1¼ cups milk

TOAD

30g/1oz/2tbsp butter

1tbsp flavourless oil (or beef dripping if you have some)

8 fat sausages

5 stalks rosemary (optional)

10 sprigs thyme (optional)

GRAVY

15ml/½oz/1tbsp butter (or oil, if you prefer)

3 small red onions, sliced into semicircles

1tsp brown sugar

2tsp Worcestershire sauce

1tbsp plain/all-purpose flour

500ml/17floz/generous 2 cups beef stock

Salt and pepper

EQUIPMENT

High-sided roasting tin, ideally one that can also sit on your hob

Tongs

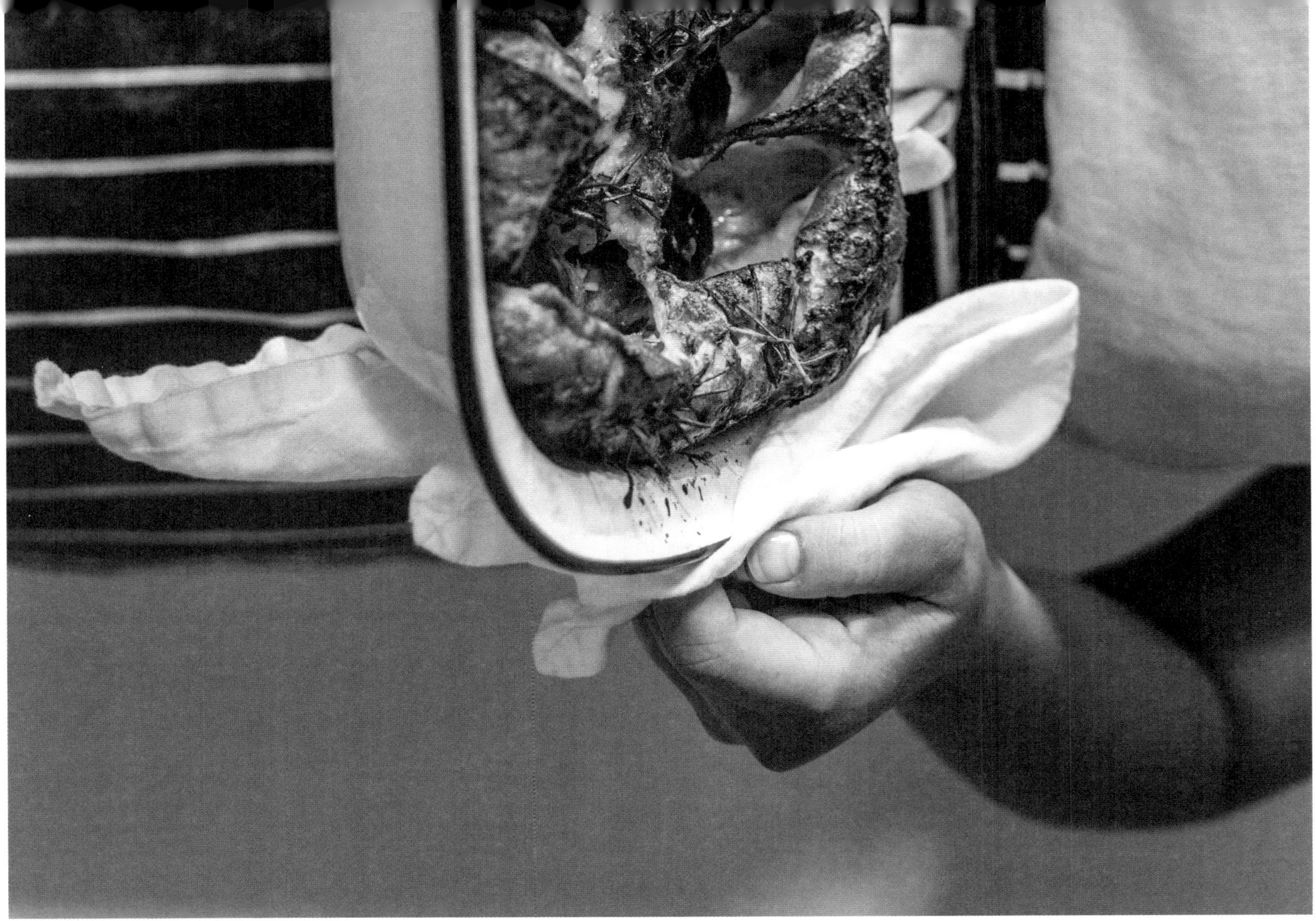

A Farmhouse Lunch for Five

'Now you'll have to take what we've got. I'm busy today and haven't had time for cooking. You can have a bit of homemade meat-pie, or a slice or two of ham and tongue, or hard-boiled eggs and salad. Bless you, you look as pleased as Punch! I'll put the lot on the table for you and you can help yourselves! Will that do? There's no vegetables though. You'll have to make do with pickled cabbage and my own pickled onions and beetroot in vinegar.'
Five on a Hike Together, Enid Blyton

As a child, I was often mistaken for a boy. I had very short hair and wore T-shirts and shorts that I could run around in. Standing next to my cherubic, ringleted sister who insisted on wearing 'swirly skirts', I can understand it. When I discovered Enid Blyton's George, a girl who loved being mistaken for one of the boys, I was thrilled.

Nowadays, I am more of an Anne than a George. My initial disdain for the girl who stayed home to make beds out of heather and prepare the supper while the others were off exploring has turned into admiration at what she managed to achieve with so little. Her housekeeping and cooking are second to none. She is forever assembling the sort of lunches that keep me coming back to Enid Blyton for inspiration – potted fish sandwiches, fresh fruit, bottles of ginger beer and thick slices of sticky cake.

This luncheon comes after a long autumnal walk on the Yorkshire moors and a sleepless night in a barn for Anne and Dick. After a day of cold food from their backpacks, they are welcomed into a farmhouse and sit down to a proper lunch. Though the meat pie in the story is probably a cold pork one, lifted from the sideboard alongside jars of pickles, I imagine this warming beef and ale version might have been a little more appealing.

Steak and Ale Pie

Serves 5

1. Warm 1tbsp of the oil in a saucepan. Brown the beef in batches, then remove to a bowl. Pour in the second tablespoon of oil, then tip in the diced carrots and onion.

2. Once softened, add the meat back in along with the flour, and stir until all ingredients are coated. Cook for 2 minutes, stirring constantly, then add the ale and beef stock. Tie the herbs together with string and drop them in. Season the pot generously with black pepper. Bring to the boil, then cover the pan, reduce to a very slow simmer and cook for 2 hours.

3. While the beef is cooking, place the frying pan over a medium heat and fry the bacon until golden. Remove from the pan, then melt the butter and fry the mushrooms. Set aside.

4. To make the pastry, rub the cold butter into the flour until it resembles breadcrumbs. Add a couple of drops of ice cold water, bringing the dough together with your hands. As soon as it forms a cohesive dough, wrap in plastic wrap and refrigerate for half an hour.

5. When the beef is cooked, remove the herbs, season with salt and combine with the mushrooms and bacon. Place in the fridge to cool.

6. Take the pastry out of the fridge and roll around two-thirds of it out into a large circle. If it's a warm day, your pastry will be sticky, so roll it out between two sheets of greaseproof paper. Use it to line the pie dish, patching up any holes or cracks, and leaving the pastry to overhang the edges. Return to the fridge. Preheat the oven to 200°C/400°F/Gas 6 and put in the baking tray to heat up.

7. Once the beef is cool, spoon it into the pastry-lined dish. Roll out the remaining pastry. Brush the underside with a bit of water, and the rim of the pie dish with some beaten egg, and put the pastry lid on, damp-side down. The water

INGREDIENTS

FILLING

2tbsp vegetable oil

600g/1lb 5oz braising steak, in 2cm/¾in cubes

2 large carrots, diced

1 large onion, diced

3tbsp plain/all-purpose flour

250ml/8½floz/generous 1 cup ale (Yorkshire, if you can get it)

300ml/½ pint/1¼ cups beef stock

3 bay leaves

10 sprigs thyme

Plenty of cracked black pepper

150g/5oz streaky bacon, diced

30g/1oz/2tbsp butter

150g chestnut/cremini mushrooms, sliced into quarters

2tsp flaky sea salt/Kosher salt

PASTRY

200g/7oz/1¾ sticks chilled butter, cubed

500g/1lb 2oz/3¾ cups plain/all-purpose flour

1 egg, beaten

EQUIPMENT

String

Pie dish (mine is 22cm/8¾in wide)

will turn into steam and help keep the lid from soaking up the gravy.

8. Trim the excess pastry from the pie, and press the edges to ensure they are sealed. Brush the top with more beaten egg, and use any offcuts to make some decorations. Make a couple of holes in the lid of the pie and place it on the baking tray in the oven. Bake for 50 minutes to an hour, until browned on top. Eat immediately.

Pickled Beetroot
Makes enough to fill a 500ml/17floz jar

INGREDIENTS
500g/1lb 2oz fresh beetroot/beets
Drizzle of olive oil
Salt and pepper
150ml/5floz/⅔ cup cider vinegar
100g/3½oz/½ cup caster/superfine sugar
5 cloves
1 star anise

EQUIPMENT
500ml/17floz sterilized jar

1. Preheat the oven to 190°C/375°F/Gas 5. Trim the beetroot of their stalks and rub them clean. Season each with olive oil, salt and pepper, and wrap individually in foil. Place each parcel on the baking tray, and transfer to the oven for an hour.

2. Allow the beetroot to cool for 15 minutes before you open the parcels. While you're waiting, put the vinegar, sugar and spices in the saucepan. Bring to a simmer over a low heat, swirling the pan every now and then to ensure the sugar dissolves.

3. Trim the beetroot tops and tails, and peel the skins – they should come away easily. Slice into halves or quarters, trying to keep the pieces relatively similar in size. Place all the pieces in the sterilized jar and pour the hot vinegar mixture over the top. You can leave it in the fridge for up to a month, or you can start eating it immediately.

Pickled Onions

Makes enough to fill 1 litre/quart jar

1. Put the shallots in a mixing bowl, and cover with boiling water. Once the water is cool enough to put your hand into, pull the shallots out, top and tail them, and peel off the skins. Wear plastic gloves here if you like – the onion skins can stain your nails.

2. Put the trimmed shallots into a bowl and add the salt. Toss together, then cover and leave to sit in the fridge overnight.

3. Rinse the shallots under running water for 5 minutes; you need to rinse off the salt, so don't do this for too short a time. Pat dry, then transfer to the sterilized jar.

4. Bring the vinegar, honey, and peppercorns to a simmer in the saucepan. Remove from the heat, add the garlic cloves and chilli, then pour the hot vinegar over the shallots. If there are any air pockets, give it a shake. Ensure that the shallots are covered – if not, add some more vinegar.

5. Leave the jar in a cool, dark place for 6 weeks. Once opened, store in the fridge and use within a month.

INGREDIENTS

600g/1lb 5oz shallots or very small brown onions
100g/3½oz/½ cup rock salt
300ml/½ pint/1¼ cups cider vinegar
150g/5oz/½ cup honey
10 peppercorns
5 cloves garlic, peeled
1 small red chilli

EQUIPMENT

1L/1 quart sterilized jar

after noon

after noon (tea)

Afternoon tea has always felt like a treat. Unlike breakfast (compulsory in our house), lunch (always scheduled into school and work days) or dinner (again, compulsory), afternoon tea slots in like a very welcome add-on. I remember tea after school with particular affection. After form room, we'd loosen our ties and race up to the shops for a parcel of hot chips with chicken salt, before running back for choir rehearsal.

As an adult, teatime is something so few of us really sit down to enjoy. A tea break at work leaves barely enough time for the kettle to boil and a cup of tea to brew. But on days when there is time – long, lazy Saturdays spent with friends from out of town, birthday parties in the park – afternoon tea is a joy. Pots of well-brewed tea, good company and a bit of something sweet – there is little better.

When I turned twenty-three, my friend Lydia and I hosted a joint birthday party picnic. It remains, to this day, one of the best birthdays either of us has ever had. We spent the day before preparing an impossibly large spread. I'd sprained my ankle that week, falling down a circular flight of stairs in the Tube (I was carrying all our fizzy wine – the bottles, mercifully, survived the fall), and so we did the prep in my tiny galley kitchen, with my foot propped up as I creamed butter and sugar and rolled out pastry.

The next day, we collected picnic blankets, baskets and straw hats, and laid out our food in the park a mile or so up the road. We were there all afternoon, greeting waves of friends from our prime position under a large tree. The sun shone all day. The drinks were plentiful. The food was glorious. That sunny May day in 2010 has taken on an almost mythical quality in our memories. It has become the bar by which all other afternoon teas have been measured. In this light, I have included only my very favourite things in this chapter – the ones I would want on that picnic blanket if we could ever re-create that day.

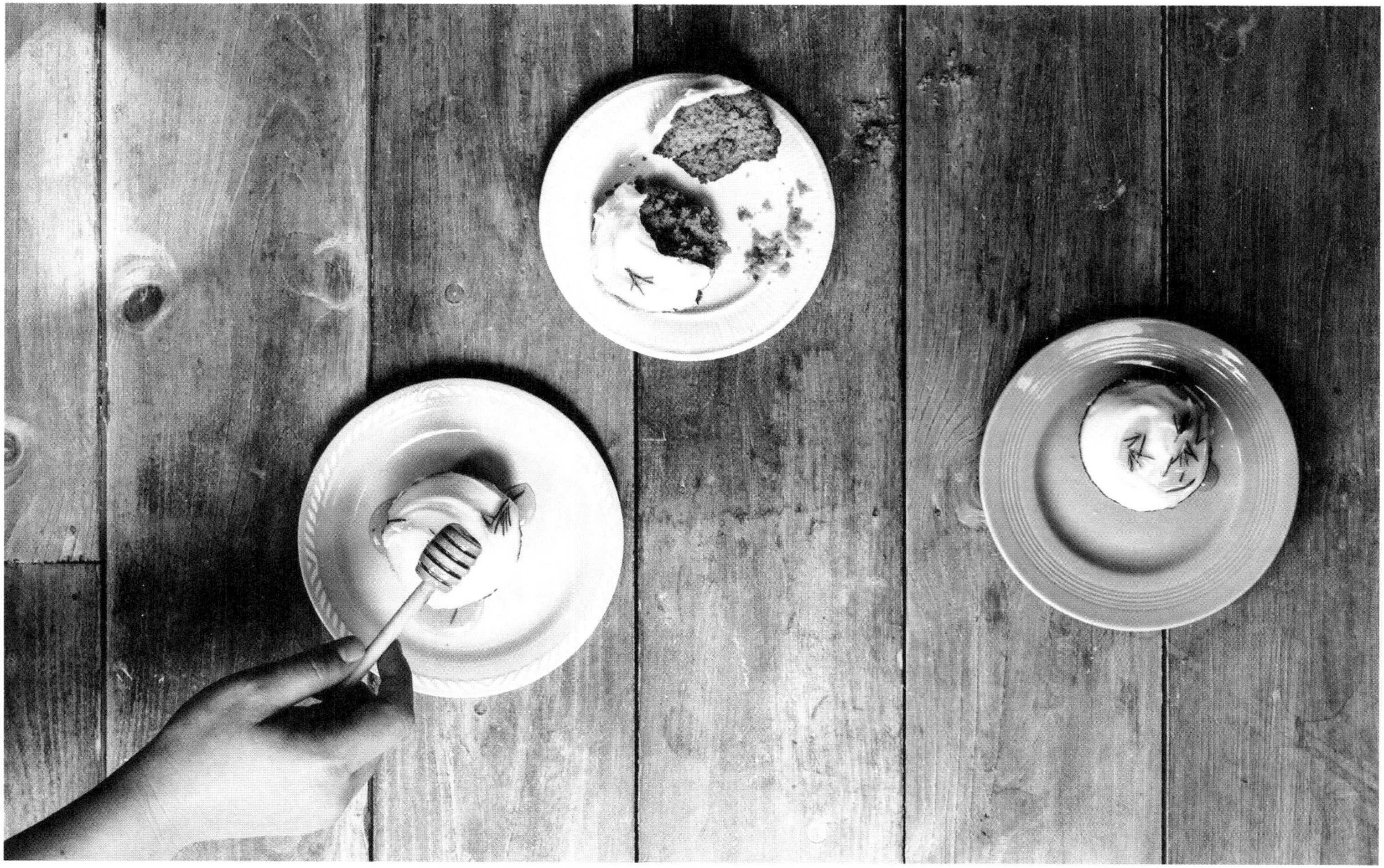

Hunny & Rosemary Cakes

'That's funny,' he thought. 'I know I had a jar of honey there. A full jar,
full of honey right up to the top, and it had HUNNY written on it, so
that I should know it was honey.'
Winnie-the-Pooh, A. A. Milne

I grew up with Winnie-the-Pooh. As well as beautiful hardback
editions of *Winnie-the-Pooh* and *The House at Pooh Corner*, and a
Hundred Acre Wood height chart on the wardrobe door, we had
cassette tapes of all the books, which we listened to countless times.

Years later, when I went to hear Alan Bennett speak about his latest
play, I spent the whole evening spellbound. His voice sent me
straight back to the back seat of our car en route to Canberra, to the
long drive filled with stories about Pooh, Piglet, Eeyore and Rabbit,
to a childhood spent playing pooh-sticks with my dad and sister,
and sneaking spoonfuls of honey straight out of the jar. Until that
moment, I hadn't made the connection; I couldn't quite believe I
was sitting in the same room as the man who'd read to me all those
years before.

I have served these honey cakes at birthdays, weddings and supper
clubs, sold them at cafés and made countless batches for friends.
Their distinctive dark yellow sponge leads many people to think
they're full of ginger. It wouldn't be a bad addition, but I love them
as they are. The recipe is originally from Tessa Kiros's *Apples for
Jam*, one of the first recipe books I had in London, and they're one
of the first things I baked from it. I've made a few changes over the
years, but their rich honey and herb flavour hasn't altered. They're
just the things I would want to make with Pooh's pot of 'hunny'.

Honey and Rosemary Cakes
Makes 10

1. Preheat the oven to 180°C/350°F/Gas 4 and grease the muffin tins with a little of the butter. Place the rest of the butter, along with the sugar, honey and 1tbsp water, into the saucepan. Heat gently, stirring only once, until the butter is melted and the sugar dissolved. It will look like it's separated, but don't stress, this is normal. Set aside to cool.

2. Sift the flour, baking powder and cinnamon together, and add the finely chopped rosemary.

3. When the honey mixture is cool, stir in the beaten eggs. Add to the dry ingredients and stir until the mixture is smooth.

4. Divide the mixture between the well-greased tins, making sure they are all around two-thirds full. Bake for around 25 minutes, until a skewer inserted in the centre comes out clean. Cool for 5 minutes in the tins, then turn out and transfer to a wire rack.

5. Whisk the cream cheese until light and airy. Sift the icing sugar and beat it into the cheese, to create a smooth and creamy icing that holds its shape.

6. When the cakes are completely cold, ice them using a palette knife to drop the icing onto the cake, then round it off at the edges.

7. To make the rosemary honey drizzle, put the honey in a saucepan with the rosemary leaves and bring to the boil. As soon as the honey starts bubbling, turn off the heat and allow the flavours to infuse for at least 20 minutes. Pour the mixture into a jar – it will keep for a good few weeks, and tastes wonderful on roasted carrots as well as cakes.

8. To serve, warm the rosemary honey in the saucepan and spoon over an iced cake. Eat immediately.

INGREDIENTS

CAKES
170g/6oz/1½ sticks butter
115g/4oz/heaping ½ cup dark brown sugar
175g/6oz/⅔ cup honey
200g/7oz/1½ cups plain/all-purpose flour
1½tsp baking powder
½tsp ground cinnamon
1tbsp finely chopped rosemary leaves
2 eggs, beaten

ICING
100g/3½oz/scant ½ cup cream cheese
300g/10½oz/heaping 2 cups icing/confectioners' sugar

DRIZZLE
150g/5½oz/heaping ½ cup honey
2 sprigs rosemary

EQUIPMENT
Deep 12-cup muffin tray
Palette knife

Bread, Butter & Honey

I shouldn't think even millionaires could eat anything nicer than new bread and real butter and honey for tea.
I Capture the Castle, Dodie Smith

Lately, I have been wrestling with the concept of 'home'. It is an intangible idea, one that speaks of family and familiarity so much more than mere bricks and mortar. I have called so many places home over the years. The tin-roofed houses I grew up in in Queensland, with the ever-present cacophony of birdsong in the trees. The renovated church we later moved into with Dad and my stepmother Cheryl, with the kitchen at its heart. A flat above a bank in Whitechapel, with an electric blue carpet. A magnolia-painted living room in Hackney, lined with shelves stacked high with books. A bedroom on the top floor of another family's home. A house built of Cotswold stone in a Gloucestershire village, full of people who have welcomed me into their lives.

The strange reality of life as an immigrant is that home will always be more than one place – the one left behind, and the new one that must be built. I am destined to be forever homesick, but for a place that no longer truly exists: a memory of the Brisbane that all my friends lived in, where we had infinite time and freedom and sunshine. When I return to those streets now, that place I so long for has disappeared. In leaving, and moving on, we have scattered it irretrievably across the world. It lies now in new cities and on new streets, impossible to rebuild into what it was.

There's a moment in *Little Women* that I have always found to have resonance. Louisa May Alcott/Jo March/Winona Ryder observes that 'some books are so familiar that reading them is like being home again'. I know that feeling precisely; on my shelf, that book is *I Capture the Castle*.

However far from home, family or comfort, however uncertain about where the next place I can call home might be, I am immediately reassured when I open it. The Mortmain family is so well known to me that they feel like old friends. It is one of the books I read every year, despite the ever-increasing pile of unread new ones that sits by my bed. It is, in fact, the literary equivalent of making bread and butter, two things I find equally soothing, predictable and familiar. There is an old wives' tale that tells you to spread your cat's feet with butter when moving home, to ensure the cat feels comfortable in the new place. It would work for me. Bread and butter, in my most homesick moments, ground me and remind me that I have made my own home.

INGREDIENTS

BREAD

450g/1lb strong white
bread flour

7g/1½tsp salt

7g/¼oz/2½tsp fast-action
yeast

340ml/11⅓floz body-
temperature water

BUTTER

600ml/1 pint/scant
3 cups double/heavy
cream

1tsp flaky sea salt/Kosher
salt

TO SERVE

Honey

EQUIPMENT

Electric hand whisk or
mixer (you can make
butter by hand, but it will
take an age)

Fine cotton, for
squeezing the butter

Bread, Butter and Honey

Makes 1 large loaf and plenty of butter

1. Place the flour in a large bowl. Add the salt on one side and yeast on the other.

2. Add the water to the dry ingredients. It should be about body temperature – if you put your finger in and can't tell whether it's hot or cold, then it's just right. Mix with your hands until everything comes together in a ball. Cover with a wet tea towel and leave in a warm place for 30 minutes until it has doubled in size.

3. Turn the dough out onto a lightly floured surface and knead until it is no longer sticky and bounces back quickly when prodded. You can knead by stretching, slapping or folding the dough – whatever works for you.

4. Shape into a ball by pinching one side of the dough, stretching it out and folding it across the rest of the dough. Continue to work your way around the dough, repeating this four times. Flip over and bring your hands together underneath, twisting as you do so. Keep twisting until the dough is a firm ball.

5. Sprinkle a baking tray liberally with flour and place the dough on it to prove for an hour. It should have doubled in size and will spring back when touched. Around 20 minutes before the dough is ready, preheat the oven to 210°C/410°F/Gas 6½.

6. Score the dough a couple of times with a serrated knife and transfer to the oven on a low shelf for around 40 minutes, until the bread is a deep golden brown and sounds hollow when tapped on its underside.

7. While the bread is baking, you can make the butter. Pour the cream into a mixing bowl and start to whisk it. It's going to take a little while – you need to take it beyond stiffly whipped until it starts separating. Eventually you'll start seeing little yellow flecks swimming in a creamy liquid.* Stop whisking at this point.

8. Reach your hand in and, using it as a sieve-of-sorts, remove the yellow solid pieces from the liquid and place them in a sieve over a bowl. Once you have collected them all, sprinkle with salt (you may like more or less, depending on your taste) and squidge the whole lot together. Squeeze in a piece of cotton to get rid of any excess buttermilk. Voila! You have butter. Place in the fridge to harden a little.

9. Serve a thick slice of the bread with your butter and the nicest honey you can find.

* The liquid left over from the butter is buttermilk – keep this in a bottle in the fridge and use within a couple of days. It's very versatile; you can use it to make cakes, soda bread or buttermilk pancakes.

Currant Buns

Then old Mrs Rabbit took a basket and her umbrella, and went through the wood to the baker's. She bought a loaf of brown bread and five currant buns.
The Tale of Peter Rabbit, Beatrix Potter

Afternoon rain in Australia is often intense – it's the kind that will drench you through to your bones in seconds. If I was caught in a deluge on my walk home from school, my backpack full of textbooks and sports kit, I could easily have reached for the umbrella underneath it all. In reality I almost never did. Instead, I took my shoes off, turned my face up towards the clouds and belted out 'Singin' in the Rain' at the top of my lungs. I jumped in puddles, and danced around, and sometimes even took the long way home. And when I finally walked through the front door, I had a hot shower, a toasted fruit bun spread generously with butter, and a cup of tea.

I still love being outside when it rains – especially when there's the promise of tea, buns and a bath at the end of it. These are my favourites: dark, moist and full of flavour. The type of thing I imagine Peter would want after a tiring day stealing vegetables in Mr McGregor's garden.

The recipe below makes wonderful hot cross buns each Easter, with a line of flour and water paste piped down the centre, but I love them unadorned through the rest of the year too. They're ones I've developed from a Dan Lepard recipe: his *Short and Sweet* is a complete baking bible.

Currant Buns

Makes 12

1. Tip the cider, yeast and rye flour into a bowl. Stir and allow to bubble away for 30 minutes while you put your feet up and enjoy the rest of the bottle of cider over ice.

2. Warm the cream, mixed spice and honey over a low heat. Remove from the heat, beat in the eggs, then pour into the cider mix. Add the currants.

3. Sift in the flour, cornflour and salt, then mix by hand to form a sticky dough. Cover and leave for 10 minutes.

4. Turn the dough out onto a work surface (grease it with a little flavourless vegetable oil first, so it doesn't stick) and knead for 10–20 seconds until noticeably smoother. This really won't take long at all, so don't over-knead it. Place the dough back in the bowl, cover with plastic wrap and leave to prove for an hour.

5. Once visibly risen (it doesn't need to double in size here), weigh the dough, and divide into 12 balls. Roll each under a clawed hand until smooth, then place on a baking tray lined with greaseproof paper. Leave about 1cm/⅜in between each – you want them to join up while they prove, so that you end up tearing them apart after they're baked.

6. Cover the tray with plastic wrap and leave the buns to prove until they've doubled in size: about an hour.

7. When the buns are approaching the end of their prove, preheat your oven to 220°C/425°F/Gas 7. Transfer the buns to the oven and bake for 15–18 minutes, until browned.

8. In a small saucepan, heat the sugar, water and mixed spice. Reduce by half and remove from the heat.

9. Remove the buns from the oven, allow them to cool for a couple of minutes, then paint the glaze over the top. Serve warm, or toasted the next day.

150ml/5 floz/⅔ cup apple cider/hard cider (at room temperature)

7g/¼oz/2½tsp fast-action yeast

75g/2⅔oz/¾ cup rye flour

150ml/5floz/⅔ cup double/heavy cream

4tsp mixed spice/ pumpkin pie spice

50g/3tbsp honey

2 eggs

300g/10¾oz/2¼ cups dried currants

400g/14oz/3 cups strong white bread flour

25g/scant 1oz/¼ cup cornflour/cornstarch

1tsp salt

GLAZE

25g/2tbsp sugar

25ml/5tsp water

1tsp mixed spice/ pumpkin pie spice

The Tale of Peter Rabbit, Beatrix Potter

Scones

The smell of scones wafted through the kitchen. I ate three before I even touched my tea. They were sweet and crumbly, and succulent with melting butter.
The Butterfly Lion, Michael Morpurgo

My grandmother – Dad's mum – was the baker in our family. Her kitchen was always rich with the smell of something buttery and sweet in the oven. Peanut butter biscuits, jam drops, Anzac biscuits and shortbread sat in jars on top of the fridge, there for afternoon tea, or for my dad to drop his hand into when he arrived to pick us up. We spent countless holiday days there, playing pick-up-sticks, spinning around the Hills Hoist washing line in her beautiful garden or eating Kool Mints from the jar in the living room.

Though I didn't do it nearly as much as I would have liked, I remember baking with her too. I remember her scones, soft and buttery, and served with very good jam. They're ideal for afternoon tea, a genuine crowd pleaser that you can have on the table in less than twenty-five minutes, when someone unexpected knocks on the door.

For the lightest possible scones, make sure all your ingredients are at room temperature, don't overwork the dough and get them into the oven as soon as possible after bringing the ingredients together.

Scones

Makes 12

1. Preheat the oven to 220°C/425°F/Gas 7. Line a baking tray with greaseproof paper and set aside.

2. Mix the buttermilk, cream and sugar together in a bowl until the sugar is dissolved. Sift the flour, baking powder and bicarbonate of soda into a mixing bowl, then rub in the butter as quickly as possible.

3. Add the buttermilk mixture to the dry ingredients, using a metal knife to stir to avoid overmixing. As soon as the mixture has come together, tip it onto a floured surface and sprinkle with flour. Push down lightly with a rolling pin until the mixture is around 4cm/1½in high. Dip a 5cm/2in biscuit cutter, or a glass, in flour and push it down firmly, without twisting. Reshape the dough with as little kneading as possible and continue cutting out scones until all the dough is used.

4. Place the scones on the baking tray, leaving at least 2cm/¾in between each one for them to spread (though most of their rise will be upwards). Brush the beaten egg onto each scone with a pastry brush.

5. Bake for 12–15 minutes, removing the tray from the oven when the scones are risen and golden on top. Eat immediately, split in half and spread with butter and raspberry jam.

INGREDIENTS

250ml/8½floz/generous 1 cup buttermilk

25ml/5tsp double/heavy cream

2tbsp caster/superfine sugar

400g/14oz/3 cups plain/all-purpose flour

4tsp baking powder

½tsp bicarbonate of soda/baking soda

50g/scant 2oz/3½tbsp softened butter

1 egg, beaten (for glazing)

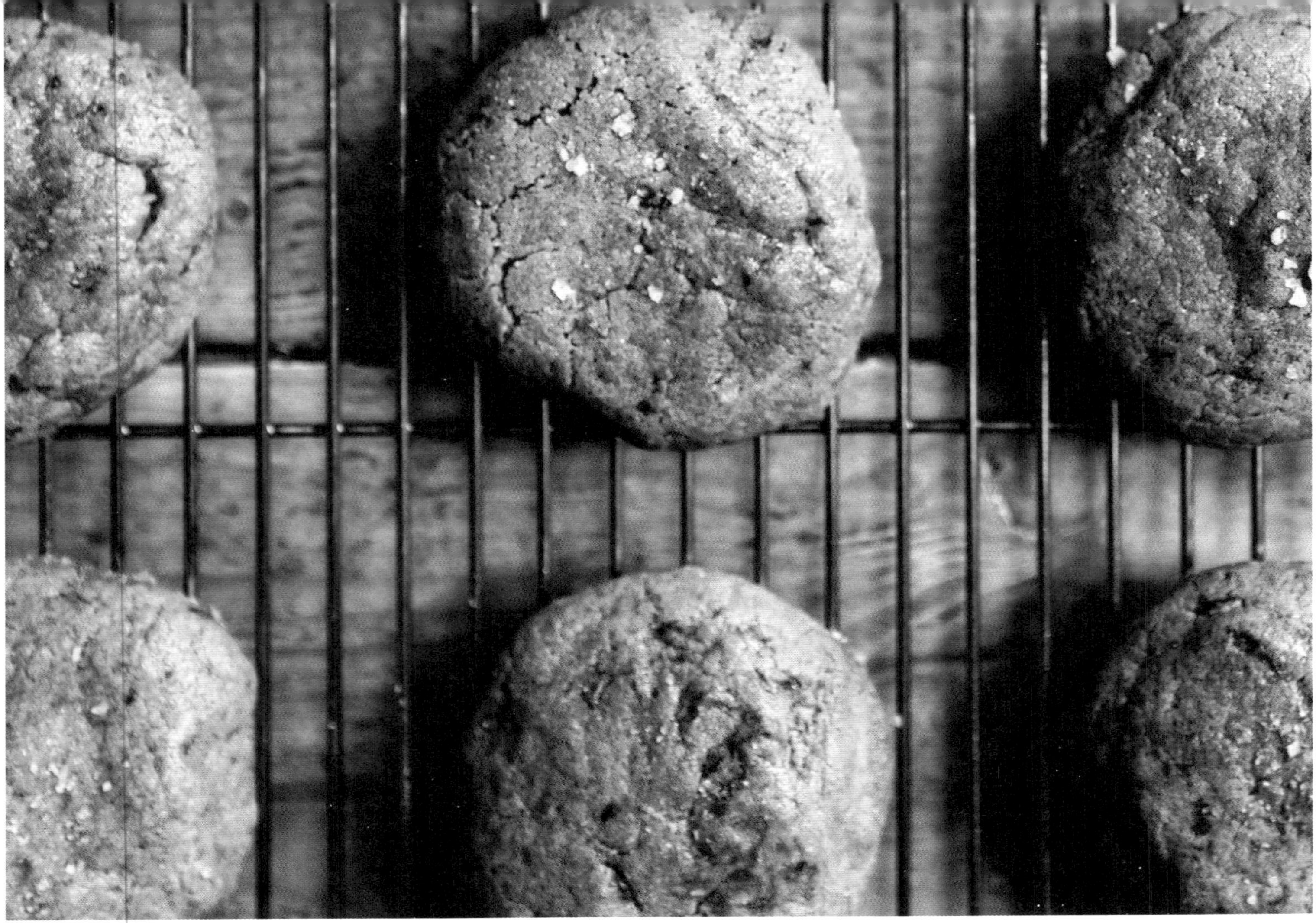

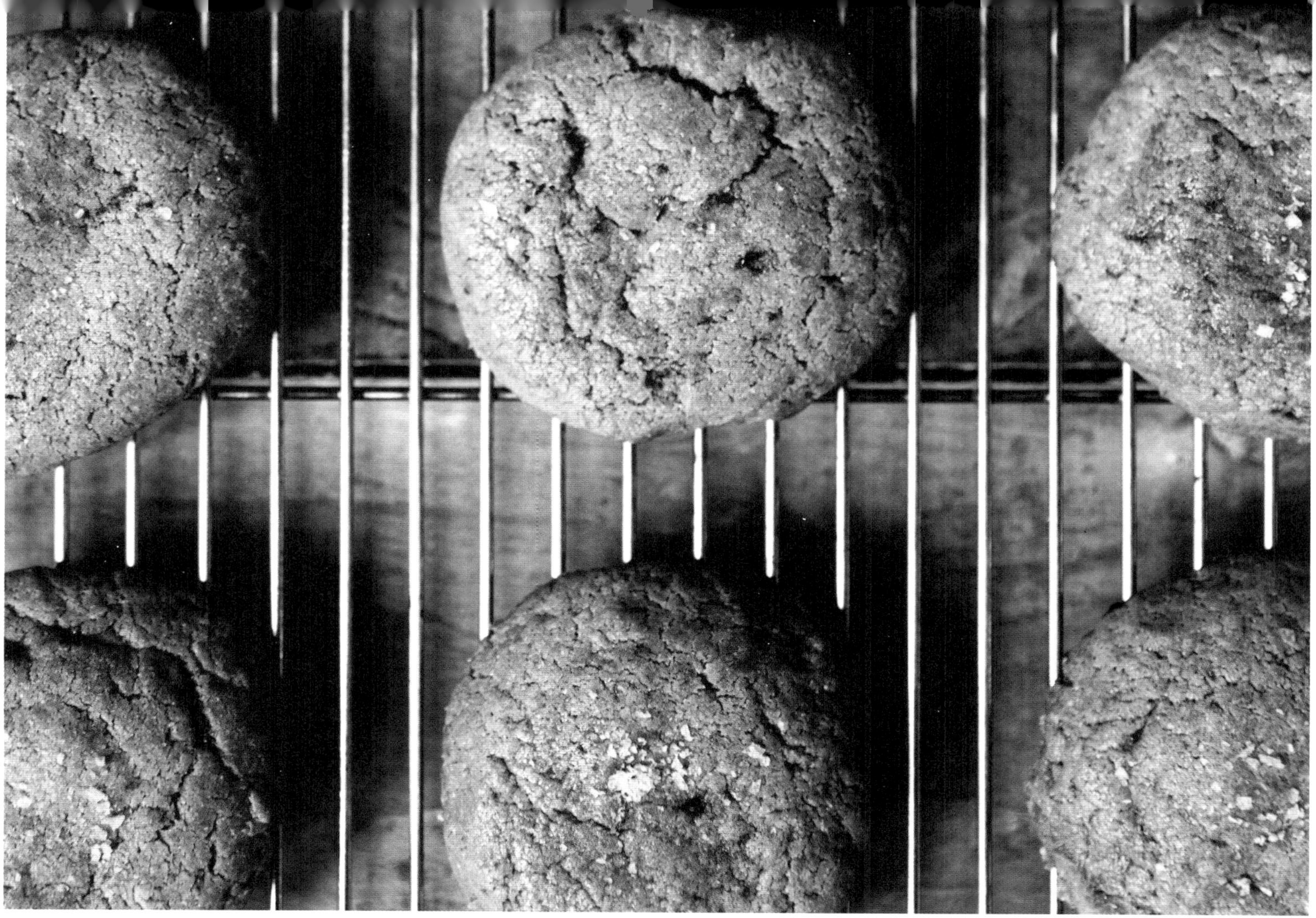

Spice Cookies

There were rows and rows of spice cookies cooling and the kitchen still smelled of cinnamon and nutmeg.
We Have Always Lived in the Castle, Shirley Jackson

I grew up with four parents and one sister. Every weekend, my sister and I packed our sheets of homework, soccer uniforms and beloved items of clothing into bags and moved back and forth between houses. Whatever else changed, Lucy and I remained the constants in each other's lives. She is the person I have spent the most time with – on the sofa watching Saturday-morning cartoons, drawing elaborate floor plans of our dream house (where we swapped our bunk beds for separate rooms with four poster beds and an interconnecting slippery slide) and sharing hundreds of favourite stories – on paper, on screen and in real life.

It is hardly surprising, then, that I have always identified with stories about sisters. Shirley Jackson's final book, a Gothic horror story that manages to be eerie without a hint of the supernatural, is one of my favourites. Merricat and Constance live with their ailing grandfather after the deaths of the rest of their family. Shunned by the local community, who are convinced that Constance murdered the family, they are almost entirely self-reliant. Merricat braves weekly trips into town, while Constance spends much of her time in the kitchen. When their estranged cousin comes to visit, Constance bakes racks and racks of spice cookies.

These cookies are a product of many I have enjoyed over the years: Tessa Kiros's gingerbread biscuits, slabs of fennel-studded Printen in Germany, and the fudgiest American cookies I have ever eaten. My darling sister lives in America now, and has just started referring to biscuits as cookies. These, a batch of cookies from a story about sisters, are for her.

Spice Cookies

Makes 12

1. If you are using cardamom pods, remove the seeds from the pods and crush them to a powder. Put all the spices (the fennel seeds should be whole, everything else will now be ground) with the treacle in a saucepan and place over a low heat. Warm through, removing from the heat at the first sign of a bubble. Leave to cool and infuse.

2. Beat the butter, tahini and sugar together until light and creamy. Add the spiced treacle and beat for a minute or so.

3. Add the egg and egg yolk, beating well after each is added. Sift the flour and baking powder into the dough, and fold in. The dough will be sticky, but don't be tempted to add more flour.

4. Line a plate with a sheet of greaseproof paper. Roll the dough into 12 balls and place them on the plate. Try to ensure they don't touch, as they will stick together.

5. Freeze the dough – overnight if you can, but for at least 2 hours. They'll keep this way for about 6 months.

6. Heat your oven to 160°C/325°F/Gas 3. Once the oven is hot, line a baking tray with greaseproof paper and place some of the frozen balls of dough on it. The beauty of this method is that you can cook as many as you want to eat. Leave room for them to spread as they cook.

7. Place the tray in the oven immediately and bake for 14 minutes. When you remove the cookies, they will still be very soft, and should have puffed in the middle and spread out to form circular cookies. Sprinkle each with some of the salt and leave to cool on the tray for 10 minutes.

8. The cookies will collapse a bit, and may crack – this is fine. Move to a wire rack and cool for a further 10–15 minutes. Eat warm, with a cup of coffee or a glass of milk.

INGREDIENTS

10 cardamom pods (or ¼tsp ground cardamom)

1½ tsp ground cinnamon

¼tsp grated nutmeg

2tsp fennel seeds

50g/2¼tbsp black treacle/molasses

110g/4oz/1 stick unsalted butter

110g/4oz/½ cup tahini

150g/5⅓oz/¾ cup light brown sugar

1 egg

1 egg yolk

230g/8oz/1¾ cups plain/all-purpose flour

1tsp baking powder

1tsp smoked sea salt (if you don't have smoked salt, plain sea salt is fine)

Coconut Shortbread

Charles commanded an awestruck girl in a white apron to bring at least a dozen of the cakes she personally liked best, and a gallon of tea. She evidently favoured coconut: there were macaroons, and speckled shortbread, and lozenges of cake doused in raspberry jam and rolled in coconut flakes.

The Essex Serpent, Sarah Perry

I have long been fascinated by Victorian literature. Growing up in a city where the books I read were older than most of the buildings, the characters seemed so unfamiliar, almost otherworldly. My country wasn't even a federated nation as their lives played out across the sea. When I moved to England, it took me years to get over the rush of pointing out buildings that had stood for centuries.

In 2016, I read a book so extraordinary that it occupied my thoughts for weeks. I consumed it in a single day, at the start of summer, completely taken with the world Sarah Perry so deftly draws for us. Hers is a Victorian England that feels at once familiar and strange. Doctors are experimenting with open-heart surgery, people ride the Underground home after a funeral, a housing crisis affects much of the working class. It could be my England. I felt instantly closer to her Victorian characters than I had felt to any before.

The characters eat meals that wouldn't be out of place on a twenty-first-century table, including a midsummer feast I can imagine serving up, and this gorgeous afternoon tea spread. Shortbread has been made in the United Kingdom for many hundreds of years. Modern recipes often substitute some cornflour for a bit of the plain flour, but for these biscuits, served in a Victorian tearoom at the turn of the century, I wanted to keep it simple.

Coconut Shortbread

Makes 16 generously sized biscuits

1. Cream the butter and sugar until the mixture is light and the sugar has dissolved. Fold in the flour, salt and coconut, then turn out and knead to a soft dough.

2. Roll the dough to around 1cm/⅜in thick. Lightly flour a 5cm/2in biscuit cutter, or glass, and cut rounds out of the dough, re-rolling the offcuts to form more biscuits. Arrange the biscuits on lined baking trays, leaving a space between each for the biscuits to spread slightly. Place the trays in the fridge for 30 minutes.

3. Preheat the oven to 160°C/325°F/Gas 3. Once the biscuits are chilled, prick the tops with a fork and place in the oven for 12–15 minutes, until golden around the edges.

4. Leave the biscuits on the trays to cool and harden for 5 minutes, before transferring to a wire rack to cool completely.

INGREDIENTS

200g/7oz/1¾ sticks unsalted butter, softened

100g/3½oz/½ cup golden caster/superfine sugar

300g/10½oz/2¼ cups plain/all-purpose flour

Pinch of salt

80g/3oz/heaping 1 cup desiccated/shredded coconut

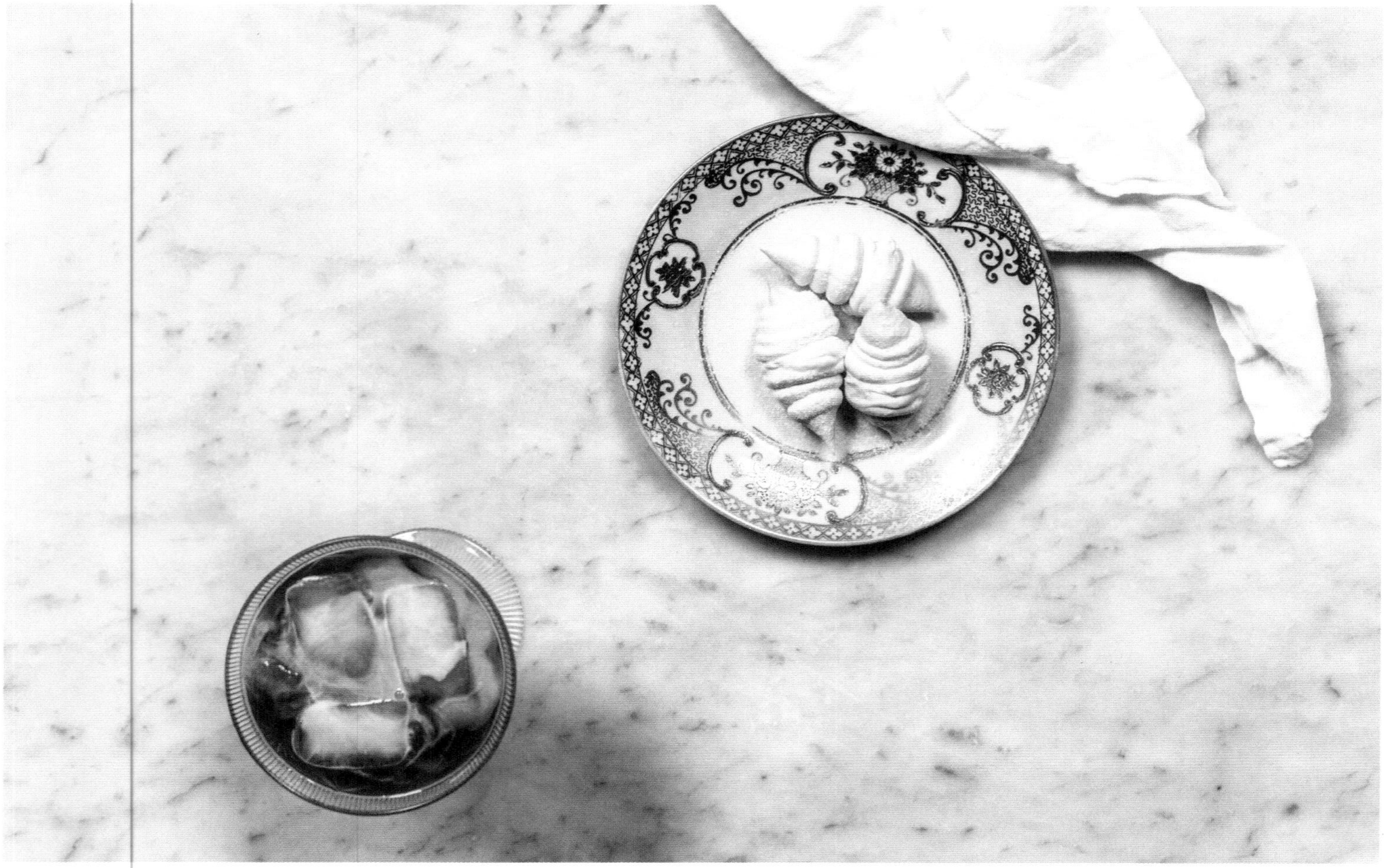

MERINGUES & ICED COFFEE { 96 } *A Room with a View*, E. M. Forster

Meringues & Iced Coffee

She loved going to concerts, she loved stopping with her cousin, she loved iced coffee and meringues.
A Room with a View, E. M. Forster

When I visited Florence with a friend from university, we stayed in a mixed dorm room that slept twelve. Our window looked over an internal stairwell. My room with a view was not as Forster had promised. But it was cheap, and we were in Italy. We rose early every morning (I'm not sure you have much of a choice when sleeping in a dorm) and explored the city, its churches and museums on foot. I thought often of Lucy Honeychurch, who religiously follows suggestions listed in her Baedeker guide, before being led astray by the wonderful Miss Lavish.

Throughout the novel, Lucy gradually abandons her well-planned life. She leaves behind the iced coffee and meringues, and the comfort of her English village, to embrace a life uncertain, but full of love, with George.

The thing is, I think meringues and iced coffee get a raw deal here. They're meant to be emblematic of the comfortable, predictable life that Lucy lives as a young woman, but I think they deserve better. Both, at their best, are wonderful. And so I'm here to advocate for meringues and coffee.

INGREDIENTS

MERINGUES
A slice of lemon
1 egg white
55g/2oz/4½tbsp golden
caster/superfine sugar
80ml/6tbsp double
cream (or other filling of
your choice)
Dash of vanilla extract

ICED COFFEE
250ml/8½floz/generous
1 cup very strong freshly
brewed coffee
60ml/2floz/¼ cup milk
Ice cubes

EQUIPMENT
Electric hand whisk or
mixer
Disposable piping bag

Meringues and Iced Coffee

Makes coffee for 2, and plenty of meringues

1. Preheat the oven to 110°C/225°F/Gas¼. Rub the slice of lemon around the inside of a bowl, to get rid of any traces of fat. Tip the egg white into the bowl and whisk until it forms stiff peaks.

2. Continue to whisk on a low-medium speed, adding the caster sugar one spoonful at a time. Once all the sugar has been added, whisk until the meringue forms stiff, glossy peaks. Transfer to a piping bag and snip a ½cm/¼in hole in the end. Line the baking tray with greaseproof paper.

3. Hold the piping bag at a 90-degree angle to the baking tray and pipe little meringues, 2cm/¾in in diameter. I think they end up looking lovely if you keep the piping bag close to the tray and allow the meringue to spread from a central point, rather than swirling it around. Make them stand proud by slowly pulling the bag away from the tray, squeezing all the time. They're not going to spread much, but do give them a little breathing room.

4. Bake the meringues for an hour, until crisp on the outside and still soft in the middle. Turn the oven off and leave the meringues to cool in the oven for another hour.

5. Make the coffee and pop it in the fridge to chill.

6. Whip the cream to soft peaks and use it to sandwich the meringues together (try to pair similar sizes if, like me, you're a bit rubbish with consistency).

7. Put some ice in a glass and pour the chilled coffee over the top. Add a dash of milk or cream, stir and enjoy with the meringues.

Éclairs

'Then, Linda dear, could one ask for a cup of tea?'
She rang the bell, and soon Davey was falling upon éclairs and
mille feuilles with all the abandon of a schoolboy.
The Pursuit of Love, Nancy Mitford

There is no better way to arrive into Paris than on the train. I
have done the journey on an eight-hour overnight bus, flown into
Charles de Gaulle and battled the traffic in a car full of suitcases,
but it is the train that fills me with real excitement. I first travelled
by Eurostar in the late Nineties, munching on a salami and cheese
baguette, completely blown away by the idea that the English
Channel was sitting somewhere above our heads. When we arrived
at Gare du Nord, I was taken with its beauty and romance; so much
more exciting than a clinical, carpeted airport.

When Linda arrives into Paris, she is running from a marriage that
has gone wrong. Having missed her connection back to London,
she is swept off her feet by a man she meets on the train platform.
At his urging, she stays. I can think of worse predicaments.

I have visited Paris more often than I have visited any other city. I
have explored the galleries, travelled up the Eiffel Tower, strolled
the Champs-Élysées, walked up to Sacré-Cœur and along the
Seine. But my very favourite thing to do is walk from pâtisserie to
pâtisserie, admiring the glorious creations behind the glass. Pastel-
hued, glossy and almost too beautiful to 'fall upon', these éclairs are
a real delight.

INGREDIENTS

PASTRY

50g/1¾oz/3½tbsp butter
100ml/3⅓floz water
40g/1½oz/4½tbsp strong white bread flour
35g/1¼oz/¼ cup plain/all-purpose flour
Pinch of salt
2 eggs

CRÈME PÂTISSIÈRE

125ml/4½floz milk
125ml/4½floz double/heavy cream
Vanilla bean, split down the middle
2 egg yolks
50g/1¾oz/¼ cup caster/superfine sugar
25g/3tbsp plain/all-purpose flour

PISTACHIO PASTE

150g/5⅓oz/1¼ cup shelled pistachio nuts
2tbsp caster/superfine sugar

ICING

150g/5¼oz/1 cup icing/confectioners' sugar
1tbsp milk
½tsp rosewater
Red food colouring paste
50g chopped pistachio nuts

EQUIPMENT

Two disposable piping bags
Food processor

Éclairs

Makes 10

1. Preheat your oven to 160°C/325°F/Gas 3. To make the pastry, place the butter and water in a large saucepan over a medium heat. Heat until the butter has melted and the water is simmering, then sift in both flours along with a pinch of salt, and beat the mixture until it forms a thick paste. Continue to cook for a minute (which will ensure the pastry doesn't taste floury), then take the pan off the heat and continue to beat with a wooden spoon until it is cool.

2. Add an egg to the cooled mixture, beating very well before adding the second egg. The dough should form a thick and glossy mixture that drops from a wooden spoon, leaving pastry hanging from the spoon in the shape of a 'v'. Transfer the dough into a piping bag, and snip the end off to create a 1.5cm/⅝in hole. Line the baking trays with greaseproof paper and flick some water onto the sheets. Pipe 10cm/4in lines of the choux dough onto the paper (about 2cm/¾in wide), allowing space for the éclairs to double in size.

3. Bake the éclairs for 20 minutes, until risen and golden brown. Remove the tray from the oven, and poke a hole in the end of each pastry with a small knife. Place the tray back in the oven for 5 minutes to dry out the insides. Place on a wire rack to cool.

4. To make the crème pâtissière, place the milk, cream and vanilla in a large saucepan over a medium heat, and bring to a slow simmer. Whisk the egg yolks and sugar together in a bowl until pale and creamy, then whisk in the flour. Slowly sieve the hot milk into the bowl, whisk thoroughly, and then pour the liquid back into the saucepan.

5. Cook the mixture over a low heat for around 10 minutes, stirring continuously, until thick and glossy. Cover with plastic wrap, pressed right onto the surface of the crème pâtissière to prevent it forming a skin. Leave to cool in the fridge.

6. Blitz the pistachio nuts with the sugar in a food processor for 10 minutes, until they form a paste.

7. Mix 6tbsp pistachio paste through the cooled crème pâtissière and transfer into a second piping bag, snipping a small hole in the end. Fill each éclair via the hole pierced in the end.

8. Finally, whisk the icing sugar, milk and rosewater together. Add a tiny amount of red food colouring to the icing, and beat again. Dip each éclair, top-side down, into the icing. Shake slightly to get rid of the excess, sprinkle with pistachios and place on a wire rack for 10 minutes or so until the icing sets.

Madeleines

She sent out for one of those short, plump little cakes called 'petites madeleines,' which look as though they had been moulded in the fluted scallop of a pilgrim's shell.
In Search of Lost Time, Marcel Proust

These delicate little cakes, barely crisp at the edges and impossibly light in the middle, are almost always the first edible mentioned in conversations about food in fiction. Forever associated with *Swann's Way*, the first part of Proust's extraordinary tome *In Search of Lost Time*, these scalloped morsels, soaked in tea, famously result in an involuntary memory of childhood.

I bought them in a supermarket, years ago, and was underwhelmed. It wasn't until I tried a plate of them, fresh from the oven, at the brilliant St John Bread & Wine in East London, that I understood just how good they can be. You need to eat them as soon as possible after pulling the tray out of the oven; if you leave them sitting around they'll dry out and lose their lovely texture. Happily, the batter, once made, can be stored in the fridge for a couple of days, so you'll only be ten or so minutes away from having a plate of them on the table. The brown butter in these is optional (you can just use melted butter if you like), but I think it turns them into something very special and memorable. Which, after all, is the point.

Brown Butter Madeleines

Makes around 20

1. Melt the butter over a low heat. Once melted, tip half into a dish and set aside. Leave the other half over the heat until the butter has turned brown and gives off a nutty aroma. Remove from the heat and add this browned butter to the dish of melted butter.

2. Beat the eggs with the caster sugar in a bowl until very thick, which should take at least 5 minutes using an electric mixer or whisk.

3. Sift the flour and baking powder into the egg and sugar mixture and fold in gently with a spatula. Fold in the butter, then cover and chill for at least 2 hours, or overnight if that's easier.

4. Preheat the oven to 200°C/400°F/Gas 6 and generously brush the madeleine tin with melted butter. Dust with a little flour, then pop the tin in the freezer for 10 minutes. Fill the tray with the batter – around two-thirds full is enough, as the sponge will spread as it rises.

5. Bake for 7–9 minutes, until brown and risen, then tip out of the tin and leave to cool on the rack. You'll have enough batter to do a second, and possibly third, batch. Dust all the madeleines with icing sugar and serve, warm, with a cup of tea.

INGREDIENTS

110g/4oz/1 stick unsalted butter
2 large eggs
100g/3½oz/½ cup golden caster/superfine sugar
100g/3½oz/¾ cup plain/all-purpose flour
1tsp baking powder
15g/1tbsp melted butter for greasing
Icing/confectioners' sugar for dusting

EQUIPMENT

Electric mixer or whisk
Madeleine tin (mine has large 7.5cm/3in moulds)

In Search of Lost Time, Marcel Proust

Halwa

'The Chinese say it's better to be deprived of food for three days than tea for one.' Mariam gave a half-smile. 'It's a good saying.'
'It is.'
'But I can't stay long.'
'One cup.'
They sat on folding chairs outside and ate halwa with their fingers from a common bowl. They had a second cup, and when Laila asked her if she wanted a third Mariam said she did.
A Thousand Splendid Suns, Khaled Hosseini

You may have noticed that there is a relatively regular use of cardamom throughout this book. When I first tasted it, I hated it. Hidden in the saffron rice served at the Indian restaurant I worked in as a teenager, it was always an unpleasant find. I would crunch down on a whole pod, then have to figure out a polite way to hide it in my serviette (turns out there isn't really a nice way to do that).

Years later, I kept coming across it: in buns, in cakes, in curries and in halwa. Ground, rather than left whole, it is rich, fragrant and completely unique. It works beautifully with chocolate, pears or nuts, and is also robust enough to serve as the central flavouring – as it is in this halwa. It is now my favourite spice.

I first ate Afghan food at a brilliant restaurant five doors down from the Tricycle Theatre in northwest London where I used to work, called Ariana 2. After shows or production meetings, our little team would head over and order so many dishes that we'd have to balance plates on top of each other to make space on the table. The food was always fragrant, delicious and perfectly spiced. It always made me think of the pickles, breads and meats in Hosseini's *The Kite Runner*, and this halwa and tea that the women share in *A Thousand Splendid Suns*.

Halwa

Makes plenty for 6 to eat with tea

1. Preheat the oven to 150°C/300°F/Gas 2. In a mixing bowl, pour the boiling water over the sugar and stir to dissolve.

2. Heat the oil in a saucepan over a medium heat until it is very hot and spits when you flick a little water into it (be very careful doing this, as you don't want it to splash or spit onto your hand). Add the semolina and stir immediately. The semolina will absorb the oil and turn golden.

3. Turn the heat off, and quickly pour half the sugar water into the pan. It will bubble and spit, but you need to stir it – a long-handled wooden spoon will be helpful here. Once the mixture is smooth, turn the heat back on to medium. Stir the mixture constantly, while you add the rest of the sugar water. Keep stirring for another 5 minutes, while the halwa thickens and darkens to a golden brown.

4. Add the ground cardamom and continue to stir for another couple of minutes. Turn the heat off, and cover the saucepan with an ovenproof lid – or foil if your lid is plastic.

5. Transfer the pan to the oven and cook for 25 minutes. Leave to cool, then spoon the halwa into a serving dish and eat with friends, your fingers and a cup of chai tea.

INGREDIENTS

500ml/17floz/generous 2 cups boiling water
220g/scant 8oz/generous 1 cup caster/superfine sugar
125ml/4⅓floz/generous ½ cup flavourless vegetable oil
220g/scant 8oz/1⅓ cups finely ground semolina
1tsp ground cardamom

EQUIPMENT

Large saucepan with a tight-fitting lid (the saucepan and lid should be ovenproof)

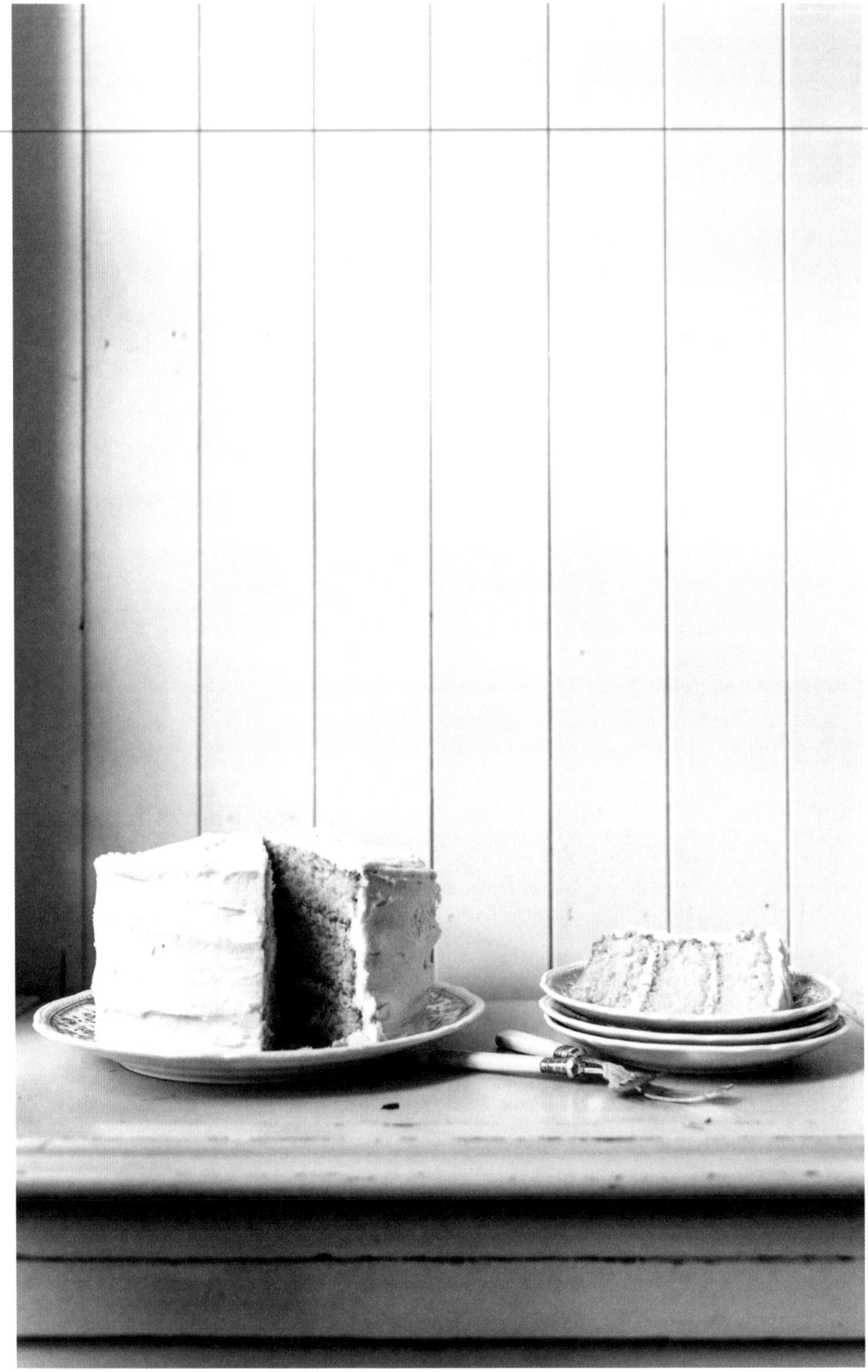

Vanilla Layer Cake

The cake did rise, however, and came out of the oven as light and feathery as golden foam. Anne, flushed with delight, clapped it together with layers of ruby jelly, and, in imagination, saw Mrs Allen eating it and possibly asking for another piece.
Anne of Green Gables, L. M. Montgomery

I have had my fair share of baking disasters. I've had cakes that have sunk (one so low that the 'top' touched the bottom), meringues that have sweated their way to a soggy mess in the humidity and custards that have scrambled. Most memorably, my sister and I once served the most disgusting crumble I have ever tasted. We were new to cooking without supervision, but we had some cookbooks and a brash confidence we hadn't yet earned. One day during the holidays, we used our pocket money to prepare a three-course dinner for our dad, stepmum and granddad.

We found a recipe for spiced apple crumble, diligently measured out the ingredients for the topping, peeled and chopped the apples, and put the huge baking dish in the oven. Unfortunately, we misread the instructions, and thought that '¼tsp' meant between one and four. So we ended up adding four teaspoons each of cinnamon, nutmeg, allspice and salt. We dished up large portions for our dinner guests, and they bravely struggled through a bite or two each before asking what on earth we'd put in it. Thankfully, there was a tub of ice cream in the freezer.

So I sympathize with poor Anne, who wants so desperately for this cake to be well received, and is foiled by a bottle of liniment that is mistakenly labelled 'Vanilla'. Her cake rises beautifully, but it is inedible, and her hopes of Mrs Allen asking for a second slice are dashed. We've all been there. Though Anne's original is layered with ruby jam (you can substitute shop-bought raspberry jam for the icing here, if you like), I wanted to make it a very vanilla-rich cake, like Anne originally intended.

INGREDIENTS

CAKE

6 eggs, weighed in their shells then the same weight of:

Unsalted butter

Caster/superfine sugar

Self-raising flour

2tsp vanilla extract (not liniment)

Small amount of milk, if necessary

ICING

120g/4oz/1 stick unsalted butter

1kg/2¼lb icing/confectioners' sugar

1 vanilla pod

4tbsp milk

EQUIPMENT

Three 20cm/8in sandwich tins/layer cake pans

Vanilla Layer Cake

Serves 10 – generously

1. Preheat the oven to 160°C/325°F/Gas 3. Grease the sandwich tins and line the bottom with greaseproof paper. Ensure all ingredients for the cake are at room temperature.

2. Beat the butter and sugar on a high speed for at least 5 minutes, until the mixture is pale in colour and very light in consistency.

3. Crack the eggs into a glass, and add them one at a time. Add a spoonful of the flour after each egg to prevent the mixture curdling. Add the vanilla and mix again.

4. Sift the remaining flour into the batter and fold in gently. Once it is incorporated (don't overmix it here – stop as soon as you have mixed in all the dry bits of flour), test the consistency. Take a spoonful of the batter and hold it above the bowl. It should drop off the spoon and back into the bowl. If it is reluctant to do this and clings to the spoon, add a tablespoon of milk and test again.

5. Divide the batter evenly between the three tins. Level out the tops, then transfer to the oven, putting them on the same shelf if your oven is big enough. Bake for 20 minutes, until a skewer inserted into each cake comes out clean.

6. Cool the cakes in their tins for 5 minutes, then tip them out and leave to cool completely on a wire rack.

7. To make the icing, beat the butter until light. Fold in half of the icing sugar, and beat on a low speed until incorporated. Add the other half and again beat on a low speed until incorporated. Split the vanilla pod and scrape the seeds into the icing. Increase the speed to high, and beat for a couple of minutes.

8. Start adding the milk, a tablespoon at a time, then beat on high for 5 minutes until the icing is light and fluffy.

9. To assemble the cake, place one of the sponges on a serving plate, and spread about a quarter of the icing over the top. Add another sponge, another quarter of the icing, and then the final sponge. Scrape a thin layer of icing around the sides of the cake, to seal the crumbs inside. Dollop the rest of the icing onto the top of the cake, then smooth it down the sides. Run a palette knife around the edge of the cake to smooth the icing. Serve in large slices, on your nicest plates, with tea.

Crumpets

Those dripping crumpets, I can see them now.
Rebecca, Daphne du Maurier

About a year after I moved to the UK, my mum came to visit. The two of us hired a car and drove down to Cornwall where we ate seafood, stayed in B&Bs and walked around National Trust gardens. We took cold, blustery walks along cliffs and up to lighthouses. At night, with matching glasses of whiskey, we sat and talked, before retiring to bed with our books. I took *Rebecca* with me on that trip, and have read it many times since.

It is a book that perfectly reflects the Cornish landscape: moody and unpredictable. The sinister Mrs Danvers, surely one of the most insidious and manipulative villains in literature, turns a story that could be romantic into one where even the crumpets seem to be a threat. Though the afternoon-tea spreads sound glorious – multiple cakes, delectable sandwiches, crumpets and buttered scones – for the second Mrs de Winter, they serve only as a reminder of how uncomfortable she felt under Mrs Danvers's judgmental eye.

My own memories of crumpets are not exactly unproblematic either. I first attempted them very late one night, suddenly taken with the idea of having them the next morning. Unfortunately, I used old metal rings as my moulds, and no matter how thoroughly I buttered them the crumpets stuck and refused to rise. I finally gave up on the batch at 2 a.m. Please do learn from my errors – I can't recommend non-stick rings more enthusiastically. Once you have the right equipment, crumpets are a total dream to make.

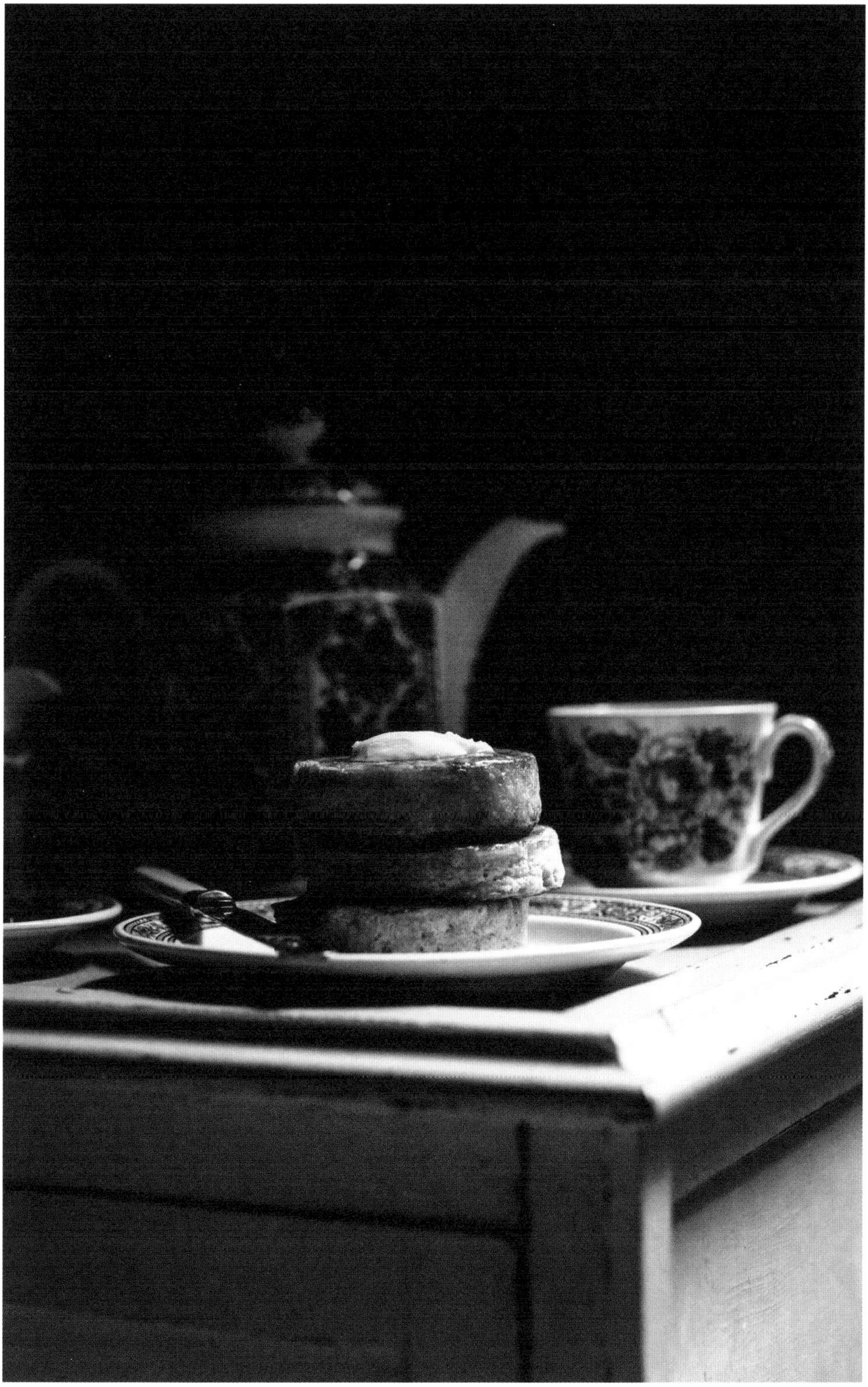

Crumpets

Makes 8

INGREDIENTS

300ml/½ pint/1¼ cups milk

1tsp caster/superfine sugar

15g/½oz/1tbsp fresh yeast (or 5g/1tsp fast-action yeast)

125g/4½oz/1 cup strong white bread flour

125g/4½oz/1 cup plain/all-purpose flour

½tsp salt

½tsp bicarbonate of soda/baking soda

100ml/3⅓floz water

EQUIPMENT

Crumpet rings or round egg moulds (non-stick really is best here)

1. Warm the milk to body temperature in a pan. Mix in the sugar and yeast. Leave for 10 minutes to activate.

2. Tip the flours and salt into a bowl. Add the liquid mix and stir. Leave, covered, for an hour. The mixture should bubble up and rise, then start to fall.

3. Mix the bicarbonate of soda with the water and fold in to the batter. Leave for 10 more minutes.

4. Put a frying pan over a very low heat. Butter the crumpet rings generously. Ladle about 1.5cm/½in of batter into each ring and cook for 10 minutes until the bubbles on top have popped – you can help them with a skewer if you like – and the holes have stopped refilling with batter. Remove the ring, flip the crumpet and cook for a further 2 minutes.

5. Let the crumpets cool a little, then toast them, and serve dripping with butter.

Mint Julep

'Open the whiskey, Tom,' she ordered. 'And I'll make you a mint julep.
Then you won't seem so stupid to yourself... Look at the mint!'
The Great Gatsby, F. Scott Fitzgerald

On the back deck of my mum and stepdad's house, they have
built a bar. The walls are covered in posters of the Rat Pack and
the Beatles, and an obscenely large collection of beer trays; you
can barely see the walls for the paraphernalia. When I picture
my stepdad, Geoff, at home, this is where I see him: in a brightly
coloured shirt, pouring drinks for friends who have dropped by
unexpectedly, while he points out a new poster he has acquired. I
have spent many happy evenings around that bar – mixing sangria
for my school friends Meg and Kirst, as we reconvened during
our university days, pouring Campari and soda for Mum and me
to drink on the back deck or filling the huge freezer chest with ice
before a party.

In fact, both my mum's house and my dad's house have bars.
Dad's shelves are lined with spirits and liqueurs that he and my
stepmother Cheryl collect on trips to far-flung locations. We'd
spend Sunday afternoons poring over recipes for cocktails,
toying with the idea of something new, before requesting our old
favourites. We'd sip them on the deck, reading books or listening to
music as we made plans for the last dinner of the weekend.

This cocktail is made under significantly less relaxed conditions.
The Great Gatsby has no shortage of glamorous parties, afternoon
teas and dinners, but I have chosen instead to focus on this moment,
my favourite scene in the book. It is a pressure cooker – one fuelled
by whiskey, the heat and a summer of poorly kept secrets. Though
Daisy attempts to diffuse the tension with cocktails, the mint juleps
can't stop the inevitable, catastrophic conclusion to their summer.

Mint Julep

Serves 2

1. To make the syrup, pour the sugar and water into the saucepan, and swirl them around over a low heat until the sugar has dissolved. Once dissolved, remove the pan from the heat.

2. Strip the mint leaves from the stalks and add them to the pan. Bruise the leaves in the syrup, pressing them around with the rolling pin. Leave this to sit for at least 20 minutes, but ideally a couple of hours, in the fridge.

3. To assemble, prepare two glasses by filling them with ice and water, and setting aside. In a large glass (or cocktail shaker), add the mint leaves and 3tbsp of the strained simple syrup and bash them around a bit with the rolling pin. Add the bourbon and a handful of ice. Stir to chill.

4. Empty the glasses and dry them. Strain the mint julep into the chilled glasses. Top with plenty of crushed ice, then add the stalks of mint for decoration and stirring purposes. Try not to encourage a fight between your husband and the man who is in love with you as you drink.

INGREDIENTS

SYRUP*
50g/1¾oz/¼ cup granulated sugar
50ml/3⅓tbsp water
10 stalks mint

COCKTAIL
20 mint leaves
100ml/3⅓floz/generous ⅓ cup bourbon whiskey
Plenty of crushed ice
6 stalks mint, to decorate

EQUIPMENT
Rolling pin or muddler
Large glass or cocktail shaker
2 serving glasses

*This makes plenty; leftovers will keep for weeks in the fridge.

Hush's Feast

They ate Anzac biscuits in Adelaide,
mornay and Minties in Melbourne,
steak and salad in Sydney
and pumpkin scones in Brisbane.
Possum Magic, Mem Fox

When I was eight, I stood on my school stage in a leotard, white tights, a tail and furry ears. Our teachers had turned one of the best-loved picture books in Australia into a musical. It included, memorably, a piece called the 'Tassie Devil Rap', tonnes of kids dressed as lifeguards and more than a couple of hats with corks hanging from the brim. I played Hush, a young possum who wishes she was invisible. For her birthday, Grandma Poss makes it so, but cannot then reverse it. Grandma Poss thinks that the remedy lies in food, so they travel around Australia, eating, until Hush is visible once more (a lamington cake in Hobart finally does the trick).

It is a charming story, and full of things I love to eat – steak, pavlova, Vegemite and these three afternoon-tea favourites: Anzac biscuits, pumpkin scones and lamingtons. In the parties of my childhood, nestled alongside platters of sausage rolls and big bowls of tomato sauce, these three were staples.

If they are unfamiliar to you, please allow me to introduce you. Anzac biscuits, originally made for the Australian and New Zealand Army Corps (Anzacs), last for many weeks, and were sent to soldiers fighting in the First and Second World Wars. The pumpkin scones in the book are eaten in Brisbane in honour of Flo Bjelke-Petersen (wife of ex-Queensland Premier Jo Bjelke-Petersen), who shared her now-famous recipe for them in the 1980s. Lamingtons are my personal favourite, and classic lunchbox fodder: a dense sponge, rolled in rich chocolate icing and desiccated coconut. I was convinced they weren't worth making myself (the shop-bought ones are great) until I made them for my friend Jess's thirtieth birthday – a gift from one Australian to another, both many miles from home. They're a joy to make and to eat.

Pumpkin Scones
Makes 10

1. Peel and chop the pumpkin into roughly even-sized pieces. Put the pieces in a saucepan, cover with water and bring to the boil. Cook for around 10 minutes, or until a skewer can be easily poked through a piece of pumpkin.

2. Drain the pumpkin and allow it to cool. Mash it with a potato masher, then place it in a sieve and squash it around to drain any excess water. Don't squash it too much – you don't want it bone dry.

3. Preheat the oven to 220°C/425°F/Gas 7. Beat the butter and sugar together in a mixing bowl until combined. Add the salt and beat in the egg. Fold in 280g/10oz of the cooked pumpkin (any leftovers are great folded through pancake batter or added to mashed potato for dinner), then sift the flour and baking powder into the mixture and fold it through gently. It's really important not to overmix, so as soon as the flour has been incorporated, stop. If the mixture is still sticky, add a little more flour (bit by bit). Stop as soon as you can comfortably pat the mixture without it sticking to your floured hand.

4. Tip the mixture onto a floured surface and push into a 2.5cm/1in-high mound. Flour a 5cm/2in biscuit cutter, or glass, and press down into the dough, without twisting or turning the cutter. Transfer the scones to the tray. Reshape any leftover dough and cut it out as before.

5. Brush the tops of the scones with milk (don't brush down the sides or they won't rise) and transfer to the oven for 15 minutes. Serve hot, with jam and cream.

INGREDIENTS

500g/1lb 2oz unpeeled pumpkin
20g/¾oz/heaping 1tbsp butter
75g/6tbsp caster/superfine sugar*
Pinch of salt
1 egg
350g/12⅓oz/3½ cups spelt flour
4tsp baking powder
30ml/2tbsp milk

* Lady Flo says 100g but, controversially, I'm going to disagree – a smaller amount is plenty and means the scones work well with both sweet and savoury toppings

INGREDIENTS

CAKE

175g/6oz/1½ sticks butter

250g/9oz/1¼ cups caster/superfine sugar

200g/7oz/scant 1 cup yoghurt

2tsp vanilla extract

5 medium eggs

300g/10½oz/2¼ cups plain/all-purpose flour

3tsp baking powder

ICING

200ml/7floz/scant 1 cup milk

300g/10½oz/1½ cups caster/superfine sugar

30g/1oz/⅓ cup cocoa powder

300g/10½oz dark chocolate, finely chopped

250g/9oz/2 cups fresh or desiccated/shredded coconut

EQUIPMENT

Square baking tin (25 x 25cm/10 x 10in)

Lamingtons

Makes 25

1. Preheat the oven to 180°C/350°F/Gas 4. Grease the base and sides of the cake tin, and line with greaseproof paper.

2. Melt the butter in a saucepan and allow to cool slightly. Pour into a bowl with the sugar, yoghurt and vanilla extract. Beat for a minute until smooth, then add the eggs one at a time, beating each one in well before the next is added.

3. Sift in the flour and baking powder and fold in with a spatula. Pour the batter into the tin and cover the top with foil. Bake for 40 minutes, then remove the foil and bake for a further 20 minutes, until a skewer inserted in the middle of the cake comes out clean. Remove the cake from the oven and cool in the tin, covered with the foil again, until the cake is cold and you're ready to use it. The cake can be made the day before you need it and left like this overnight.

4. While the cake is cooling, make the chocolate icing. Whisk the milk, sugar and cocoa powder together in the saucepan and bring to the boil. Remove from the heat, then pour over the finely chopped chocolate and stir to melt. Allow to cool to body temperature before using.

5. Using a ruler if you're pedantic (like me), slice the cake into 25 even squares. Each should be 5cm/2in wide, 5cm/2in long and 5cm/2in high. Obviously this isn't actually important, and if your cake rises like mine, your middle ones will be very slightly taller. But it's nice to imagine you're aiming for perfect cubes.

6. Spread the coconut on a tray – if you have one with a lip around the edge, to contain the mess, that would be ideal. Place the tray next to your bowl of chocolate and place

another rack, with a layer of baking paper underneath, on the far side of the coconut tray. Dunk each cake in the chocolate, shake a little to get rid of the excess icing, then roll in the coconut and place on the rack to set. Doing this in a production line is ideal (one person rolls in chocolate, the next in coconut), but if you're doing them on your own, roll them a couple at a time, and wash your hands in between each step, or your coconut will be covered in chocolate.

7. Allow the chocolate to set for an hour (on your worktop, rather than in the fridge, unless you're making them during an Australian summer) before eating.

Anzac Biscuits
Makes 16

1. Preheat the oven to 180°C/350°F/Gas 4. Melt the butter and golden syrup over a low heat and stir to combine. Put the flour, oats, coconut and sugars into a bowl and mix.

2. Add the bicarbonate of soda and water to the golden syrup and butter, and stir. Pour the liquid over the dry ingredients and mix with a wooden spoon. The mixture should come together in clumps.

3. Shape ping-pong-ball-sized balls of the mixture and place onto baking trays lined with greaseproof paper. Flatten slightly with the back of the spoon. If the biscuits crack at the sides, don't worry, just squidge them back together again – the mixture is incredibly forgiving.

4. Bake in the oven for 10–12 minutes until golden brown. The biscuits will feel underbaked when you take them out of the oven, but will harden on cooling. Err on the side of slightly underdone; an Anzac biscuit should be chewy.

INGREDIENTS

125g/4½oz/1⅛ sticks butter

3tbsp golden syrup

150g/5¼oz/heaping 1 cup plain flour

100g/3½oz/1 cup rolled oats (or porridge oats)

80g desiccated/shredded coconut

90g/7tbsp dark brown sugar

60g/5tbsp caster/superfine sugar

½tsp bicarbonate of soda/baking soda

1tbsp water

the *dinner* table

the *dinner* table

The table in our dining room at my mum's house is the heart of
our home. It seats ten comfortably, sixteen at a push. As a family of
four, it has always felt extravagant. The final third is like a separate
piece of furniture, forever covered with half-read newspapers, the
beginnings of a science project and a pile of books one or another
of us is working our way through. This table has been used for
everything from party preparations and late-night conversations, to
the cutting-out of my high-school formal dress.

It journeyed with us from England to Australia when I was two – it
has been in my mum's life for longer than I have and has seen her
through thousands of dinners. Quick ones we grabbed before choir
competitions. The Christmas Day buffet, where we'd fill our plates
before carrying them outside into the sun. My early experiments
with cooking, served up to the family. It also supported everything
I owned as I tried to squash it all into the backpack I brought with
me to London.

When I was a teenager, my mum and stepdad hosted a dinner
party every fortnight or so. They'd often be a week or more in the
planning – a menu drawn up, shopping trips organized, one of the
courses prepared in advance. On the day itself, as we watched back-
to-back police procedurals, we'd spend time setting the table, and
help Mum prepare whatever she had planned for dinner. Her food
was rarely fussy or fiddly – she likes to put a big dish on the table
and encourage everyone to dive in. On these nights, a place was
set for us too – our glasses received a dribble of wine, and we were
expected to join in with conversations. After dinner, we'd disappear
to watch *The Sound of Music* (again) and the adults would sit and
drink wine until at least midnight.

That table still sits there, covered with newspapers and a blue
tablecloth. Every time I go back to Australia, it's the place where we
all come together, after long days, to debrief and to eat dinner. The
dishes in this chapter are ones I can imagine us all sharing around it.

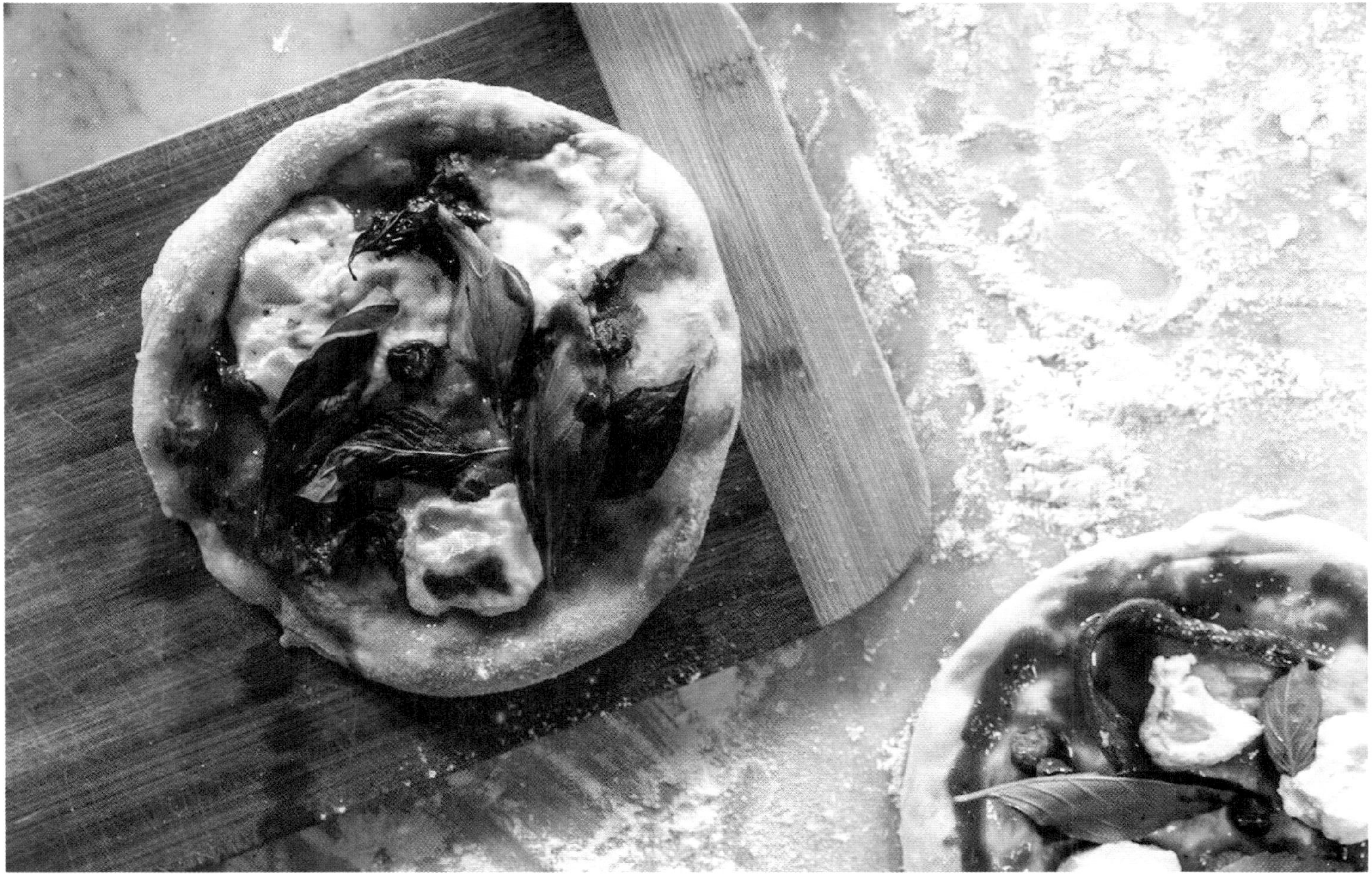

Neapolitan Pizza

I was overwhelmed by the names, the noise of the traffic, the voices, the colours, the festive atmosphere, the effort of keeping everything in mind so that I could talk about it later with Lila, the ease with which he bought me a pizza melting with ricotta, the fruit seller from whom he bought me a yellow peach.
My Brilliant Friend, Elena Ferrante

In Bloomsbury, in central London, lies a bookshop that I love: the London Review Bookshop (LRB). I hope that you have an equivalent near you; a shop full of passionate, knowledgeable staff, a well-curated selection of books and a café full of cake worth travelling for. I met Natalia, who manages the shop, at an afternoon tea in March 2015, when I was still working in theatre. Natalia asked what I did, and I told her about my blog. She was one of the first people 'in the business' who said it needed to be a book.

I met her again at the bookshop a couple of months later, and asked if there was anything she thought I should read. She pressed the first of the Neapolitan novels into my hands. I was hooked five minutes into the bus ride home, and stretched out the rest of the quartet over the six months that followed, desperate for them not to end. Set in post-war Naples, the books explore the complex relationship between two childhood friends: Elena and Lila. We follow them through their schooling, marriages, careers and motherhood, in a story that plays out across Italy.

The book is also full of food I am desperate to eat. Crisp pastries, bowls of homemade pasta and this: a classic Neapolitan pizza. The pizza demands time (days of it, in fact), but very little of it is hands on. Once you have made the dough, it will sit quietly in your fridge, rising imperceptibly until you have delicate balls, filled with bubbles. Perfect for pizza with a crisp base and a chewy interior.

Neapolitan Pizza

Makes 6 small pizzas

1. Prepare the ricotta. Line a sieve with the muslin and place over a bowl. Pour the milk and buttermilk into a saucepan and heat to 80°C/175°F, stirring constantly. If you don't have a thermometer, don't worry, just make sure you prevent it from boiling. The liquid will separate into white curds and a yellowish whey. The curds will float on the top once the temperature hits 80°C/175°F. Skim the curds off the top, and place in the lined sieve. Strain for 3–20 minutes, depending on how firm you want the ricotta (I like it soft, so do mine for only a couple of minutes). Transfer to a jar/bowl and stir the salt through. Refrigerate until you're ready to use it.

2. To prepare the dough, crumble the yeast into the mixing bowl and add the water.* Whisk to soften the yeast. Add the flour and salt and mix with your hand. Tip onto your work surface and knead for 10 minutes, until the dough is soft, smooth and elastic.

3. Clean the mixing bowl and return the dough to it. Cover with plastic wrap. Leave to rise in a warm place for 90 minutes (fast method) or at room temperature for half an hour, then the fridge for 24 hours (slow method).

4. Split the risen dough into 6 even pieces and shape into balls. Place on a baking tray lined with greaseproof paper, sprinkle with flour and cover with plastic wrap. Return to a warm place for a further hour (fast method) or place in the fridge for a 2 days (slow method).

5. If you've made your dough using the fast method, it will be ready to use. If you've made it using the slow method, remove your dough from the fridge about 90 minutes before you want to use it so it can come to room temperature and finish rising. Place a cast-iron pan/pizza stone/baking tray in your oven and turn it onto the hottest setting. It will never be as hot as a true pizza oven, but preheating for a good length of time is a start.

INGREDIENTS

DOUGH
20g/¾oz/heaping 1tbsp fresh yeast (or 7g/¼oz/2½tsp fast-action yeast)
300ml/½ pint/1¼ cups water (at body temperature)
500g/1lb 2oz/scant 3 cups '00' (pasta) flour
1tsp salt
Handful of semolina

RICOTTA
1L/¾ pint milk
250ml/8½floz/generous 1 cup buttermilk
Large pinch of salt

TOPPINGS
Olive oil
Passata or home-made tomato sauce
Anchovies
Capers
Fresh basil leaves

EQUIPMENT
Thermometer (optional)
Piece of muslin/ cheesecloth
Pizza stone, cast-iron pan or baking tray
Paddle/cake lifter/thin bread board

6. Each ball of dough will now be full of irregular holes; this is exactly what you're looking for. Sprinkle your work surface with some semolina and, handling the dough with kid gloves to try to retain as many of these holes as possible, push and pull each piece into shape with your hands. If you can spin it in the air, do – mine would inevitably end up on the floor. Ensure that you leave the crust a little thicker than the centre.

7. Trickle some olive oil into the centre of the pizza, and spread it over with your fingertips. Spoon a tablespoon of passata onto the base, then add your toppings – some ricotta, a couple of anchovies, a small handful of capers, and some basil leaves works well.

8. Slide your pizza onto a paddle/cake lifter/thin board that you've sprinkled with semolina. Shake the pizza onto the stone in the oven and close the door quickly. Bake for around 7 minutes, until the base is puffed and blackened in places.

9. Drizzle with olive oil and serve. Continue making pizzas with the rest of the dough and toppings, but keep it simple – the dough can become stodgy if you load it with ingredients.

*I like to let this dough rise slowly over three days – a long time, I know, but it gives a real depth of flavour, and makes for a gloriously light dough filled with uneven pockets of air. If you cannot wait three days, don't worry. You can make the dough in an afternoon and the pizza will still be delicious. I have provided the 'slow' three-day method along with the 'fast' single afternoon method for you to choose whichever suits your timetable.

My Brilliant Friend, Elena Ferrante

Spaghetti & Meatballs

'Is Clemenza out there?' Sonny asked.
Michael grinned. 'He's cooking up spaghetti for the troops,
just like the army.'
The Godfather, Mario Puzo

I thought I was Italian for much of my childhood. A strange miscommunication and a series of assumptions meant that I always imagined our big, generous family, our love of Tuscan red wine and Campari, our adoption of words like *mangiare* (eat up) and *salute* (cheers) and our regular consumption of lasagnes represented something more than just my mum's taste. Though I was confronted with the English/Irish/Danish reality when filling in a family tree at the end of primary school, it was a difficult affiliation to let go of.

When my stepfather, Geoff, moved in, he brought with him a box-set of *The Godfather* on VHS, and a vast collection of friends he made in high school. Both had an indelible impact on me. His friends became part of our extended family, and it was not long after Geoff arrived that I met Mrs G, his friend Viv's mother. If I couldn't be Italian, I could at least have an Italian grandmother in my life – and Mrs G is one of the best.

Although I've watched *The Godfather* countless times with Geoff, I didn't read the book until many years later. It now sits on my bookshelf in London, reminding me of my brilliant stepfather. And my non-Italian family.

Mrs G's Spaghetti and Meatballs

Serves 4

1. Put the beef mince, garlic, parsley, egg, breadcrumbs, salt, pepper and wine into a bowl. Mix by hand until combined. The mixture should be sticky but not wet – add more breadcrumbs if it is too wet, or wine if it is too dry. Cover and leave in the fridge for an hour.

2. Shape the mince into tablespoon-sized balls, then roll each in the flour to coat. The mixture should make 20–24 meatballs.

3. Heat a couple of tablespoons of oil in a frying pan. Add the meatballs, frying until browned on each side. Check one to ensure it is cooked all the way through, then turn off the heat. Set the meatballs aside.

4. To make the sauce, clean out the frying pan, then warm a tablespoon of olive oil over a medium heat. Once hot, add the tin of tomatoes. Stir until bubbling, then add the tomato purée, salt and sugar. Turn the heat down and stir occasionally until thick. Add the meatballs, stir to coat and leave on a very low heat while you cook the pasta.

5. Fill your largest saucepan with water and bring it to the boil. Add a generous pinch of salt (the water you cook pasta in should be as salty as the sea) and cook the spaghetti until al dente. Reserve a mug of the cooking water and drain the pasta. Add it to the sauce and stir through, along with some of the cooking water to lubricate the spaghetti. Serve immediately with Parmesan and basil, if you like.

A NOTE: The meatballs won't be dry or dense inside, so they may be a little delicate. Stir carefully once they're in the sauce or, if you'd like to ensure they stay whole, pull them out of the pan before combining the pasta and the sauce, and add them in again afterwards.

INGREDIENTS

MEATBALLS
500g/1lb 2oz beef mince/ground beef
1 clove garlic, finely chopped
A handful of flat-leaf parsley, finely chopped
1 egg
2tbsp soft breadcrumbs
Salt and pepper
125ml/4floz/½ cup white or red wine (whatever is open)
3tbsp plain/all-purpose flour
Olive oil

SAUCE
400g/14oz tin chopped tomatoes (or around 600g/1lb 5oz fresh tomatoes, if it is summer where you are and the tomatoes are delicious)
2tbsp tomato purée/paste
Pinch of salt
Pinch of sugar

AND
300g/10½oz dried spaghetti
Grated Parmesan cheese
Fresh basil leaves

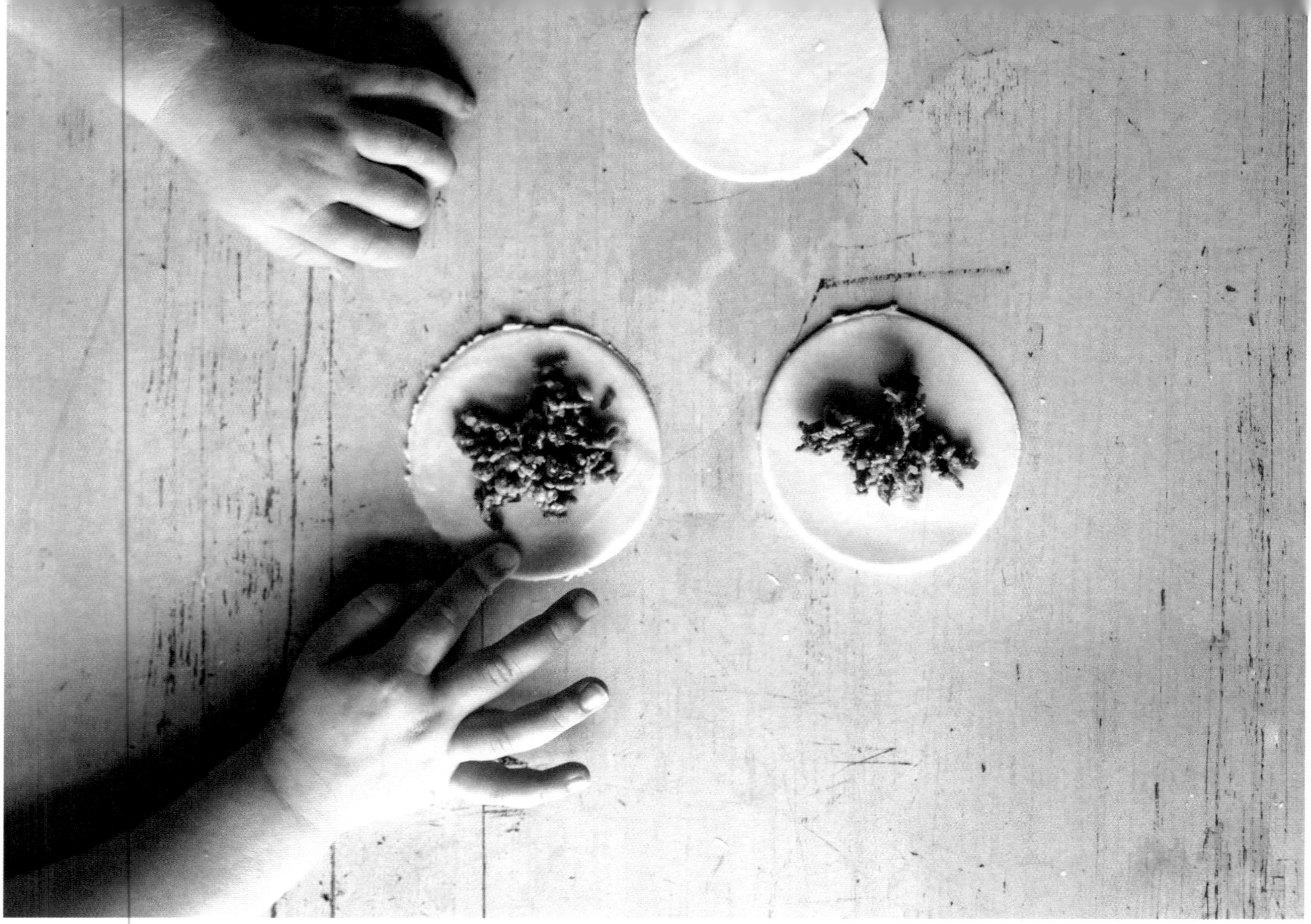

A Thousand Pork & Ginger Dumplings

Back home, I told the cook girl to boil enough pots of water and to chop enough pork and vegetables to make a thousand dumplings, both steamed and boiled, with plenty of fresh ginger, good soy sauce, and sweet vinegar for dipping.
The Kitchen God's Wife, Amy Tan

People often ask what I miss most about Brisbane. Every time the mercury drops, someone will mention the fact that I made the move from a hot country to a cold one, and tells me I must miss the weather. But I'm a winter person at heart, far happier wrapped in a blanket than sitting on a beach.

What I do miss are the little things, like preparing food with my family. I miss our dinner parties. I miss making cocktail party food for eighty people. I miss the production line that we would set up around our island bench. Cooking is, after all, such a social activity. Your hands are occupied, but otherwise you are free to converse with those around you. It is this that I love about Amy Tan's books: the conversations that happen over food, the time spent in kitchens and in dining rooms.

These dumplings are ideal for making with family but, far away from mine, I am much more likely to be making them on my own. An added bonus: as an anxious person, I have to tell you that these are extraordinarily therapeutic. Once you get the hang of the fold and pinch, they are very easy to make. The slow, calm repetition, while you watch your pile of dumplings grow, has been a lifeline for me on more than one occasion.

Pork and Ginger Dumplings

Makes a more modest 30

1. First, make the dough for the wrappers. Put the flour and salt in a bowl, then pour in the water. Stir with a wooden spoon to combine and then, once cool enough, continue to mix with your hands. Cover and allow the dough to rest for half an hour.

2. For the filling, warm the sesame oil in a frying pan over a medium heat. Fry the garlic for a minute, stirring to ensure it doesn't brown. Add the spring onions, ginger and chilli, cook for a minute, then add the pork. Cook for 5 minutes, moving the meat around to ensure it all cooks through. Add the lime zest, lime juice and soy sauce, cook for a final minute, then remove from the heat. Set aside to cool.

3. Once the dough has rested, knead it for around 10 minutes until smooth. At the start, it will be hard to manipulate, but keep working, stretching the dough out with the heel of your hand. If the dough is too hard to work with, add some extra water, a teaspoon at a time. It will get there. Once smooth and pliable, cut into 6 pieces and return 5 of these to the fridge, covered in plastic wrap.

4. Flour your work surface, roll the piece of dough out to around 2mm/⅛in thick, then cut into rounds with an 8cm/3¼in biscuit cutter. Set each wrapper aside, covered with a tea towel. You might like to put a bit of greaseproof paper between each one to ensure they don't stick, but I just layer them, then peel carefully when I come to use them. Repeat with the rest of the dough. Keep any scraps, re-knead, and cut out again.

5. Once your filling is cool, mix the flour and water into a paste and set up a bit of a production line. To fill the dumplings, place a generous teaspoon of the mixture into the centre of the wrapper. Run a finger, moistened with the flour paste, along the top edge of the wrapper, and fold the other side over to create a semi circle.

INGREDIENTS

WRAPPERS*
180g/6⅓oz/1⅓ cups plain all-purpose flour

Pinch of flaky sea salt/ Kosher salt

80ml/about 5tbsp just boiled water**

1tbsp flour and 2tbsp water (for sealing the wrappers)

FILLING
1tbsp sesame oil

5 cloves garlic, finely chopped

2 large spring onions/ scallions, finely chopped

1½tbsp finely chopped ginger

1 large green chilli, finely chopped

200g/7oz minced/ ground pork

Zest and juice of a small lime

1tbsp soy sauce

SAUCE
1tbsp sesame oil

80ml/5tbsp rice wine vinegar

1tbsp sweet chilli sauce

2tbsp soy sauce

Pinch of sugar

*You can buy the dumpling wrappers if you prefer. I often do when short of time.

** On a hot day, you may need as much as 140ml/4½floz to get the dough pliable enough.

135

6. Working from the edge of the mixture, push the wrapper closed, ensuring there are no air holes, then seal the edges. Starting at one corner, crimp the dough between your thumb and forefinger, with your middle finger supporting the dough underneath. Repeat at close intervals along the edge. Store each finished dumpling under a cloth and continue with the rest of the wrappers and mixture.

7. To prepare the sauce, put all the ingredients in a small saucepan and bring to the boil. Reduce the heat to low, and leave to simmer away quietly while you cook the dumplings.

8. Bring a large pot of water to the boil, then reduce to a confident simmer. Drop the dumplings into the water in batches, giving them room to move. Cook for 5–6 minutes, then remove with a slotted spoon. Allow to drain, then transfer to a serving plate. Spoon the sauce over the top and serve immediately.

Spanakopita

Desdemona went up and down the line, adding walnuts, butter, honey, spinach, cheese, adding more layers of dough, then more butter, before forging the assembled concoctions in the oven.
Middlesex, Jeffrey Eugenides

I tried making filo once. After a frustrating afternoon with a broom handle, my pasta machine and more than a few tears, I am happy to report that you never need to. This pastry, assembled in layers around sweet and savoury fillings, needs to be paper-thin to crisp up properly in the oven. You are not a machine – and neither am I – and so the good stuff from the supermarket will serve you much better. Pleasingly, shop-bought filo turns this pie from a full-day challenge into a mid-week supper or a simple weekend lunch.

The key here is the butter: be generous with it between each layer, as pallid, soft filo is such an unattractive prospect. And, most importantly, the spinach needs to be drained very well. Squeeze it, squelch it, press it, leave it to drain, and then do the same again. It really will make a world of difference.

In *Middlesex*, Desdemona lays her pastry out all over the house, but she is cooking in the 1920s, long before the Greek pastry she grew up with was readily available in American supermarkets. When using shop-bought, keep it covered for as much time as possible. Laying supermarket filo all over your sitting room will cause it to dry out faster than you can fill it, and it will end up all over your carpet, rather than round your spinach.

INGREDIENTS

1 brown onion, finely chopped

1tbsp flavourless oil

1kg/2¼lb frozen spinach

1tbsp chopped dill

3tbsp chopped flat-leaf parsley

1 egg

100g/3½oz feta cheese

Freshly grated nutmeg

Salt and pepper

100g/3½oz/scant 1 stick butter

10 sheets filo/phyllo pastry

Sesame seeds, to decorate

Spanakopita

Serves 4

1. Preheat the oven to 180°C/350°F/Gas 4. Fry the onion in a large saucepan with the oil. Once translucent, tip in the spinach and stir constantly while it defrosts. Cook over a relatively high heat to try to encourage some of the water to evaporate.

2. Tip the spinach and onion into a sieve and squelch them around with your hand, squeezing out as much of the water as you can. The more you can remove here, the crisper your pastry will be. Leave to cool.

3. Once cool, add the chopped herbs and the egg, and crumble in the feta. Grate in some nutmeg and add salt and pepper to taste.

4. Melt the butter in a saucepan. Lay 2 sheets of filo on your work surface, with their longest edges parallel to where you are standing, and overlapping by 2cm/¾in. Brush generously with butter. Add two more sheets on top, butter again and repeat until all the filo is used up. Lay a long line of filling about 5cm/2in from the long edge of pastry closest to you. Roll the pastry up into one long sausage. Coil it into a spiral.

5. Transfer the spanakopita to a lined baking sheet, brush generously with butter, sprinkle with sesame seeds and bake for 25 minutes until golden brown.

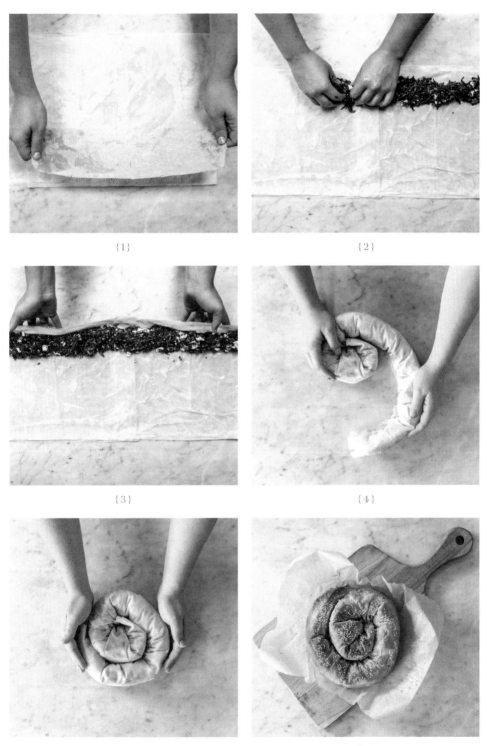

{1}

{2}

{3}

{4}

{5}

{6}

Jollof Rice

She made him the kind of jollof rice he liked, flecked with bits of red and green peppers, and as he ate, fork moving from the plate to his mouth, saying, 'This is pretty good,' as he always had in the past, she felt her tears and her questions gathering.
Americanah, Chimamanda Ngozi Adichie

I love family recipes. We have books of them printed in my mum's careful hand – writing down the recipes that my granny and great-grandmother dictated to her. When I moved to England, Mum handed me a box full of handwritten recipe cards, ones I have used innumerable times since. We also have family recipes that have been passed down without ever being committed to paper. Our bolognese, which includes inauthentic mushrooms alongside the tomatoes, beef and herbs. Our egg-fried rice, which we make with whatever we find at the bottom of the fridge. They are recipes I still use now.

In *Americanah*, Ifemelu makes this jollof rice for comfort, many miles from where she grew up. When I started developing a recipe for it, I asked friends, and friends of friends, for advice. People were keen to speak at length about every detail of the dish – from the brand of stock cube, to the best way to cook rice, to the consistency of the sauce. When researching this recipe, I knew I needed to speak to people for whom it is a staple; families who eat it like mine eat fried rice: regularly, and with whatever is available.

The recipes they shared were filled not only with lists of ingredients and directions, but with anecdotes: 'My mum chops up whatever vegetables she can find to add in – hiding them from my brothers', 'My aunt crumbles a Maggi stock cube into hers – it has to be Maggi'. This is an amalgam of those recipes. I can't claim it as a definitive version, but it is the one I like the best. For a recipe made a thousand different ways, in millions of different households, that will have to do.

Jollof Rice

Serves 4 as a main – or more as a side

1. Remove the seeds from the red peppers and chillies, then chop into large chunks. Slice the tomatoes into quarters and remove their seeds. Slice the onion into large chunks. Place these, along with the salt, into a food processor/pestle and mortar and blitz/pound to a paste.

2. Warm the oil in a frying pan over a high heat and tip in the paste. Lower the heat and reduce it until thick (around 10 minutes), stirring regularly to prevent it sticking.

3. Meanwhile, cook the rice. Rinse it three times in cold water, tip into a saucepan and then add enough fresh water to cover the rice by 2cm/¾in. Place a lid on the pan. Put it on to boil, reducing to a simmer once the water is bubbling. Allow to cook (with the lid on) until the water has evaporated to the level of the rice. Turn the heat off and leave the rice to steam in the pan while you finish the sauce.

4. Add the tomato purée, crumbled stock cube, spices and chopped red and green peppers to the paste mixture. Continue to cook for 5 minutes over a low heat, until the pepper has softened to your taste. Remove from the heat, stir through the cooked rice and serve immediately with meat, fish, or on its own.

INGREDIENTS

SPICE PASTE

2 small red peppers

2 scotch bonnet chillies (this is very much to taste – add more or less as you fancy)

600g/1lb 5oz tomatoes (or one 400g/14oz tin chopped tomatoes if you can't find ones that smell like tomatoes)

1 red onion

Large pinch of salt

3tbsp rapeseed/canola oil

TO SERVE

250g/9oz/heaping 1½ cups long-grain rice

4tbsp tomato purée/paste

1 chicken stock cube

2tsp curry powder

Pinch of grated nutmeg

1 small red pepper, finely diced

1 small green pepper, finely diced

EQUIPMENT

Food processor/stick blender/pestle and mortar

A Fine Curry

Now we have heard how Mrs. Sedley had prepared a fine curry for her son, just as he liked it, and in the course of dinner a portion of this dish was offered to Rebecca. 'What is it?' said she, turning an appealing look to Mr. Joseph.

'Capital,' said he. His mouth was full of it: his face quite red with the delightful exercise of gobbling. 'Mother, it's as good as my own curries in India.'

Vanity Fair, William Makepeace Thackeray

There's a little Indian restaurant across the road from my dad's house. It sits between a fish and chip shop that's changed owners more times than I can count, and a shopfront that had nothing behind it for most of my teenage years. But the Indian restaurant thrived. It was (and, I am assured by my family, still is) fantastic.

Through school and much of university I had a job there, spending my Thursday and Saturday nights packing fragrant saffron rice into boxes, blitzing sweet mango lassis, and delivering steaming bowls of butter chicken to the heaving dining room. The range of curries on offer was extensive, but when the chefs cooked their own for dinner after service, they were quite unlike the saucy curries I was serving to the customers. Drier, full of different vegetables, and flavoured with even more spices, these were curries we ate with our hands and a pile of roti before locking up for the night.

This moment in *Vanity Fair*, when Becky Sharp tries curry for the first time, brings my own memories into focus. She tucks in, determined to feign an interest in all things from India to impress Joseph Sedley. Already struggling with the heat of cayenne pepper, she takes a bite out of a shiny green chilli, an action she comes, of course, to regret. My experience of those early curries was similar. My teenage determination to prove I could handle the heat would often end with me sitting with a mouthful of yoghurt, desperately trying to cool my protesting tongue. Nowadays, my threshold is slightly higher, so do adjust this to suit your own palate.

Goat and Potato Curry

Serves 4 – generously

1. Blitz or bash the ginger, garlic and chillies to a paste. Warm the ghee in the pan over a low heat and fry the paste for 5 minutes, until very fragrant. Keep it moving so that it doesn't stick to the pan and burn.

2. Add the cumin and coriander, along with the stick of cinnamon. Fry on a low heat for a further 5 minutes. Stir the onions through the spices, frying for 10 minutes until soft and translucent.

3. Tip in the meat. Increase the heat to medium. Add the turmeric and cayenne pepper and coat the meat in the spices while browning it on all sides. Stir in the flour, and coat the meat with it.

4. Add the stock and bring to the boil. Reduce to a low simmer, cover with a lid and cook for an hour until the meat is tender. Add some more stock if the goat is drying out at any point.

5. Add the diced potato. Stir, then cook, with the lid on, for a further 20 minutes. The potato should be tender and the meat meltingly soft.

6. Serve the curry with chapatis, naan or rice, and some chutney or hot lime pickle.

INGREDIENTS

Thumb-sized piece of ginger, peeled

4 cloves garlic

2 long green chillies, deseeded

30g/1oz ghee (or rapeseed oil)

2tsp cumin seeds, ground to a powder

1tbsp coriander seeds, ground to a powder

1 stick cinnamon

2 brown onions

700g/1½lb goat meat, cut into 2cm/¾in pieces (shoulder is good use mutton or lamb if you can't find goat)

1tsp turmeric

1tsp cayenne pepper

2tbsp plain flour

500ml/17floz/generous 2 cups vegetable stock

400g potatoes, peeled and diced into 2cm/¾in cubes

EQUIPMENT

Pestle and mortar or food processor

Fish & Chips

When Mrs Broom and her fish and chips arrived home, they received a fine welcome.
The Bear Nobody Wanted, Janet and Allan Ahlberg

Having decided, aged twelve, that I was going to move to London as soon as humanly possible, I committed myself to finding a job the minute I was legally old enough. In Australia, that minute was when I turned fifteen. One night, just before my fifteenth birthday, as we were picking up our fish and chips, Mum convinced me to ask behind the counter for a job. I started a week later.

Dressed in a Hawaiian shirt and cargo shorts, and smelling fetchingly of oil and fish, I spent the next six months in front of a deep-fat fryer. I learnt about keeping batter cold, about the best condiments to serve with chips (salt and cider vinegar or cheap, thick mayonnaise), and which chocolate bars from the shop across the road would stand up to being battered and fried (Nigella is right: Bounty bars are, hands down, the best). I moved on relatively quickly to a waitressing job at our local Indian restaurant, always having preferred the smell of curry to that of oil, but this first job had a big impact on me. I discovered I loved working with food.

The Bear Nobody Wanted is set in late-1930s London, where a teddy bear with an unfortunate expression is passed from household to household. He survives the threat of being 'recycled' for parts, being left out in the rain, the Blitz and, on his first day of life, a trip home in a shoulder bag with a parcel of fish and chips.

Fish and Chips
Serves 2

1. Peel the potatoes and slice them lengthways, about 1cm/½in wide. Boil for 5 minutes until just tender enough to pierce with a knife. Keep a good eye on them, as you don't want to overcook them. Drain, and leave to cool.

2. Heat the oil to 150°C/300°F in a high-sided saucepan. If you don't have a thermometer, put the handle of a wooden spoon into the oil. If tiny bubbles fizz around it, it's ready. If bubbles move to the surface, it is too hot, and you should turn it down a little. Tip the chips into the oil and cook for around 5 minutes until pale golden. Drain on some kitchen paper, and leave to cool while you cook the fish.

3. Turn the oil up slightly, until it reaches 180°C/350°F. At this stage, the bubbles around the wooden spoon should be moving enthusiastically and be varied in size. Get the batter ingredients out of the fridge. Whisk the flour and baking powder together. Pour in the fizzy water, whisking vigorously. You should have a thick, bubbling batter. Put the extra 3tbsp flour in a shallow dish.

4. Press a piece of fish into the flour, then shake off and dip into the batter, ensuring it is completely coated. Allow the batter to drain off slightly, then place it into the oil, moving it back and forth a little as you do so to start the batter puffing and ensure it floats. Repeat with the rest of the fish. If your pan is too small for this, cook it in stages.

5. Turn the fish over once or twice as it cooks, removing it to a plate lined with kitchen paper when it is golden brown (5 or 6 minutes). Leave to drain while you finish the chips.

6. Tip the cool chips back into the oil for another 2 minutes until golden. If you fancy some scraps (stray, puffed bits of batter), dribble some leftover batter in too. Drain the chips on some kitchen paper. Serve immediately, sprinkled with lots of salt and vinegar, and condiments of your choosing.

INGREDIENTS

CHIPS
200g/7oz Maris Piper potatoes
2L/3½ pints/8½ cups vegetable oil

FISH
300g/10½oz sustainably sourced white fish (I used cod loin fillet, but haddock or pollock would do well here too)

BATTER
100g/3½oz/¾ cup plain/all-purpose flour, plus 3tbsp
1tsp baking powder
125ml/4floz/½ cup soda or fizzy mineral water

AND
Salt and vinegar
Mayonnaise/tartare sauce
Mushy peas
Pickled onions
Lemon wedges

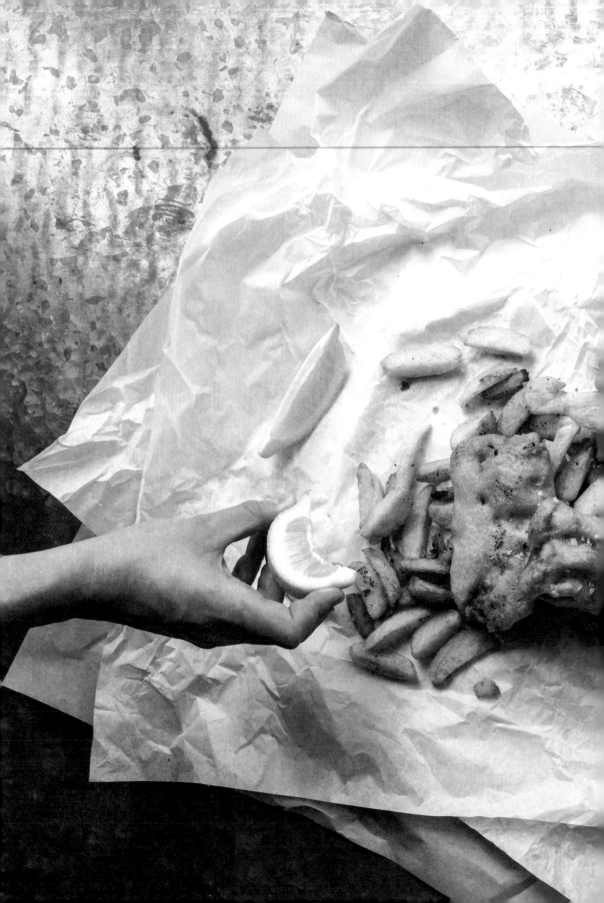

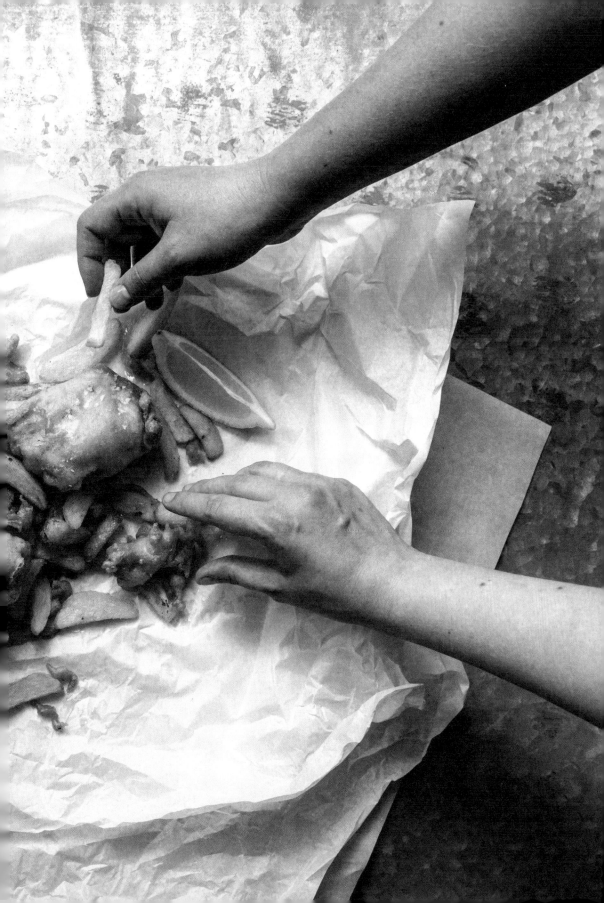

Chicken Casserole

'I think it might be time to see to that casserole,' I said, getting up.
'It's just on half past seven.'
It turned out to be a very nice bird and I am sure that even William's
could not have been better.
Excellent Women, Barbara Pym

I didn't imagine I'd be single at thirty. Growing up, I assumed that
by this age I would have a partner, and children would be just
around the corner. I didn't think I'd be glancing around at a series
of friend's weddings, noticing that I was one of the only ones there
without a plus one.

So the discovery of Mildred, the titular 'excellent woman' of
this book, came as a breath of fresh air. This phrase is used
(condescendingly) in the book to describe the sort of unmarried
woman who is useful to have around when planning church
rummage sales and the Christmas bazaar. Though she is
undoubtedly good at those things, Mildred is really rather excellent
in other ways too – wonderfully dry, witty and heart-breakingly
honest. I read the book with a nod of recognition: the lunches and
dinners for one, the inevitability of being the spare at a dinner of
couples, the freedom of being beholden only to oneself, and the
challenges that come with that.

This casserole is a good option when you have a few friends
coming round for dinner. It requires very little of your attention
once you transfer it from the worktop into the oven; just leave
it to bubble away while you and your guests crack open a bottle
of wine. Mildred eats this chicken casserole with Everard, the
anthropologist she eventually marries. It is, however, equally
delicious made for one. If you are eating alone, do what I do: halve
the ingredients, replace the whole chicken with four small thighs
and take the leftovers for lunch the next day.

Chicken Casserole

Serves 4

1. Preheat the oven to 200°C/400°F/Gas 6. Melt the butter in a large frying pan. Once it is foaming, add the chicken pieces, skin-side down. If they won't fit in one layer, with some space between each piece, then cook in batches. Remove and set aside.

2. Fry the onions, celery, leek, and carrots in the remaining melted butter for around 5 minutes, until they start to soften. Stir in the flour, and cook for 2 minutes. Add the wine and cook for another minute. Tip the vegetables and wine into a casserole dish, then add the lemon slices, garlic, salt, pepper and thyme. Pour in the stock, then nestle the chicken, skin-side up, in amongst the liquid.

3. Cover and transfer to the oven for 20 minutes. Remove the lid and roast for a further 5 minutes, or until the juices that escape a pierced thigh run clear. Serve the chicken with the vegetables and a generous spoonful of the juices that sit underneath it.

INGREDIENTS

30g/1oz/2tbsp butter

Whole chicken, jointed*
(around 1.5kg/3¼lb)

2 brown onions, finely sliced

2 stalks celery, finely sliced

1 leek, finely sliced

2 carrots, finely sliced

2tbsp plain/all-purpose flour

125ml/4floz/½ cup white wine

2 lemons, sliced into thick rounds

4 cloves garlic, left whole, crushed with a knife

Salt and pepper

20 sprigs thyme

125ml/4floz/½ cup chicken stock

EQUIPMENT

Large casserole dish (or roasting tray)

* Ensure your chicken is at room temperature. Place on its back, legs towards you. Open the legs wide, find the joint that connects the thigh to the body and cut through. Then find the joint between the drumstick and thigh and cut straight through. Repeat on the other leg. Turn the chicken over. Find where the wing meets the body. Cut straight through on both sides. Finally, turn the chicken breast-side up, find the middle of the breast, and slice through. Either slice the breast away from the bones, or slice right through the bones.

Curried Sausages

'Delicious,' said Ted, taking another mouthful. 'Best curry I've had in ages. Really like the glacé cherries.'
Two Weeks with the Queen, Morris Gleitzman

We had an unprecedented year of hospital visits when I was thirteen. On all sides of our extended family, people we loved faced cancer diagnoses. Mum became a champion at batch cooking. We'd always have four or five options ready for reheating when we got home from the hospital. On weekends, my sister and I would help her prepare enough to stock our freezer, and to box up for anyone else she suspected of needing some support, and some sausages.

I have put these curried sausages in the microwave more times than I can count. They speak to me of comfort in a way that no other dish does; I've cried into them, had difficult conversations over a bowl of them, and have made them for myself when feeling horribly homesick. They're great with rice, but they're just as good on toast, or on their own if the idea of boiling rice is more than you can face.

Morris Gleitzman's brilliant *Two Weeks with the Queen* tackles big questions: death, cancer, family, AIDS, loneliness, and does so with such obvious affection for its strange collection of characters. It is still capable of reducing me to tears. Colin, who is sent from Australia to England when his brother is diagnosed with terminal cancer, makes this dish twice, both times for someone struggling with grief and the anticipated loss of a loved one. I had forgotten about his curried sausages, and coming across them again recently (albeit with the presence of very unwelcome glacé cherries) made me burst into tears. Colin's family, and mine, coping with the help of curried sausages. The recipe below is, verbatim, my mum's.

Curried Sausages

Serves 6

1. Simmer the sausages in water for around 3 minutes, until cooked, then skin them and cut into 1cm/½in slices. Warm the oil in the saucepan, and add the onion, carrot and celery. Cook until soft, but not brown, stirring constantly.

2. Add the curry paste and cook for 2 minutes. Tip in the flour and cook over a low heat for 3 minutes, stirring constantly. The vegetables should be coated in curry paste and flour. Add the milk gradually; start with about 200ml/7floz, and then continue to add, stirring all the time, until the mixture forms a thick white sauce.

3. Add the sausages and peas and heat gently until they are cooked through. Season with salt and pepper to taste. Serve with rice or on toast. Don't worry about presentation here – this is beige comfort food of the highest order, to be eaten while curled up on the sofa.

INGREDIENTS

1kg/2¼lb fat pork sausages

750ml/1¼ pints water

2tbsp vegetable oil

2 medium brown onions, diced

1 large carrot, diced

1 stick celery, diced

1tbsp curry paste (korma or madras)

4tbsp plain/all-purpose flour

600ml/1 pint/2½ cups milk

75g/scant 3oz/heaping ½ cup frozen peas

Salt and pepper

Two Weeks with the Queen, Morris Gleitzman { } CURRIED SAUSAGES

Steak & Onions

Is it possible to fall in love over a dish of onions?

...

I said, 'It's a good steak,' and heard like poetry her reply, 'It's the best I've ever eaten.'

The End of the Affair, Graham Greene

A couple of years ago, I started to reduce the amount of meat in my diet; eating fish and vegetarian meals during the week, and keeping meat for the weekend. When I did buy my meat, I could afford to spend a little more on something from the butcher or the market.

Visiting a market stall on Broadway Market in East London became a beloved Saturday-morning ritual. I would pick up a parcel of chicken thighs, or a piece of black pudding, or a bit of pork belly, for my meaty dinner that evening. Steak was reserved for special weekends, when I was feeling a bit more flush. As I was usually cooking for one or two, I rarely had cause to buy anything larger, until the Christmas my mum and granny came to stay. Granny had planned to make her 'duvet beef': a fillet of beef that is cooked quickly, at a very high temperature, and then, quite literally, wrapped in a duvet for six or seven hours to continue cooking in the residual heat. It is perfect – meltingly tender and blush pink all the way through.

I was in charge of ordering the meat before they arrived, and was thrilled to have an excuse to order a huge cut from my regular stall. Foolishly, I ordered the wrong thing, but my error left me with eight eye fillet steaks in my freezer that I could eat over the next few months. I soon recovered from the feeling of mortification; a steak cooked very rare is one of my favourite things, and these really were the best I had ever eaten.

This is, in my opinion at least, the sexiest dish in this book. I wholeheartedly recommend serving it to someone you fancy. Sarah's thoughts on the steak in *The End of the Affair* are exactly the response you are aiming for, so keep it simple, and don't forget to let it rest. And, I guarantee you, it is possible to fall in love over these onions.

INGREDIENTS

ONIONS
Around 16 small, round
shallots
50g/1¾oz/3½tbsp butter
30 sprigs thyme
Salt and pepper

STEAK
2 pieces rump steak
Salt and pepper
Olive oil

EQUIPMENT
Griddle pan or heavy-
based frying pan

Steak and Onions
Serves 2

1. Heat the oven to 180°C/350°F/Gas 4. Remove the steaks from the fridge to bring them to room temperature.

2. Top and tail your shallots and peel off the outer layer of skin. Arrange them with one of the cut sides up in a small ovenproof dish. Place a small pat of butter on each one, then add a couple of sprigs of thyme and a generous pinch of salt and pepper. Transfer the dish to the oven for 50 minutes, until golden and soft.

3. In the last 15 minutes of the onion cooking time, start your steaks. Heat a griddle pan or heavy frying pan until water evaporates immediately when flicked onto it. Sprinkle some salt and pepper on one side of the steaks and put them, seasoning-side down, into the pan.

4. Flip each steak every 30 seconds or so. I'm loath to give cooking times here, because it is so dependent on the thickness of your steak. I use the hand test I was taught at school instead.* Once your steaks are cooked to your liking, wrap them in foil and leave to rest for 5 minutes.

5. Slice the steak into strips, place on your plate, and season with salt, pepper and a little drizzle of olive oil. Serve with the dish of onions.

*THE HAND TEST: Touch your forefinger to your thumb (don't pinch, just touch). Prod the heel of your thumb with a finger from your other hand, and then prod your steak. You're looking for a similar tenderness in your rare cooked steak. Once it reaches this tenderness, take it off the heat immediately. If you want your steak cooked differently, it should resemble:

Rare: Index finger
Medium rare: Middle finger
Medium: Ring finger
Well done: Little finger

Clam Chowder

Our appetites being sharpened by the frosty voyage, and in particular,
Queequeg seeing his favourite fishing food before him, and the
chowder being surpassingly excellent, we despatched it with great
expedition...
Moby-Dick, Herman Melville

I have spent many holidays by the seaside. If you drive an hour
north or south from my hometown, Brisbane, you will arrive
at some of the most beautiful beaches in the world. My teenage
summers were spent on these beaches; in the surf early each
morning, and then on the patio with a book each afternoon. We ate
more seafood during these weeks than at any other time of the year;
usually parcels of fish and chips so hot that we burnt our mouths,
or bowls of coral-pink prawns that we diligently peeled and then
stuffed into fresh bread rolls with seafood sauce.

This is a dish for a different kind of beach holiday; one where the
wind is always blowing a gale, and the salt and sand whip your face
as you walk along the cliffs. I've been on this holiday too, on the
south-west coast of Wales, where the wind was rushing in so fast
off the Atlantic it was impossible to walk in a straight line. We had
steaming bowls of mussels that night, but this would have been just
as welcome. It is a dinner for a cold night, warming you from the
inside out. It is simple and hearty and is described in such detail
in *Moby-Dick* (an entire chapter is given over to its ordering and
consumption) that I have little work to do on the recipe opposite.

You can, of course, increase the quantities, but I like cooking this
dinner for one. Good clams are a luxury – one that my budget
dictates I selfishly keep for myself. That said, this is a generous
portion and the quantities could stretch to a starter for two.

Clam Chowder

Serves 1

1. Rinse the clams and place them in a saucepan, along with the water. Cover and bring to the boil. Allow to steam for a couple of minutes until the shells have opened – try to resist peeking too often. Once open, drain the clams, reserving the liquid. When cool enough, remove the clams from their shells and set aside.

2. Fry the pancetta over a medium heat. It will release its own fat, so you don't need to add any at this point. Remove the pancetta to a bowl, then fry the shallot in the fat left in the pan. Cook for 5 minutes until golden, but keep the shallot moving; you don't want it crisp.

3. Return the pancetta to the pan, then add the leaves from the sprigs of thyme, along with the bay leaf and flour. Cook for a minute, stirring constantly.

4. Strain the clam liquid through a sieve lined with a piece of muslin. Slowly pour it into the pan, stirring constantly. Add the diced potatoe and simmer over a medium heat for around 10 minutes, or until they're cooked.

5. Stir the clams through the chowder and allow them time to warm through. Remove the pan from the heat, stir through the cream and butter, a generous grind of pepper and a pinch of salt. Serve with bread or crackers for dunking.

INGREDIENTS

500g/1lb 2oz clams (weighed in their shells)
200ml/7floz water
75g/2½oz pancetta
1 shallot, finely chopped
3 sprigs thyme
Bay leaf
1tbsp plain/all-purpose flour
1 medium waxy potato, diced
40ml/scant 3tbsp double/heavy cream
10g/⅓oz/2tsp butter
Salt and pepper

EQUIPMENT

Piece of muslin

Black Ice Cream

Everything tasted of pepper, even the ice cream – which was black.
The Hundred and One Dalmatians, Dodie Smith

My granny is a truly extraordinary woman; she can cackle on cue,
and had two black cats for much of my childhood. Some part of me
spent my early years wondering whether she might be a witch, a
suspicion that she and my mother actively encouraged. She is also
a wonderful cook. My mum taught me to cook, but my granny was
the one who encouraged me to taste new and challenging things.
Under her watchful eye, I discovered mole sauce, increasingly
hotter chillies, crumbed lamb's brains and caviar.

When the calendar gave us a Friday 13th, she would host a black
food dinner, where plate after plate of ebony-hued dishes would
delight her guests. I remember eating squid-ink pasta followed by
the darkest of chocolate gelatos for dessert, which always made me
think of Cruella de Vil's black ice cream.

As delicious as dark chocolate gelato is, it doesn't taste like pepper,
and so I developed this one. It's not for everyone – despite the
honey, it does taste quite savoury – but I have a feeling granny will
love it. I hope it's one she makes next Friday 13th.

INGREDIENTS

1¼tbsp black sesame
seeds

150ml/5floz/⅔ cup milk

150ml/5floz/⅔ cup
double/heavy cream

3 egg yolks

80g/scant 3oz/heaping
¼ cup honey

½tsp black peppercorns,
coarsely ground

1tsp flaky sea salt/Kosher
salt

EQUIPMENT

Pestle and mortar or
spice grinder

Freezer-proof bowl or ice
cream maker

Black Sesame Ice Cream

Makes 8 scoops

1. Grind the sesame seeds to a paste in a pestle and mortar.

2. Bring the milk and cream to simmering point on the hob/stove. Whisk together the egg yolks and honey until they are light and foamy. Slowly pour the cream and milk over the top, whisking constantly to avoid the yolks scrambling. Add the sesame paste, the pepper and the salt.

3. Return the custard to the saucepan and stir constantly over a low heat until it is thick enough to coat the back of a wooden spoon.

4. Strain through a fine sieve (you can discard the larger chunks of peppercorn and sesame seed that will get caught) and allow to cool. Pour into an ice-cream maker and freeze according to the machine instructions. Alternatively, pour into a freezer-proof bowl and place in the freezer for an hour, then remove and whisk vigorously to prevent ice crystals forming. Return to the freezer, and then repeat hourly for the next 3 hours. Freeze overnight.

5. Serve with a sprinkle of black sesame seeds.

Bread & Butter Pudding

The main course plates had long been cleared away and Betty had returned with the bread and butter pudding.
Atonement, Ian McEwan

The first chapters of *Atonement* are imbued with an almost tangible sense of summer; the oppressive heat seems to radiate right off the page. On impossibly hot days, when the heat sits so heavily on the city that it is difficult to think, I drift towards cold fresh fruit, plenty of iced fizzy water and bowls filled with ice cream or sorbet. I'm not good in the heat. I grumble, sweat and shy away from tackling difficult tasks. While others flock to parks and beer gardens, I'm happier searching for a shady spot with a breeze, or sitting by a swimming pool. I much prefer the park for a long walk on a brisk autumn day.

The very idea of a bread and butter pudding on the warmest day of the year makes me slightly queasy. In the book the pudding follows a roast and some particularly cloying chocolate cocktails, so I can't imagine the assembled party have much stomach for it. The men have removed their dinner jackets by the time it arrives on the table, thank goodness, but the atmosphere is still stifling.

Do yourself (and your guests) a favour, and save this one for a cooler evening. Though you can obviously buy bread specifically for this recipe, it's one of the best ways of using up any you might have lying around; I often end up making it with leftover panettone and brandy butter in the week after Christmas.

Bread and Butter Pudding

Serves 6

80g/3oz/¾ stick salted butter, at room temperature

1 loaf of slightly stale bread, sliced into triangles (brioche or panettone work particularly well)*

5 eggs

2tbsp light brown sugar

375ml/12½floz milk

125ml/4floz/½ cup double/heavy cream

1 tsp vanilla extract

75g/scant 3oz/½ cup sultanas/golden raisins, soaked overnight in rum (optional)

1tbsp demerara/ turbinado sugar

EQUIPMENT

Deep ovenproof dish – mine is 26 x 18 x 10cm/10¼ x 7 x 4in

*A note on the bread. If you have a hankering for bread and butter pudding, but no stale loaf in the bread bin, lay out fresh slices of bread for an hour or so before making the dessert, so that they dry out a little. They'll soak up the custard much more efficiently than fresh bread will.

1. Butter each slice of bread generously. Stand them up in the dish, layering the slices so that their corners poke up in various directions.

2. Whisk the eggs and light brown sugar together. Heat the milk and cream almost to boiling point in the saucepan, and then pour over the eggs and sugar, whisking constantly to avoiding scrambling the eggs. Whisk in the vanilla.

3. Pour the custard over the bread, squelching the slices down into the liquid if they pop up and out of place. If you're using them, sprinkle the sultanas over the top. Set aside to soak for 20 minutes, while you heat the oven to 160°C/325°F/Gas 3.

4. Sprinkle the demerara sugar over the pudding, then place the dish in a roasting tray and transfer to the oven. While the oven door is open, fill the roasting tray with boiling water, so that the sides of the ovenproof dish are surrounded by water. This will ensure your custard is really silky.

5. Bake for 35 minutes, until the bread is golden brown. Leave to sit for 5 minutes, before dishing up in generous portions.

Blueberry Pie

'Just in time for a piece of blueberry pie,' said Mrs. Zuckerman.
'Look at my frog!' said Avery, placing the frog on the drainboard and
holding out his hand for pie.
Charlotte's Web, E. B. White

This blueberry pie is not quite like the more perfectly formed pie in *Charlotte's Web*, a piece of which can be placed in Avery's hand. It is made with a pastry so rich in butter and sugar, any attempt to lattice it would inevitably end in tears. It is also nearly impossible to get it out of the pie dish in slices – it's one to scoop out with a spoon instead. Yet, despite the aesthetic challenges, I love this pie.

I love the blueberries, sharp with lemon juice, that work perfectly against the sweet, biscuity pastry. I love the way that the pastry closest to the fruit turns an extraordinary purple as it soaks up its juice. I love that it is the sort of pie that you keep returning to with a spoon; good hot from the oven, warm on the table or cold from the fridge. I hope it would be welcome on the Zuckerman's table.

It is a simple pie. The pastry is slightly hard to work with, but it doesn't react badly to being rolled and re-rolled, so you can play with it until you get it right. If you find it too tricky to roll out, don't. Just push the slightly softened pastry into your pie dish in bits instead. Then all you need do with the top is crumble the mixture over; no trimming, fancy pastry leaves or straight lines. This is a pie that the phrase 'easy as pie' is wholly appropriate for.

500g/1lb 2oz blueberries

2tbsp lemon juice

150g/5⅓oz/1¼ sticks
butter

150g/5⅓oz/¾ cup golden
caster sugar

1 egg

250g/8¾oz/2 cups plain/
all-purpose flour

1tsp baking powder

20g/¾oz/scant ¼ cup
ground almonds

TO SERVE
Vanilla ice cream

EQUIPMENT
Pie dish

Blueberry Pie
Serves 8

1. Place the blueberries in a bowl and sprinkle with the lemon juice. Squash some of the fruit with a potato masher or fork, leaving most of them whole. Toss with your hands and leave to sit while you make the pastry.

2. Cream the butter and sugar until very light and fluffy. Beat in the egg. Once incorporated, sift the flour and baking powder into the butter mixture and fold in until you have a soft dough.

3. Lightly butter your pie dish. Flour your work surface and lightly knead the pastry for a minute or so. Split in half and place one piece between two sheets of greaseproof paper. Wrap the other in greaseproof paper and store in the fridge for later. Roll the pastry out to around the thickness of a pound coin. Peel the paper back and flip the pastry into the pie dish – allowing it to overhang the edge a little. Press lightly into the corners to ensure there is no air underneath. Sprinkle with the ground almonds, which will soak up some of the blueberry juice as the pie cooks. Rest the pastry in the fridge for at least an hour, or overnight if you like.

4. Preheat the oven to 180°C/350°F/Gas 4 and place a baking tray on the middle shelf to heat up. Bring the still-wrapped half of the pastry to room temperature. Pour the blueberries into the pie dish. Crumble the other half of the pastry over the top of the blueberries.

5. Place the pie on the baking tray in the oven and bake for 40 minutes, or until golden on top. The pastry has a lot of sugar in it, so keep an eye on it, covering it with foil if it browns too quickly. Remove from the oven and allow to cool a little before serving. Don't expect your slices to be neat and clean; this pie should be spooned out of the dish and eaten with generous scoops of vanilla ice cream.

Figs & Custard

… a companion dish on which lay a solid rectangle of Smyrna figs, a dish of custard topped with grated nutmeg…
'The Dead', *Dubliners*, James Joyce

I have spent countless nights in my friend Jen's living room. She was in the same one-bedroom flat on Newington Green for seven years, an anomaly amongst my friends, most of whom had to move every couple of years thanks to sharply rising London rents. We painted the walls when she first moved in, but as we got steadily drunker and the ABBA tunes got steadily louder, our painting skills became steadily worse. Our slightly dodgy brushwork was still visible in the bathroom when she moved out. We had long parties, and sleepovers, and lovely dinners in her living room. Someone else owns it now, but it will always be Jen's flat to me.

It was Jen who bought me a copy of *Dubliners*, and reminded me of 'The Dead': of Miss Kate, and her meltdown in the kitchen. Jen has watched me go to pieces over a much too thin béarnaise, burn myself on caramel and fall apart after dropping a cake on the floor. We have shared dinner innumerable times and, of course, always recovered with aplomb (or a takeaway) from every disaster faced in her kitchen. What I have realized in her company is that the way to ensure that cooking is relaxing, calming and fun is to do it for people you love. The good ones won't care that you split the sauce.

These figs have their origins in Nigella Lawson's 'Figs for a Thousand and One Nights', which I have eaten many times at Jen's. The flavours used here are entirely different; more Irish than Middle Eastern, but no less enjoyable. They're the ideal, very grown-up partner for plain, sweet, nursery custard.

Figs and Custard

Serves 6

1. First, make the custard. Pour the milk into the saucepan, then split the vanilla pod, scrape it out and add both the pod and the seeds. Bring it almost to the boil over a medium heat, then set aside to infuse for 10 minutes.

2. Whisk the eggs, yolks and sugar together in a mixing bowl. Once the milk is cool, add the cream, then pour it through a sieve into the egg mixture. Whisk well, but avoid creating big bubbles. Carefully pour the custard into the ovenproof dish and set aside to settle.

3. Preheat the oven to 120°C/250°F/Gas ½. Grate a little nutmeg over the custard. Place the dish inside a roasting tray and place the tray on a shelf in the centre of the oven. Add enough hot water to the tray to come halfway up the sides of your dish, ensuring that you don't pour any into the custard.

4. Bake for an hour, until the custard is set, but still has a slight wobble. Remove from the oven, and from its water bath, and set aside to cool for 30 minutes.

5. For the figs, in a small saucepan, warm the butter and honey until they are melted and combined. Add the water from the soaked tea bags and the whiskey. Set aside.

6. Slice the figs through the tip, almost down to the base, but ensuring both halves remain attached. Make another slice to create a cross. Pinch the fig at the base to open it up. Repeat with the rest of the figs and sit them on their bases in an ovenproof dish; one where they need to be packed together would be best.

7. Preheat the oven to 200°C/400°F/Gas 6. Spoon a little of the honey mixture over each fig, and add a generous sprinkle of demerara sugar. Transfer to the oven for 15 minutes. Serve the figs hot, with a scoop of baked custard, and some of the fig juice from the bottom of the dish.

INGREDIENTS

CUSTARD
500ml/17floz/generous 2 cups milk
1 vanilla pod
2 eggs
2 egg yolks
50g/1¾oz/¼ cup golden caster sugar
100ml/3⅓floz/generous ⅓ cup double/heavy cream
Grated nutmeg

FIGS
30g/1oz/2tbsp butter
1tbsp honey
2 Irish Breakfast tea bags, soaked for 4 minutes in 2tbsp boiling water
1tbsp Irish whiskey
12 fresh figs
40g/1½oz/3¼tbsp demerara/turbinado sugar

Treacle Tart &
Rosemary Ice Cream

A moment later the desserts appeared. Blocks of ice cream in every flavour you can think of, apple pies, treacle tarts, chocolate eclairs and jam doughnuts, trifle, strawberries, jelly, rice pudding... As Harry helped himself to a treacle tart, the talk turned to their families.
Harry Potter and the Philosopher's Stone, J. K. Rowling

It all started with treacle tart. Back in 2014, I cooked up a three-course meal for friends: homemade ravioli, shoulder of lamb and treacle tart. The tart was a first for my (Australian) friends, and they were intrigued – why treacle tart? Well, I explained, it's Harry Potter's favourite. They were tickled that I could remember that sort of detail, and even more so that it would inspire me to cook. And so my blog was born.

I had grown up dreaming of Harry's treacle tart, and Edmund's proper Turkish Delight (nothing like the stuff covered in chocolate from the corner shop – see p. 265 for a recipe), and the eggs roasted in their shells that Mary and Dickon eat in *The Secret Garden*; the foods my favourite characters were eating. I was desperately homesick, and simultaneously loving England (it seems that this is destined to be my permanent state of being)   cooking something quintessentially English that reminded me of my childhood in Australia seemed perfect. And so Harry's treacle tart it had to be.

I've tried many ice creams with it over the years – this one is the best. You need something woody, salty and rich to cut through the sweetness of the tart. Though, to be completely honest, good shop-bought vanilla, or a spoonful of crème fraîche, works too.

INGREDIENTS

PASTRY

250g/8¾oz/2 cups plain/
all-purpose flour

2tbsp icing/
confectioners' sugar

Zest of 1 lemon

Pinch of salt

175g/6oz/1½ sticks
butter, chilled and cubed

1 egg yolk

FILLING

600g/1lb 5oz golden
syrup

¼tsp ground ginger

150g/5½oz/2½ cups
fresh fine breadcrumbs

Zest and juice of 1 lemon

1 egg, beaten

EQUIPMENT

23cm/9in fluted tart tin
(or similar)

Treacle Tart

Serves 10

1. To make the pastry, combine the flour, icing sugar, lemon zest and salt in a bowl. Rub in the cold butter until the mixture resembles breadcrumbs. Add the egg yolk and 1–2tbsp of very cold water. Combine with your hands until the mixture comes together into a dough. Turn onto a lightly floured work surface and form into a ball. Don't work the mixture too much or your pastry won't be crisp. Wrap in plastic wrap and pop in the fridge for half an hour. Don't be tempted to skip the chilling: it prevents the pastry from shrinking in the oven.

2. Roll the pastry out on a lightly floured surface (if the pastry is sticking – as it is wont to do in a warm kitchen – roll it between two pieces of greaseproof paper). You want a 30cm/12in circle that is around the thickness of a pound coin/about ⅛in.

3. Transfer your pastry to a fluted tart tin. Use a small ball of spare dough (rather than your fingers – your nails may cut the pastry) to push it into place, making sure it goes right into the corners. If there are any tears, patch them up with extra dough. Time the pastry just above the tin. Lightly prick the base with a fork and return to the fridge to chill for a further 30 minutes. Preheat your oven to 190°C/375°F/Gas 5 and insert a baking sheet in the middle of the oven to heat up.

4. Line the chilled case with greaseproof paper and fill with baking beans or uncooked rice. Place in the oven, on the baking sheet, for 15 minutes, then remove the baking paper and beans and bake for a further 5 minutes, until golden.

5. For the filling, heat the golden syrup and ground ginger in a saucepan over a low heat until hot, but not boiling. Remove from the heat. Stir in the breadcrumbs, lemon zest and juice and beaten egg until just combined, then pour into the pastry case.

6. Bake the tart in the oven for 30–35 minutes until the filling is set and the pastry golden. Cool on a wire rack for 15 minutes before removing from the tin and serving warm. Leftovers (should there be any) should be reheated a little in the oven before eating, or you risk losing a tooth!

Rosemary Ice Cream
Makes 10 scoops

1. Place the milk and cream in a saucepan. Bring almost to the boil over a low heat. Whisk the egg yolks with the golden caster sugar until light and creamy. Once the milk and cream are just under boiling point, pour it over the yolks, whisking constantly so that the yolks don't cook. Rinse the saucepan, then pour the custard back in. Add the rosemary and stir over a very low heat until it coats the back of a wooden spoon.

2. Once the custard is thick, add the salt, then strain it into a large bowl to remove the rosemary. Press a layer of plastic wrap onto the surface (which prevents it from forming a skin) and allow to cool completely.

3. Once cold, pour the custard into the ice-cream maker and freeze according to the machine instructions. Alternatively, pour into a freezer-proof container and freeze for 2 hours. Once partially set, remove from freezer, beat until smooth with a whisk and return to the freezer for another hour. Repeat for 3 hours and then freeze overnight. Serve with treacle tart. Or on its own, with a spoon.

INGREDIENTS
475ml/16floz/2 cups milk
225ml/7½floz/scant 1 cup double/heavy cream
5 egg yolks
100g/3½oz/½ cup golden caster/superfine sugar
Four 15cm/6in sprigs rosemary
1tbsp flaky sea salt/ Kosher salt

EQUIPMENT
Ice-cream maker and/ or freezer-proof box and electric hand whisk

Dinner for Two at the England

'... turbot... poulard à l'estragon, macédoine de fruits... etc.,' and then instantly, as though worked by springs, laying down one bound bill of fare, he took up another, the list of wines, and submitted it to Stepan Arkadyevitch.

Anna Karenina, Leo Tolstoy

For something that reads like an extravagant menu, the food that Oblonsky and Lëvin eat here, in *Anna Karenina*, is deceptively simple to cook. In fact, part of it could function well as an 'after-work dinner party' meal – on the table quickly, with very little input from you. Of course, to re-create it in full, you'd need a budget larger than the one I normally allocate to dinner; the men start with three dozen oysters, drink the best champagne and order turbot, which is prohibitively expensive in the twenty-first century. But, with a few modern tweaks, it can work.

My friends Nic and Max are two of the best dinner party hosts I know. I have often sat at their kitchen table, wine in hand, while they bustle about, filling bowls with salads and pulling roasting trays out of the oven. They both have jobs that consume a good deal of their time, but have mastered the art of the 8 p.m. dinner: arriving home with ingredients, opening the door to friends and then calmly getting dinner on the table while we catch up.

The key here is to make life easy for yourself: use the oven for only one course, so you don't have to juggle or adjust temperatures; make at least one dish that involves no cooking at all; and keep the grocery shop to a minimum. Normally, I'd go for something that can be made in advance, but when the meal is this simple, you don't need to. In its entirety, it's an impressive three-course feast. But the main and dessert (or starter and main, or starter and dessert) are plenty for a mid-week dinner – one you can dish up less than an hour after walking through the door.

Turbot in Lemon Sauce

Serves 2

INGREDIENTS

FISH

2 x 120g/4oz turbot fillets*

2 shallots, sliced lengthways

2 spring onions/scallions, sliced lengthways

300ml/½ pint/1¼ cups white wine

300ml/½ pint/1¼ cups water

SAUCE

20g/¾oz/1⅓tbsp butter

20g/¾oz/2⅓tbsp plain/all-purpose flour

60ml/2floz/¼ cup milk

1 egg yolk

60ml/2floz/¼ cup single/light cream

Salt and pepper

Juice of ½ a lemon

TO SERVE

8 asparagus spears

EQUIPMENT

Fish knife (if skinning)

* I have yet to find an affordable fillet of turbot so do feel free to substitute John Dory, halibut or sole fillets here, as I often do. Fillets may be different thicknesses, so keep an eye on the texture of the fish; when cooked, it should be springy when pressed, rather than flaking away under your touch.

1. Skin the fillets, or ask your fishmonger to do this for you. If you are doing it yourself, a very sharp, flexible fish knife will be best here. Put the fish, skin-side down, on a board and, keeping the knife parallel to the board, but angling slightly downwards, work the flesh away from the skin.

2. Line the base of a pan with the sliced shallots and spring onions, then place the fillets of fish on top. Cover with the wine and water. Bring the pan to a simmer over a low heat, allow to bubble gently for 2 minutes, then turn off the heat. Keep an eye on the fish; the flesh will turn white as it cooks, but scoop it out of the liquid while the flesh is still springy and firm. Reserve the cooking liquid and keep the fillets on a warm plate while you make the sauce.

3. Break the woody ends off the asparagus, and steam the spears over a pan of boiling water. Set aside.

4. Melt the butter in a saucepan and add the flour. Stir over a medium heat for 2 minutes to cook the flour. Pour in 100ml/3⅓floz of the fish cooking liquid and whisk. It will thicken almost immediately. Take it off the heat and whisk in the milk. Set aside for a moment, while you whisk together the egg yolk and cream in a mixing bowl, then dribble in a little of the thickened sauce, and whisk. Continue to do this, bit by bit, until it is all incorporated.

5. Place the sauce over a low heat and bring to the boil. Taste it, and season with salt and pepper. Remove from the heat, and whisk in the lemon juice.

6. To serve, lay 4 asparagus spears on each plate, then sit the fish on top. Spoon a very generous amount of the sauce over the fish and serve immediately. You will have some sauce left over – you can keep this in the fridge for a day or so; it's delicious warmed through, served with steamed vegetables.

Chicken with Tarragon

Serves 2

1. Preheat the oven to 180°C/350°F/Gas 4. Melt the butter in a frying pan until foaming, then fry the chicken legs, skin-side down, until golden and crisp. Flip over and fry on the other side.

2. Place the onion slices in the bottom of a roasting dish, then add the wine and 3 sprigs of the tarragon, finely chopped. Season with salt and pepper and stir. Lay the chicken on top of the onions and pour any leftover butter from the pan over the top. Transfer the uncovered dish to the oven for 40 minutes.

3. Once roasted, remove the legs to a dish and keep warm. Tip the onions and juices into a frying pan. Bring to a simmer, reduce a little, then whisk in the crème fraîche. Cook for a minute, then spoon some of the onions and sauce onto each plate, top with a chicken leg and some fresh tarragon leaves. Serve with boiled new potatoes and green leaves.

INGREDIENTS

60g/2oz/½ stick butter
2 chicken legs (thighs and drumsticks)
2 brown onions, sliced into semicircles
200ml/7floz white wine
5 sprigs tarragon
Salt and pepper
2tbsp crème fraiche/sour cream

INGREDIENTS

1 pear

8 cherries

1 flat peach

4 stalks redcurrants

6 physalis/Cape gooseberries

100ml/3⅓floz/⅓ cup kirsch (or other fruit liqueur you fancy)

4tbsp caster/superfine sugar

Fruit in Liqueur

Serves 2

1. Prepare your fruit. Slice the pears into thin wedges, the peaches into small slices, the cherries in half, pull the redcurrants off their stalks and remove the husks from the physalis.

2. Pour the kirsch into a bowl and stir the sugar in until it is dissolved. Place the prepared fruit into the bowl to macerate for 20 minutes, while you get on with the other courses, or making coffee for your guest.

3. Arrange all your fruit in serving bowls/glasses, and then spoon 2tbsp of the sugary kirsch over each portion.

The Women's Meal

*Here was the soup... One could have seen through the transparent
liquid any pattern that there might have been on the plate itself. But
there was no pattern. The plate was plain.*

...

*Next came beef with its attendant greens and potatoes – a homely
trinity, suggesting the rumps of cattle in a muddy market, and sprouts
curled and yellowed at the edge, and bargaining and cheapening and
women with string bags on Monday morning...*

...

Prunes and custard followed.
A Room of One's Own, Virginia Woolf

I had been writing about food in literature for about a year when
I hosted my first supper club. It was a baptism by fire: a tiny café
kitchen, twenty guests and an oven the size of a microwave. I
learnt so much, and after I had the first couple of dinners under my
belt, I sat down with a friend to brainstorm other possible menus
that would work well. I was lamenting that the men's dinner in *A
Room of One's Own* was out of reach in terms of budget – I couldn't
stretch to a Dover sole and a partridge for everyone around the
table, especially not with a 'retinue' of salads and sauces. But then
we remembered the women's meal. And, despite the disparaging
paragraphs written by Woolf, it does have appealing components.

It needed a little work before we could serve it to a room of people.
The thin soup, so transparent that a pattern could be viewed
through it, became an onion consommé, served with fresh spring
vegetables. The beef was cooked rare, coupled with roasted new
potatoes and served alongside an old favourite: Etti's herb salad
from Ottolenghi's first book. The custard was frozen into a rich ice
cream, and the prunes were improved by the addition of Armagnac.

This is now my dream Sunday-lunch meal; just the main, most of
the time, with all three courses reserved for very special occasions.
The meal is fresh, full of flavour and delicious; just the sort of thing
I hope Woolf's women might have enjoyed – and more than the
equal of the men's fish, birds and pudding.

INGREDIENTS

SOUP

3 carrots

1 large leek

2 brown onions

3 stalks celery

5 bay leaves

8 peppercorns

2.5L/4¼ pints/2⅔ quarts water

1kg/2¼lb brown onions

50g/1¾oz/scant ½ stick butter

150g/5½oz/2¼ cups mushrooms

3 egg whites

Salt and pepper

TO SERVE

4 mangetout/snow peas

24 small or 12 large asparagus spears

2 spring onions/scallions

20 leaves coriander/cilantro

20 sprigs dill

EQUIPMENT

2 large saucepans, that can hold 3L/5 pints/3¼ quarts of liquid

A piece of muslin

Vegetable Consommé

Serves 4

1. Peel and roughly chop the vegetables for the stock. Put them in your second-biggest saucepan along with the bay leaves, whole peppercorns and water. Bring to the boil and then simmer over a low heat, with the lid on, for 2 hours.

2. While the stock is bubbling away, prepare the onions. Peel and finely slice them, then melt the butter in a frying pan and add the onions to the pan. Cook over a low heat, stirring frequently, for around an hour. They should be soft, golden and caramelized. Strain the stock onto the onions and simmer for 20 minutes over a low heat.

3. Strain the stock into a bowl, then pour back into the large pan. Clean and dice the mushrooms. Whisk the egg whites until frothy, then add the mushrooms. This will look a little gross, and if you have never made a consommé before, adding it to the stock will seem ridiculous. Just go with it.

4. Bring the stock almost to a simmer, and keep on a gentle heat. Pour the egg whites and mushrooms into the stock. Whisk constantly until the protein in the eggs starts to cook and rise to the surface. This is the magic bit. The egg and mushroom will form a 'raft' on top of the soup, drawing out any impurities from the stock below. As it forms, gently push a wooden spoon against the side of the raft, so you can see the stock below. Once the stock looks clear, turn off the heat. If you accidentally disrupt the raft, and it splits, don't panic: strain the stock, then add more egg and mushroom and start the clarifying process over.

5. Line a sieve with a piece of muslin. Carefully push a small ladle through the gap in the raft you have created, and draw up a ladleful of stock, trying not to get any of the egg or mushroom into the ladle. Strain it through the muslin. Continue with the rest of the consommé. Taste it, and season with salt and pepper.

6. Warm the clarified stock slowly in a spotlessly clean pan. Slice the mangetout, asparagus and spring onions, and arrange them in your bowls along with the herbs. Ladle the clear consommé over the top of the raw vegetables. Eat immediately.

Beef, Greens and Potatoes
Serves 4

1. Preheat the oven to 200°C/400°F/Gas 6. Lay the sliced onions in the base of a roasting tin. Rub the beef with the olive oil, and sprinkle generously with salt and pepper. Place it on top of the onions and transfer to the preheated oven. Cook for 25 minutes if you want it very rare, 45 minutes for medium, or up to an hour for well done. If you have a meat thermometer, you can easily check this – poke it into the middle of the roast: aim for 46°C/115°F for very rare, 56°C/133°F for rare, 66°C/150°F for medium and 76°C/170°F for well done. A note on the cut: this is a relatively inexpensive cut of beef – you need to cook it fast, rest it well, and eat it pink to ensure its tenderness.

2. Put the potatoes in a saucepan, and cover with cold water. Bring to the boil with the lid on, and cook until just tender. This should take around 10 minutes, but it is very dependent on the size of your potatoes. Drain, and tip into another roasting tin. Pour over a generous glug of olive oil, add the rosemary stalks and bash the garlic cloves with the heel of a knife (though don't bother to peel them) and add them too. Season and set aside until the beef comes out of the oven.

3. Remove the beef from the oven. Wrap it in foil and leave to rest under a tea towel for 30 minutes. Strain the cooking juices from the pan into a small saucepan and leave to simmer slowly on the hob. Place the potatoes in the oven to roast for around 25 minutes.

INGREDIENTS

BEEF
2 brown onions, thinly sliced
800g/1¾lb beef top rump, at room temperature
Olive oil
Salt and pepper

POTATOES
600g/1lb 5oz small new potatoes, unpeeled
Olive oil
4 rosemary stalks
6 cloves garlic
Salt and pepper

GREENS
25g/scant 1oz/1⅔ cups coriander/cilantro leaves
30g/1oz/1 cup flat-leaf parsley leaves
15g/½oz/1¾ cups dill fronds
25g/scant 1oz/2½ cups tarragon leaves
20g/¾oz/¾ cup basil leaves
30g/1oz/1½ cups rocket/arugula leaves

DRESSING
100g/3½oz/¾ cup whole almonds
35g/generous 1oz/¼ stick butter
Salt and pepper
Juice of ½ lemon

4. To prepare the salad, pick all the herb leaves off their stalks. Pick away until you have enough herbs, then toss them together in a bowl. This is time-consuming, but worth it.

5. For the salad dressing, brown the almonds in a warm, dry frying pan. Do watch them carefully, as they can catch and burn incredibly quickly. Tip them onto a board, and chop roughly.

6. Melt the butter in the frying pan until foaming, and then tip in the chopped almonds. Season with salt and pepper, then add the lemon juice and take off the heat.

7. Once the beef has rested, unwrap it from its parcel, and slice it thinly. Place some slices of beef on each plate, along with a few potatoes, and spoon over some of the warm cooking juices. Pour the warm dressing over the herbs, toss it through gently and add a handful of salad to each plate. Serve immediately.

A NOTE: If you have leftovers, all of these components are brilliant in sandwiches the next day.

Prunes in Armagnac with Brown Bread and Butter Ice Cream
Serves 4

1. First, prepare the prunes. These last in the fridge for months, and are best if left for at least a week, so do start well in advance if you can. Pour the water, sugar and split vanilla pod into a saucepan and bring to a simmer, swirling to dissolve the sugar. Once simmering, tip in the prunes.

2. Simmer for a couple of minutes, until the prunes are glossy and a little plumper looking. Remove the pan from the heat and add the Armagnac, before stirring to combine. Pour into a jar and store in the fridge.

INGREDIENTS

PRUNES
250g/9oz prunes
250ml/8½floz/generous 1 cup water
40g/3¼tbsp dark brown sugar
1 vanilla pod
100ml/3⅓floz/⅓ cup Armagnac

ICE CREAM
150ml/5floz/⅔ cup milk
150ml/5floz/⅔ cup double/heavy cream
1 vanilla pod
3 egg yolks
45g/3½tbsp golden caster/superfine sugar
2 slices brown bread

3. To make the ice cream, bring the milk, cream and split vanilla pod to simmering point on the stove. Meanwhile, whisk the egg yolks and sugar together in a bowl until sticky. Whisking constantly to prevent the mixture from scrambling, pour the milk and cream into the yolks.

4. Rinse the saucepan, then pour the custard, including the vanilla pod, back in. Place over a low heat and stir until it is thick enough to coat the back of a spoon. Do keep an eye on it the whole time. Once it is thick, pull out the vanilla pod, pour it into a bowl, cover with plastic wrap and leave in the fridge until cool.

5. Preheat the oven to 160°C/325°F/Gas 3. Tear the bread into small chunks. Melt the butter in a pan on the hob, keeping it over a medium heat until it starts to brown and gives off a warm, nutty scent. Swirl it around every now and then. Once it is an almondy brown, add the sugar, stir, and then add the bread. Toss until the bread is coated in the butter. Lay it out in one layer in an ovenproof dish, and place in the centre of the oven for 15 minutes, tossing it once during cooking, until brown and caramelized.

6. Transfer the cooled custard to an ice-cream maker, or to a freezer-proof container. Follow the manufacturer's instructions for your ice-cream maker, or remove the container from the freezer every hour for the first couple of hours to give it a brisk whisk to break up any ice crystals. Once the ice cream has nearly set, fold the chunks of bread into it and freeze until solid.

7. Serve scoops of the ice cream with a couple of prunes and some of the Armagnac syrup.

30g/1oz/¼ stick unsalted butter
15g/½oz/4tsp dark brown sugar
Pinch of salt

EQUIPMENT
Sterilized jar
Freezer-proof container or ice-cream maker

midnight *feasts*

midnight *feasts*

I still experience an illicit thrill when preparing a midnight feast. Eating rich or sweet treats at midnight is something we've been told from childhood not to do. It's something terrifically fun and a little bit naughty that we have to hide from the grown-ups.

The whispered-conversations-in-the-dormitory feeling is one I have carried with me, not from my own childhood, but from those of Enid Blyton's schoolgirls, of J. K. Rowling's Gryffindors, and of Mary Lennox and Colin Craven in Misselthwaite Manor. The role of adults in these stories – physically absent, but lurking somewhere up the corridor – adds to the belief that rules are being broken. As a nervous follower of the rules, I relished the excitement (and safety) that living vicariously through my favourite characters provided.

In truth, my midnight feasts as a child were infrequent and quite tame – snacking on marshmallows in my sleeping bag at sleepovers, or eating ice blocks with Mum when we couldn't sleep in the Queensland heat. Nowadays, they're not that unusual; I am, by nature, a night owl. I've had dinner parties that get off to a very relaxed start, the oven only turned on once evening has darkened into night. Left to my own devices, I often experience late-night enthusiasm for whipping out a baking tray at 11 p.m.

The food in this chapter is for sleepovers: ones that happen in bunk beds and forts, and for adult sleepovers too. This food can, of course, be eaten during the day: sausage rolls will make a great lunch, ramen is perfect for dinner, and the seed cake works well for afternoon tea. But I recommend them for midnight feasting. Though I'm not one for food guilt, I will say that there is something about midnight feasts being 'forbidden' that makes the food taste even better.

Chocolatl

In my first year in the UK, I would take the tube across London
every Saturday to visit my mate Reilly. She had emigrated a couple
of months before I did, and discovered a chocolate shop near her
she was mad about. Every weekend, we sat on the pavement, or
perched on stools at the bar, and talked while we drank rich, thick
hot chocolate. As I was still finding my feet, the routine of visiting
somewhere weekly grounded me.

Just down the road, there was a well-stocked second-hand
bookshop. I had arrived with only three books: a collection of
Roald Dahl short stories, a second-hand paperback I hadn't realized
was missing its final chapter, and my much-read copy of *To Kill
a Mockingbird*. I used these trips to build up a collection again. A
couple of weeks in, I spotted Philip Pullman's *Northern Lights*,
which I hadn't read since I was twelve, and picked it up, excited to
immerse myself in Lyra's world. What I didn't expect was to love
it so much more as an adult. Will and Lyra, the Gyptian boats, the
journey to the North were all still there, but the book now seemed
so much richer.

This hot chocolate, which Mrs Coulter uses to lure children away
from their homes in the dark of night, needs to be delicious. So
warm and rich and comforting that you'd willingly follow a strange
woman and her very sinister monkey. It is, in short, a drink that
needs to be as seductive as she is.

Chocolatl

Serves 2

1. Pour the milk and cream into a saucepan. Bash the cardamom pods to release the seeds. Add the pods and seeds to the milk, along with the cinnamon stick and bay leaf. Place over a low heat.

2. Bring almost to the boil, then remove from the heat and allow to sit for a minute to cool. Break the chocolate into pieces and add to the pan – the heat of the milk will melt the chocolate. Leave, undisturbed, for 10 minutes. Whisk vigorously, then add the salt and sugar to taste. Reheat over a low heat. Serve immediately.

INGREDIENTS

300ml/½ pint/1¼ cups milk

75ml/2½floz/⅓ cup double/heavy cream

4 cardamom pods

1 cinnamon stick

1 bay leaf

75g/generous 2½oz dark chocolate (I use 60–70%)

Pinch of salt

1tsp golden caster/ superfine sugar

Creamed Haddock on Toast

'You said something about finnan haddock, but you wouldn't like it in the bedroom. It leaves a smell. I'm giving it to you for your supper, creamed on toast.'
Sleeping Murder, Agatha Christie

Sleeping Murder was my first Agatha Christie. My mum bought a set of six of her mysteries when I was twelve, and I made my way through the lot in my final year of primary school. They ignited a lifelong love of the Queen of Crime. In years to come I would work my way through the entire canon; I scared myself silly reading the darker ones late at night, and relied on the company of innumerable radio dramatizations to see me through menial office tasks. I still pull at least one down from the shelf every Christmas. These are comfort books of the highest order – the ones I take into the bath, want by my side when I am poorly and desire as my companions on winter evenings.

Re-reading *Sleeping Murder* recently, I felt twelve again. I had the same shiver up my spine when Gwenda opens the wardrobe to find the floral wallpaper she has been picturing, and the same irrational desire to eat fish in bed. The latter is unquestionably a terrible idea. Instead, do allow me to echo Mrs Cocker, and suggest the haddock as a late evening meal instead – on the sofa, with a book, a blanket and a mug of tea.

Creamed Haddock on Toast

Serves 4

1. Pour the milk into a wide, deep-sided frying pan with the peppercorns and bay leaves. Add the fish and onions to the milk, and place the pan over a medium heat.

2. Bring to a slow simmer. As soon as it starts to bubble, turn off the heat. Leave the fish in the milk for 5 minutes; it will cook as it cools.

3. When the milk is cool enough to touch, remove the fish. Flake it by hand into a bowl.

4. Melt the butter in a saucepan over a low heat and then stir in the flour. Once they are combined, stir for a couple of minutes over the heat to cook the flour. Strain the milk into the pan, reserving the onions, and stir until thick.

5. Add the onions to the bowl of fish, picking out any peppercorns. Tip the fish and onions into the white sauce, and stir through. Place back over the heat to warm.

6. Serve on toasted rye bread, with plenty of cracked pepper and coarse sea salt. This will feed a few friends for a midnight feast, or you can reheat the leftovers on the stove in the morning – they're brilliant with a poached egg on toast, so long as you don't eat them in bed.

INGREDIENTS

300ml/½ pint/1¼ cups milk

5 peppercorns

2 bay leaves

400g/14oz smoked haddock, skinned, cut into large chunks

2 small brown onions, finely sliced

40g/1½oz/3tbsp butter

3tbsp plain/all-purpose flour

4 slices rye bread

Salt and pepper

MARMALADE ROLL   { 194 }   *The Lion, the Witch and the Wardrobe*, C. S. Lewis

Marmalade Roll

And when they had finished the fish, Mrs Beaver brought unexpectedly out of the oven a great and gloriously sticky marmalade roll, steaming hot, and at the same time moved the kettle onto the fire, so that when they had finished the marmalade roll the tea was made and ready to be poured out.

The Lion, the Witch and the Wardrobe, C. S. Lewis

I didn't see snow until I was twenty-two. It was my first December in London, and I was sitting in the office at the King's Head Theatre. I glanced outside and did a double take. It was snowing. In real life, it looked nothing like I had imagined – more like slowed down footage of white rain. I wanted to be outside in it immediately. I abandoned my computer and my colleague, dashed across the road and spent the next hour running around like a small child. I thought of Narnia, and of Lucy Pevensie, and of fur coats. Of course, this was London, so the snow didn't stay on the ground. Within an hour, it had melted away to slush.

Since that day, I am unable to stay inside when snow starts. I will abandon work, trolleys full of shopping, half-wrapped Christmas presents or the warmth of my bed at midnight to frolic around in the cold. But as much as I love being outside in it, that first hour back inside again – the long bath, the clean, warm socks, the hot meal – is just as wonderful. This marmalade roll, served to the Pevensie children by the beavers as the snow lies thick on the ground under an ink-black sky, is just the ticket. Custard is the ideal accompaniment.

INGREDIENTS

ROLL

250g/8¾oz/2 cups plain/
all-purpose flour

50g/1¾oz/¼ cup light
brown sugar

1tsp baking powder

40g/1½oz/3tbsp butter

40g/1½oz/⅓ cup
vegetable suet

60g/4tbsp soured cream

60ml/2floz/¼ cup milk

1 egg

450g/1lb marmalade
(whatever flavour you
fancy)

25ml/1½tbsp whiskey

CUSTARD

300ml/½ pint/1¼ cups
milk

100ml/3⅓floz double/
heavy cream

1 vanilla pod

4 egg yolks

40g/1½oz/3¼tbsp caster/
superfine sugar

EQUIPMENT
String (optional)

Marmalade Roll with Custard

Serves 6

1. Preheat the oven to 190°C/375°F/Gas 5. Sift the flour, sugar and baking powder into a mixing bowl. Rub the butter and suet into the mixture with your fingertips until it resembles breadcrumbs.

2. Whisk the soured cream, milk and egg together in a cup, then tip the liquids into the dry ingredients. Mix everything together with a fork until it comes together in a dough. Generously flour the work surface and tip the dough out. Push it out into a rough rectangle, around 18cm/7in wide, 30cm/12in long and 1½cm/⅝in thick.

3. Spoon two-thirds of the marmalade onto the dough, spreading it over the whole surface. If your marmalade is hard set and not very spreadable, warm it over a low heat to melt a little.

4. Using a spatula to help you, roll the dough up from the short end into a scroll. Pinch the ends together, and roll tightly in greaseproof paper. Tie the ends with string, or twist them and tuck them under the marmalade roll. Place a rack in the base of an oven dish, and place the roll on top. Transfer to the oven and, before you close the door, tip a little boiling water into the bottom of the dish, being careful to ensure that the water does not touch the roll. Bake for 1 hour, until a skewer inserted into the roll comes out with no bits of uncooked dough clinging to it.

5. To make the custard, pour the milk and cream into a saucepan with the split vanilla pod and place over a low heat. Heat until almost simmering, stirring occasionally to prevent the milk burning on the bottom. Remove the vanilla pod.

6. Whisk the egg yolks and sugar together and, while still whisking, slowly pour the hot milk and cream on top.

7. Pour the custard back into the saucepan. Place over a very low heat and stir continuously until thick enough

to coat the back of a wooden spoon. If you're not going to serve it immediately, cover the top with plastic wrap, pushing it down until it sits on the top of the custard, to prevent it from forming a skin.

8. Remove the roll from the oven. Place the rest of the marmalade and the whisky in a small saucepan and heat until liquid. Paint the top of the roll with the marmalade glaze and serve hot with the custard.

Marshmallows

We ended up having to make some tough decisions, between the Vita Brits and the marshmallows, the pita bread and the jam doughnuts, the muesli and the chips. I'm ashamed to say what won in each case...
Tomorrow, When the War Began, John Marsden

I come from a family of planners. On Sunday afternoons, as we relaxed in front of a film, one of us would have the list book (a fat wad of paper held together with a bulldog clip), brainstorming plans for our next big meal, event or holiday.

The lists for our camping trips were always the most epic. We were inevitably heading off in convoy with another family or two, so meals were often planned for upwards of ten people. Very occasionally, we'd manage to catch our own fish, but more often than not we would light up a barbecue, throw on an assortment of meat from the Esky and serve the whole lot with a big bag of bread rolls and some salads.

For Ellie and her friends in *Tomorrow, When the War Began*, camping trips were a time for treats. We felt much the same; excited to pack little boxes of cereals we were never allowed in our kitchen at home, packets of biscuits that actually had chocolate on them (rather than plain digestives), and bags and bags of pink and white marshmallows. We ate these marshmallows, toasted on sticks in the fire, once the sun went down. Then, later, we filled our cheeks with them in our sleeping bags, long after we were supposed to be asleep.

Marshmallows

Makes about 80 marshmallows – plenty for 7 happy campers

1. Pour 125ml/4½floz of the cold water into the bowl of your mixer. Sprinkle the powdered gelatine on top. Stir, then leave to sit while you get on with the rest of the recipe.

2. Put the caster sugar, glucose syrup and salt into a saucepan, along with the remaining 125ml/4½floz water. Bring to the boil over a medium heat, stirring to dissolve the sugar at the start, but stop stirring before it boils (or it can crystallize). Boil until it reaches 116°C/240°F or 'soft ball stage' – when the syrup forms a ball/clump if dribbled into a glass of cold water. Once it reaches this stage, remove from the heat.

3. Turn the mixer to a medium speed and slowly pour the syrup down the side of the bowl, ensuring you don't pour it onto the whisk, or you will end up with spun sugar. Once you have added all the syrup, turn the speed to high and whisk for around 12–15 minutes, until the mixture is very stiff and full of air, and the bowl has cooled. This 12 minutes is proper alchemy. I am always sure it won't work, as it remains a sloppy liquid for the first few minutes, but keep beating and eventually it puffs up like a big white cloud. Once thick, add the vanilla, and a little spot of food colouring if you like.

4. Working relatively quickly, pour the marshmallow mix into the prepared tin (see equipment note). Help it along with a wet spatula, flattening the top as you go. Sprinkle with more of the icing sugar mix, then leave to rest at room temperature for at least 4 hours (or overnight).

5. Once it has rested, cut your marshmallow into cubes, dusting your knife with cornflour between cuts to combat the stickiness. Toss the marshmallows in the icing sugar mix. Serve toasted, dropped into hot chocolate or boxed up between layers of greaseproof paper to give away as gifts.

INGREDIENTS

250ml/8½floz/generous 1 cup cold water
20g/6tsp powdered gelatine
400g/14oz/2 cups caster/superfine sugar
170g/6oz/scant ½ cup glucose syrup
Pinch of salt
Vegetable oil
50g/1¾oz/½ cup cornflour/cornstarch
50g/1¾oz/heaping ⅓ cup icing/confectioners' sugar
1tsp vanilla extract
Food colouring gel (optional)

EQUIPMENT

20cm/8in square cake tin*
Mixer or electric hand whisk (this is tricky to do by hand)

* To prepare the tin: smear with a tiny amount of oil, then line the base and sides with aluminium foil. Mix the cornflour with the icing sugar. Sprinkle into the lined tin, then turn it around, tapping, to ensure the powder covers the base and sides. Tip the excess back into the bowl for later.

Posset

The posset came, steaming, sweet, and delicious, and Pattern's gentle hands removed Sylvia's travelling clothes.
The Wolves of Willoughby Chase, Joan Aiken

On cold winter nights, arriving home late from work, or a dinner, or a walk in the snow, I find my way into the kitchen before going to bed. At the end of a long journey, the promise of a hot drink is a welcome one; something that won't wake me up, but will warm me up from the inside. This posset, given to Sylvia late at night as she arrives, after an eventful journey, at Willoughby Chase, is just the ticket. This is more extravagant than my usual cup of tea, but for special evenings, it's one to try. The addition of brandy here is ideal; not quite appropriate for a child of Sylvia's age, perhaps, but a very agreeable pre-bed drink for those of us no longer at school.

Before you start, a little note on posset. Modern posset – which you may be more familiar with – is a dessert, rather than a drink. But in centuries past, making a posset involved adding alcohol to milk to curdle it. The curds and whey separate; the curds were then sweetened and eaten with a spoon, then the whey was drunk. This drink is somewhere inbetween the old and the new: sweet and smooth, but still warm and alcoholic, and just on the edge of curdling. It is completely inauthentic – but perhaps right in the world of Willoughby Chase.

Posset

Serves 2

1. Place the milk, lemon zest, sugar and almond extract into a saucepan. Bring to simmering point over a medium heat.

2. Whisk the egg white in the bowl until frothy. Add to the hot milk and whisk well. Add the rum and brandy, and whisk again.

3. Serve hot. If you look closely, you will notice that the milk has split, but drink it while it is hot and well whisked – it is creamy and delicious.

INGREDIENTS

150ml/5floz/⅔ cup milk

Zest of 1 lemon

40g/1½oz/3¼tbsp golden caster sugar

½tsp almond extract

1 egg white

40ml/1⅓floz/2tbsp rum

50ml/1⅔floz/3tbsp brandy

Ramen

I chopped vegetables. Here in my favourite place, I suddenly thought: ramen! What a coincidence! Without turning around I said playfully, 'In my dream you said you wanted ramen.'
Kitchen, Banana Yoshimoto

I have never been much of a 'night out on the town' fan. I'd almost always rather be at dinner with friends and a few bottles of wine, than drinking and dancing in a club. At university, apart from a few notable and memorable exceptions, I generally cast myself as the sensible friend. I was the one who kept the money for taxis and beer separate, and who tried to ensure that we all had our assignments finished before we headed out to a party.

Living in London in my twenties, that didn't change; but as we no longer had any assignments to submit, I had to find a different focus. When there's the inevitable suggestion to find a late-night dinner, I pounce on it. I love making food at midnight: a croque monsieur after a gig, a batch of biscuits after a night dancing or a bowl of ramen, using whatever I can find in a friend's fridge.

I have made this dish (or a variation of it) more than any other. It is my staple when arriving home late, or when I fancy an easy lunch. It is full of flavour, but isn't too rich or heavy. It is also endlessly adaptable – don't panic too much about ingredients or toppings that you're missing. I have made this without tofu, or with prawns and chicken in its place, with all sorts of different vegetables, and with none at all. It isn't the most authentic ramen you'll ever eat, but being able to put it on the table in less than twenty minutes makes it pretty appealing as a midnight feast.

INGREDIENTS

BROTH

500ml/17floz/generous 2 cups vegetable stock (chicken or beef stock also works well here)

2tsp grated ginger

3 cloves garlic, crushed

2tsp soy sauce

5 dried shiitake mushrooms

1 nest dried ramen noodles

2 tbsp white miso paste

TOFU

2tsp soy sauce

2tsp mirin

80g/scant 3oz soft silken tofu

1tbsp sesame oil

TO SERVE

1 egg

Baby spinach leaves

Chopped vegetables (use whatever you have in your fridge)

Pickled ginger

1 spring onion/scallion

Sesame seeds, to serve

Ramen

Serves 2

1. Bring the vegetable stock, ginger, garlic, soy sauce and mushrooms to the boil in a saucepan. Allow them to bubble away for 5 minutes while you get other things ready.

2. For the tofu, mix the soy and mirin together in a dish, cut the tofu in half lengthways and put both pieces in to marinate. Turn a couple of times. Heat a small frying pan, add the sesame oil and, once it is hot, add the tofu. Fry until crisp on each side, then add the marinade to the pan. Turn the heat off, and set the tofu aside.

3. Bring a small pan of water to the boil. Once boiling, gently lower the egg in and simmer for 6 minutes. Rinse the egg immediately under cold water, then peel it by cracking the shell all over, pulling one bit off and sliding a teaspoon between the membrane and the egg. Run the spoon around the whole egg and the shell should pull off easily.

4. Drop the ramen noodles into the hot stock for a minute or so (follow the packet instructions), then remove with tongs and divide between the bowls.

5. With the stock still hot, but not boiling, stir in the miso. Once it is dissolved, remove from the heat.

6. To serve, add some baby spinach leaves and any other vegetables you fancy to the noodles, then divide the stock between the bowls. Put one piece of tofu in each bowl, then arrange the pickled ginger, the finely sliced spring onions, half the egg and the sesame seeds on top.

Soup & Muffins

Imagine, if you can, what the rest of the evening was like. How they crouched by the fire which blazed and leaped and made so much of itself in the little grate. How they removed the covers of the dishes, and found rich, hot, savory soup, which was a meal in itself, and sandwiches and toast and muffins enough for both of them.

A Little Princess, Frances Hodgson Burnett

A Little Princess is a book about the power of stories, about works of fiction that can warm and feed you almost as much as hunks of bread. When Sara Crewe finds herself suddenly orphaned and penniless, at the mercy of the cruel and heartless Miss Minchin, the stories she tells – to herself, and to Becky on the other side of the thin attic wall – help them survive the long, cold, hungry winter. After countless evenings without supper, they wake one night to find that the feast they fell asleep dreaming of has materialized in front of them. They dine on it late into the night.

Though Sara and Becky's situation is many worlds away from my own, I have also spent long winters in England, buoyed up by stories and by soup. My first January was a cold one; I had single-glazed sash windows, and not quite enough money to keep the heating on. I regularly dressed under my duvet, my body still far from acclimatized to the winter mornings.

When I felt the cold in my bones, and was missing my family so much that every day was a struggle, I was comforted by good books and simple, warming food. This soup (and these muffins, if you have the time) fits the bill.

INGREDIENTS

40g/1½oz/3tbsp butter

1kg/2¼lb brown onions, cut in thin semicircles

10 sprigs thyme

Salt and pepper

2tbsp plain/all-purpose flour

400ml/14floz/1¾ cups vegetable stock (home-made is best)

VEGETABLE STOCK*

Please note, the amounts below are a suggestion – add or subtract depending on what is in your fridge:

2 carrots

2 sticks celery

1 small brown onion

1 red onion

3 spring onions/scallions

Handful of parsley stalks

5 whole peppercorns

1.5L/2¾ pints/6¼ cups water

*Or use a stock cube

Onion Soup

Serves 2 very generously – or 1, with leftovers

1. First, if you're using home-made, make the stock. Throw the vegetables (cleaned and chopped, but not peeled), parsley, peppercorns and water into a large saucepan. Bring to a gentle simmer, and allow to bubble away for around an hour with the lid off. Sieve and set the stock aside.

2. Melt the butter in a saucepan until it foams. Add the sliced onions and fry over a moderate heat for 10 minutes. Once they are soft and translucent, strip the leaves from the thyme stalks, and add to the pan, along with 2 generous pinches of salt and some pepper.

3. Once the onions are golden in places, add the flour and stir through for 2 minutes. Pour the stock into the pan and stir again. Bring the soup to the boil, reduce the heat and then simmer, uncovered, until it is as thick as you'd like.

Muffins

Makes 8

1. Put the flour into the bowl of your mixer (or mixing bowl). Add the salt on one side and yeast on the other, then add the sugar, butter, egg and milk. Using a dough hook, mix the dough until it is smooth and stretchy (around 5 minutes). If you don't have a mixer, combine the ingredients in the bowl, then tip onto a lightly floured surface and knead for around 10 minutes. Shape into a ball.

2. Wash out your bowl and lightly grease with oil. Pop the dough in the bowl, cover with plastic wrap and allow to prove until doubled in size. A little hint in terms of dough 'doubling': take a quick snap on your phone. I find it really hard to remember what it originally looked like.

3. Once doubled in size, tip the dough onto a floured surface. Roll it out to around 2.5cm/1in thick. Cut out your muffins with a floured biscuit cutter or glass.

4. Scatter two baking trays with half the polenta, and carefully transfer the muffins to the trays. Scatter the rest of the polenta over the tops. Cover loosely with plastic wrap and allow to prove again, for around 30 minutes. Don't be concerned if the muffins haven't grown much, as they'll puff up beautifully once on the heat.

5. Heat a heavy-based frying pan over a low heat. Transfer a few muffins into the pan; they'll spread and grow, so don't overcrowd them. Cook for around 5 minutes before flipping over and cooking for a further 5 minutes, until golden brown on both sides.

6. To serve in the style of *A Little Princess*, cut the muffin in half, spear with a fork and toast over a fire (or a gas hob, in my case). Butter liberally and use to scoop up onion soup.

NOTE: Any leftover muffins will keep for a couple of days in a paper bag, and should be toasted before eating. Perfect for a packed lunch with some homemade baked beans (p. 32), for breakfast with grilled cheese and chilli jam or for a late-night snack.

INGREDIENTS

300g/10½oz/2⅛ cups strong white bread flour

6g/heaping 1tsp salt

6g/2tsp fast-action dried yeast

15g/½oz/4tsp caster sugar

15g/½oz/1tbsp softened butter

1 egg

170ml/generous 5floz/scant ¾ cup milk

15g/scant 2tbsp polenta

A Little Princess, Frances Hodgson Burnett

Sausage Rolls

'It was someone being tortured!' said Neville, who had gone very white, and spilled sausage rolls all over the floor. 'You're going to have to fight the Cruciatus curse!'
Harry Potter and the Goblet of Fire, J. K. Rowling

Harry Potter came into my life when I was ten. As a bookish girl with unruly hair, it should come as no surprise which character I identified with most. In truth, it's impossible for me to convey how important it was to see a clever, interesting girl, unafraid to put her hand up in class, as a hero in these stories I so loved. Hermione is brave, brilliant and loyal, and I spent most of my teenage years trying to live up to her example.

While I love and admire Hermione, Neville Longbottom is, I think, my favourite character. Clumsy, awkward and perpetually anxious, he spends most of the first three books as the butt of everyone's jokes. By the end of the series, though, Neville has come into his own. No longer laughed at, sneered at or dropping trays of pastries, he leads the Hogwarts students against an impossible enemy, and continues the fight when it seems all is lost.

I first read *Goblet of Fire* in my granny's house, trying to ignore my sister hovering at my shoulder, desperate for me to finish so that she could have her turn. These sausage rolls started as granny's, made in their hundreds for every party we've ever had. They are perfect for doing in bulk – the mince needs little more than a squidge and a stir, and can easily be doubled or tripled in quantity. And Granny would scoff at me if she thought I'd do anything but buy the puff pastry. The shop-bought stuff is great here, and ready-rolled even better. It makes the whole thing a much easier prospect at midnight.

INGREDIENTS

3 brown onions, finely diced

3 carrots, grated

500g/1lb 2oz sausage meat

250g/9oz pork mince/ ground pork

250g/9oz chicken mince/ground chicken (or more pork mince)

125g/4½oz/2¼ cups soft white breadcrumbs

Lots of freshly ground pepper

Large pinch of salt

3tbsp Worcestershire sauce

2tsp hot mustard powder

Handful of chopped flat-leaf parsley

4 sheets ready-rolled puff pastry (or a batch of homemade rough puff)

1 egg

1tbsp sesame seeds

Sausage Rolls
Makes around 12 rolls

1. Preheat your oven to 200°C/400°F/Gas 6. In a mixing bowl, squidge together all ingredients, except the pastry, egg and sesame seeds.

2. Roll/lay out a sheet of pastry. About 2cm/¾in from the edge closest to you, lay a quarter of your meat in a long line, about 4cm/1½in high.

3. In a small bowl, whisk the egg with a fork. Using a pastry brush, paint some egg along the edge of the pastry furthest from you, parallel to the sausage. Tightly roll a quarter of the sausage meat up in the pastry, using the line of egg to seal the roll closed. Place the roll on the work surface so that the sealed edge is sitting underneath. Slice the roll into three large pieces (you can, of course, make smaller ones if you like). Transfer each to a lined baking sheet. Paint the tops with more egg wash, sprinkle with sesame seeds, then score the pastry. Repeat with the rest of the pastry.

4. Bake for 30 minutes until a deep golden colour. Allow to cool slightly before serving with Worcestershire sauce.

Seed Cake

'Lots!' Bilbo found himself answering, to his own surprise; and he found himself scuttling off, too, to the cellar to fill a pint beer-mug, and to the pantry to fetch two beautiful round seed-cakes which he had baked that afternoon for his after-supper morsel.
The Hobbit, J. R. R. Tolkien

Brisbane, where I grew up, is a short drive from Lamington National Park, home to more than 500 waterfalls, trees that first sent their roots into the earth over 5,000 years ago, and the unique sound of whipbirds. After a period of rain, it is so green that your eyes can barely take in all the shades. It is a beautiful part of the world. On weekends with Dad and my stepmother Cheryl, we would set out in walking boots, stopping only to hear birdsong, take in the sweeping views at the summit, and occasionally when my sister Lucy would sit down in the middle of the track, pointing at her legs and diagnosing them 'broken'. Luckily, all she really needed to get going again was the promise of a story from Dad – and a reminder that spiders are far more likely to climb on you if you're sitting on the ground.

Dad is a great teller of stories. As we walked, we would provide him with characters (an elephant, a brave girl called Annie, a flea) and he would spin them into something fantastic. Back home, footsore but happy, he would set up a chair in our room and read to us until we couldn't keep our eyes open any more. The books he chose were full of adventure: *Treasure Island*, *The Hobbit* and *The Mirrorstone*.

We adored *The Hobbit*; the riddles in the dark, clever Bilbo, and the wonderful dwarves. We were terrified of Smaug, convinced that the band of thieves couldn't possibly triumph against him. Tolkien continued to feature in our lives as we grew older; Dad encouraged us to embrace *The Lord of the Rings*, and Peter Jackson's films have been projected onto a white wall in our house on more than one evening. But it is *The Hobbit* I love best; from the unexpected late-night party, where Bilbo's enviable cellar comes in handy, to his arrival back in Hobbiton one very eventful year later.

Seed Cake

Serves 8

1. Line the base of the baking tin with butter and greaseproof paper and preheat the oven to 160°C/325°F/Gas 3. Make sure all your ingredients are at room temperature.

2. Beat the butter and sugar until light and creamy. In another bowl, whisk the eggs with the brandy, nutmeg and mace, then beat into the butter and sugar.

3. Sift the flour and baking powder into the mixture, and gently fold in along with the caraway seeds. Spoon carefully into the tin, flatten the top with a spatula and sprinkle with demerara sugar.

4. Bake in the oven for 50 minutes, or until a skewer inserted in the centre comes out clean. Cool on a wire rack, and serve cold and unadorned for an after-supper morsel, or elevenses.

INGREDIENTS

225g/8oz/2 sticks butter

170g/6oz/scant 1 cup caster/superfine sugar

3 medium eggs

60ml/2floz/¼ cup brandy

½tsp grated nutmeg

½tsp ground mace

225g/8oz/1¾ cups plain/all-purpose flour

1tsp baking powder

1tbsp caraway seeds

1tbsp demerara/turbinado sugar

EQUIPMENT

20cm/8in round baking tin

parties & celebrations

parties & celebrations

Memories of my childhood birthday parties have melded together somewhat. I remember them in snippets: biting Cheezels off a string in the back garden, an early-morning exploration of the creek behind my dad's house, my mum ordering a pizza for a sleepover so oversized it couldn't fit through our front door.

In my family, as in many others I know, these celebrations were always built around food. Lots of it. My mum and granny are completely unfazed in the face of feeding thousands – I have never seen last-minute changes throw them. Our house was an open one, often teeming with guests. My eighteenth birthday party lasted for over thirty hours; the guests who woke up at my house took one look at brunch and decided to stay for as long as possible.

As children who didn't grow up in a dessert house (we ate a lot of fruit after dinner), my sister Lucy and I naturally became fascinated with baking. We were the first to volunteer to make the sweet things for a party – Mum was always much more interested in the savoury offerings. We quickly found that if we made it ourselves we were more likely to be allowed to eat it.

Our paternal grandmother, the only really enthusiastic baker in our family, passed away just as I started secondary school and so, for the most part, we taught ourselves to bake. We saved up book tokens to buy cookbooks and baked the things we'd always lusted after in shop windows and cafés. Muffins, banana bread and crumbles came first, followed by cupcakes and biscuits, and, eventually, layer cakes, intricate icing and pastry.

Now that I have grown up, my sweet tooth has taken a back seat. I am just as likely to celebrate with a steak as with a cake. But I still love the ritual of a show-stopping dessert: the visual spectacle, the cutting of it, the ceremony. And they are such fun to make.

The desserts, breads and cakes in this chapter are designed to be eaten by a crowd. They could be covered with lit candles for a birthday, sliced at weddings, or brought out to wow guests at a dinner party. In short, they are perfect for a celebration.

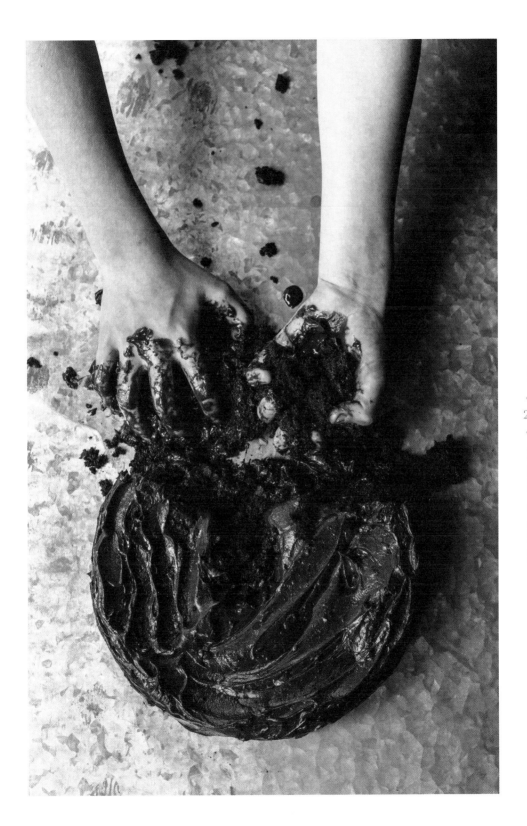

An Enormous Round Chocolate Cake

Almost at once she was back again staggering under the weight of an enormous round chocolate cake on a china platter. The cake was fully eighteen inches in diameter and it was covered with dark-brown chocolate icing.
Matilda, Roald Dahl

This is a cake I have thought about since childhood, a cake of dreams, and of nightmares. Used as an instrument of torture, and eaten by a solitary primary-school-aged boy, the cake is an extraordinary piece of writing from Dahl – the very thing every child thinks they want morphed into a grotesque ordeal, as Bruce Bogtrotter clears the platter. It is the one scene that always comes up when I am discussing this book: people want to talk about how they imagine every detail of this cake.

I have a very clear recollection of reading *Matilda* – if not for the first time, then certainly the first time without an adult. I was seven, and had been grounded by my dad – the first (and last) time I was ever grounded. Once in my bedroom, where I was to stay for four hours, I pulled *Matilda* off the bookshelf and read it cover to cover. Being grounded, it seemed, wasn't nearly as bad as I had feared.

When I think now of Bruce's cake, this is the recipe I imagine. It is dense, fudgy and rich; monstrous in size and in sweetness. The sticky icing and barely-cooked sponge find their way under fingernails, onto clothing and all over faces. When first trialling this recipe I iced it straight on the serving platter, picked it up and genuinely staggered underneath its extraordinary weight.

Chocolate Cake

Serves at least 30 children – or 1 Bruce

1. Preheat the oven to 150°C/300°F/Gas 2. Grease and line the cake tin with greaseproof paper. Melt the chocolate and butter in a bowl over a saucepan of boiling water, and allow to cool.

2. Combine the flour, baking powder, bicarbonate of soda, sugars and cocoa powder in a large mixing bowl.

3. Whisk the eggs and buttermilk together, and add to the cooled butter and chocolate. Pour in the coffee, and mix through. Tip the wet ingredients into the dry ones and fold through until combined.

4. Pour the cake batter into the tin and transfer to the oven. Bake for 90 minutes. Remove the cake from the oven once a skewer inserted comes out with clumps of cake attached to it, rather than raw batter. The cake is too sugary to 'bounce back' – it is really more akin to a giant brownie than a sponge.

5. Cool the cake in the tin for 10 minutes, then remove the sides of the tin, leaving the cake on the base until completely cool. The cake is delicate, so transfer it carefully to a serving plate. The easiest way to do this is to place a plate on top of the cake, flip it over confidently, so that the plate is underneath, and then remove the base of the tin. Flipping it over like this will help disguise any dip in the centre too. It's heavy, so is liable to break in half if you pick it up without support, but you can squidge it back together on the serving plate.

6. To make the ganache icing, bring the cream almost to the boil. Place the chocolate in a mixing bowl, and pour the piping hot cream over the top. Leave to stand for 5 minutes, then stir. Leave it in the fridge for 10 minutes to thicken – don't leave it too long, or it will solidify – then smooth over the top and sides of the cake.

INGREDIENTS

300g/10½oz dark chocolate

300g/10½oz/2¾ sticks unsalted butter

250g/8¾oz/2 cups plain/all-purpose flour (gluten-free works too)

2tsp baking powder

½tsp bicarbonate of soda/baking soda

300g/10½oz/1½ cups golden caster/superfine sugar

300g/10½oz/1½ cups light brown sugar

60g/2¼oz/generous ½ cup cocoa powder

4 eggs

100ml/3⅓floz/generous ⅓ cup buttermilk

125ml/4¼floz/generous ½ cup strong brewed coffee, cooled

GANACHE

250ml/8½floz/generous 1 cup double/heavy cream

150g/5¼oz dark chocolate, finely chopped

100g/3½oz milk chocolate, finely chopped

EQUIPMENT

25cm/10in loose-based or springform cake tin (important as the cake is too dense to 'turn out' of a traditional tin)

The Queen of Hearts' Tarts

'The Queen of Hearts, she made some tarts,
All on a summer day:
The Knave of Hearts, he stole those tarts,
And took them clean away.'
Alice's Adventures in Wonderland, Lewis Carroll

I moved to England in the month of March. It was the perfect time to arrive. I spent the next few months watching London shake off its winter coat and come back to life. Everything changed; the parks were full of flowers and fresh green leaves, and the produce from the greengrocer kept me returning almost daily. To my joy, the berry season started in earnest in June; like tomatoes, strawberries, raspberries and redcurrants never taste quite right out of season. Red berries in England speak of Wimbledon, summer picnics and sunny evenings. Though wonderful in ice cream, or jam, or pies, they're never better than when they're used fresh from the garden.

The filling inside the tarts stolen from the Queen of Hearts is unknown. The Dormouse suggests that they might be treacle, but no one seems to be able to agree. Some imagine jam tarts, which could certainly be a beautiful rich red, but they aren't quite as decadent as I imagine our Queen would want. And so I have given her these: crumbly pastry, filled with sweet, vanilla-scented custard, and topped with all the red berries you can find. I imagine the Queen of Hearts, who demands that everything be crimson-hued, would be very upset about these being stolen from under her nose.

Summer Tarts

Makes 6 individual tarts – or 1 large one

1. Preheat your oven to 200°C/400°F/Gas 6. To make the pastry, cream together the butter and sugar, beat in the egg yolk and then fold through the almonds and flour. Form into a dough (add 1tbsp cold water if it is not quite wet enough) and fashion into a thick log. Chill in the fridge, wrapped in greaseproof paper, for at least 20 minutes.

2. Remove the pastry from the fridge. Instead of rolling it out, slice into 5mm/¼in thick rounds and push into the tart tin, ensuring there are no gaps. The pastry should come all the way up the sides of the tin. Chill for a further 15 minutes.

3. While the pastry is chilling, you can make the filling. Start by beating the egg, egg yolks and sugar in a bowl until light and creamy. Sift the flour and beat in as well. Leave to stand.

4. Remove the tart shell/s from the fridge. Place in the centre of the oven and bake for 15 minutes, until very lightly browned. Leave to cool completely.

5. Bring the milk and butter almost to the boil in a saucepan over a low heat, then pour over the egg mixture, whisking briskly by hand as you do. Pour the mixture back into the saucepan (give your pan a brief wash and dry first) and cook over a low heat, stirring frequently with a wooden spoon, for around 10 minutes.

6. Once thick enough to cling to the spoon, transfer to a clean bowl, cover with plastic wrap and leave to cool. To prevent a skin from forming, push the plastic wrap right into the bowl and ensure it makes contact with the top of the custard.

7. When both the filling and shell are cool, assemble the tart. Spoon the filling into the tart shell and leave it to stand, either in the fridge or in a cool place, for around

INGREDIENTS

PASTRY
100g/3½oz/scant 1 stick butter
2tbsp golden caster/superfine sugar
1 egg yolk
100g/3½oz/1 cup ground almonds
200g/7oz/1½ cups plain/all-purpose flour

FILLING
1 egg
2 egg yolks
125g/4½oz/scant ⅔ cup golden caster/superfine sugar
40g/1½oz/heaping ¼ cup plain/all-purpose flour
500ml/17floz/generous 2 cups milk
40g/1½oz/3tbsp unsalted butter

TOPPING
250g/9oz red fruit (redcurrants, raspberries, strawberries)
Icing/confectioners' sugar

EQUIPMENT
20cm/8in tart tin (preferably at least 3cm/1¼in deep), or six 8cm/3¼in tartlet tins (2cm/¾in deep)

30 minutes. (Doing this ensures that you will be able to cut neat slices of your tart, rather than the custard mixture leaking out everywhere.) Once the tart has chilled, remove the redcurrants from their stalks with a fork, wash the raspberries and slice the strawberries, and tumble them all over the tart. Dust with icing sugar and serve.

Pear & Lemon Birthday Cake

*Moominmamma was in the kitchen decorating a big cake with pale
yellow lemon peel and slices of crystallised pear.*
Comet in Moominland, Tove Jansson

I attended quite a few weddings when I was a child, including both
my mum and dad's second ones. I remember wandering around at a
cousin's wedding, long past my bedtime, finding plates with whole
abandoned slices of cake on them, and dutifully wrapping these up
in napkins to take home. A lifelong cake fan, I couldn't understand
it. Who would leave their piece untouched?

I made my first wedding cake in June 2015. Although I had been
making and transporting cakes for the café at work for a while, I felt
nervous; this cake needed to live up to the occasion. It also needed
to be something you couldn't bear to leave on a side plate.

Every wedding cake I have made since is a variation of that first
one: dense, richly flavoured sponge (honey and rosemary, lemon
and thyme, elderflower and white chocolate), covered with
buttercream and decorated with something edible. This pear,
lemon and cardamom cake is one of my favourite variations. It is
a cake made with love by Moominmamma for a birthday, but it
would suit a wedding just as well. It's a long, involved bake, so I'd
recommend doing it for someone you love too. I promise, it will
absolutely make their (wedding/birth) day.

INGREDIENTS

SPONGE
300g/10½oz/2¾ sticks
unsalted butter
260g/9⅓oz/generous 1¼
cups light brown sugar
6 pears, peeled, cored
and diced
400g/14oz/1⅓ cups
golden syrup
400g/14oz/1⅓ cups
sour cream
6 eggs
600g/1lb 5oz/4½ cups
plain/all-purpose flour
4tsp baking powder
1tsp bicarbonate of soda/
baking soda
1tsp ground cardamom
2tsp ground cinnamon

CRYSTALLIZED PEARS
2 pears
50g/1¾oz/¼ cup caster/
superfine sugar

ICING
100g/3½oz/scant 1 stick
butter
1kg/2¼lb golden icing/
confectioners' sugar
50g/2¾oz/⅓ cup soured
cream
Zest and juice of 2
lemons

EQUIPMENT
20cm/8in loose-based
cake tin
15cm/6in loose-based
cake tin
13cm/5⅛in loose-based
cake tin
Mandoline or sharp knife
Scrap cardboard and foil
or cake plates
Wooden skewers

Pear and Lemon Cake

Serves at least 40*

1. Preheat your oven to 160°C/325°F/Gas 3. Grease and line three loose-based baking tins.

2. First, cook the pears for the cake. Melt 60g/2oz/½ stick of the butter in a frying pan until bubbling. Add 60g/5tbsp of the light brown sugar and stir until it starts to dissolve. Tip in the diced pears and cook over a low heat for 15 minutes, turning regularly. Set aside to cool.

3. Melt the golden syrup, and the rest of the sugar and butter together in a saucepan. Leave to cool, then beat in the soured cream and eggs.

4. Sift the flour, baking powder, bicarbonate of soda and spices into a large mixing bowl. Add the wet ingredients, then fold through until all the flour is incorporated.

5. Finally, fold the pears through. Leave any excess caramel in the pan (this sauce is great on ice cream). Divide the batter between the tins, ensuring they are all relatively even in height.

6. Bake in the oven until a skewer inserted in the cakes comes out clean. Start gently checking the smallest one after 35 minutes or so. The middle one should take around 50 minutes. The biggest one will take around an hour. If they're browning too quickly on top, cover with a little foil.

7. Leave to cool in the tins for 10 minutes, then on a wire rack until stone cold. You won't be able to ice them until they're completely cold, so leave them overnight, or go and have a long bath.

8. To make the crystallized pears, thinly slice the pears using a mandoline or very sharp knife. Pour the sugar into a dish, and press each side of the pear in to cover. Lay out on a baking tray lined with greaseproof paper and bake (at 160°C/325°F/Gas 3) for 20 minutes, until golden and

crisp at the edges. Keep an eye on them so they don't burn. Leave to cool for a minute or two, then gently pull the slices off the paper. Leave on a rack to cool completely.

8. For the icing, beat the butter until very pale. Add half the icing sugar, and beat until incorporated. Tip in the soured cream and the rest of the icing sugar, and beat again. Finally, add the lemon zest and juice, and beat for 5 minutes on a high speed until the icing is very light.

9. To prevent your three-tiered cake sinking into itself, I'd recommend using cake plates between each layer. You can buy these in baking supply stores, but I tend to make them myself. To make your own, trace around the base of the two smaller cake tins onto a piece of thick cardboard. Cut out, then cover each with foil.

10. To assemble, place the biggest cake on the serving plate. Put a generous amount of icing on top, and smooth it down over the sides. Poke 4 wooden skewers into the cake, and cut them off just below the level of the icing. Balance the middle cake plate and cake on the skewers. Ice this too, ensuring you ice around the cake plate to hide it. Put 4 skewers into the middle cake, then balance the smallest cake plate on top. Ice the smallest cake, and decorate each tier with the crystallized pear slices.

*Do halve this recipe if you fancy a smaller, one-tier cake

Spongy Trifle

... and Bad Harry showed my naughty little sister a lovely spongy trifle,
covered with creamy stuff and silver balls and jelly-sweets on the top.
My Naughty Little Sister, Dorothy Edwards

If my mum did make dessert, she'd either make Nigella Lawson's
superlative orange and almond cake, or a trifle. This sweet, boozy,
familiar dish was a staple at big events and Sunday lunches. Less a
recipe than an impressive assembly job, it involves layer upon layer
of sliced supermarket jam roll, sherry, red Aeroplane jelly, tinned
peaches, thick yellow custard from a carton and softly whipped
cream, topped with slivered almonds and a drizzle of chocolate.

My own trifle is an evolution of this. Though I have a great love for
supermarket jam roll, I have included a recipe for you to make it
from scratch here, as it allows you to include a jam of your choosing.
If this demands more time than you have, then you should not
hesitate to buy the jam roll instead. I'm always keen to get plenty
of fruit into the trifle bowl and, in my house at least, jelly is non-
negotiable. You can, of course, make your own with cordial and
gelatine, but I find sweet packet jelly terribly appealing.

My dear friend Jenny gave me a copy of Dorothy Edwards's book,
with a dedication in the front directing me towards the picture of
this trifle. She and her sister had dreamed of it since childhood, and
I have since found that many other friends did the same. This trifle,
then, is for all of them.

Trifle

Serves up to 12 – enough for a dinner party, or family, with leftovers

1. Make your jelly according to the packet instructions, and leave to chill in the fridge.

2. Next, make the jam. Heat the oven to 160°C/325°F/Gas 3. Place the blackberries in an ovenproof dish, and pour the sugar into another. Place both dishes in the oven for 15 minutes. Keep an eye on them (you don't want the sugar to become caramel), then remove from the oven and tip the sugar into the fruit. Be incredibly careful here, as the sugar will be very hot. Leave for a minute or two, and then stir. The blackberries should break down into a mush, mixing with the sugar to become a jam. Leave to cool.

3. Turn the oven up to 180°C/350°F/Gas 4. Line the Swiss roll tin with some flavourless oil and then greaseproof paper. Beat the eggs and sugar until pale, and tripled in size. This should take 8–10 minutes with an electric whisk, so do be patient. Sift the flour into the mix, and very gently fold it in, stopping as soon as the flour is incorporated, being careful not to knock too much air out.

4. Spoon the batter into the tin, smoothing out the top. Transfer to the oven and bake for 8 minutes, until golden. Just before it is done, sprinkle a piece of greaseproof paper large enough to fit the cake with caster sugar. When the cake is baked, allow to cool for a minute then, while still hot, flip onto the sugary sheet. Peel away the greaseproof paper the cake was cooked on. Make a shallow cut across the width of the cake, 2cm in from one of the short edges, then roll the cake up, rolling the greaseproof paper underneath with it. Allow the cake to sit, rolled up, until it is completely cool.

5. Unroll the cake and spread with the jam. Roll up again, without the greaseproof paper this time. Cut into 1.5cm/⅝in thick slices and line the base and side of the trifle dish.

INGREDIENTS

JELLY
Enough raspberry jelly powder or squares to make 600ml/1 pint/2½ cups jelly

JAM
200g/7oz blackberries
200g/7oz/1 cup caster/superfine sugar

SPONGE
4 eggs
125g/4½oz/scant ⅔ cup caster/superfine sugar (plus extra for sprinkling)
125g/4½oz/scant 1 cup plain/all-purpose flour

CUSTARD
300ml/½ pint/1¼ cups milk
300ml/½ pint/1¼ cups double/heavy cream
1 vanilla pod
6 egg yolks
60g/5tbsp caster sugar
2tbsp cornflour/cornstarch

AND
50ml/3½tbsp kirsch (or liqueur from the cherries)
150g/5½oz/ pitted cherries (ideally ones that have been preserved in something delicious)
200g/7oz blackberries
500ml/17floz/generous 2 cups double/heavy cream
Small handful of edible silver balls
50g/1¾oz jelly sweets/candy

EQUIPMENT
Swiss roll tin or large rectangular baking dish (36 x 24cm/15 x 10in)
Large glass serving dish

6 To prepare the custard, warm the milk, cream and split vanilla pod in a saucepan over a low heat. In a mixing bowl, whisk the egg yolks with the sugar and cornflour until frothy and sticky. When you can see the first couple of bubbles appear in the milk pan, whip it off the heat. Remove the vanilla pod. Whisking constantly to prevent the mixture from scrambling, pour the milk over the yolks. Rinse out the saucepan and pour the custard back into it.

7. Place over a low heat and cook the custard, stirring constantly, until it noticeably thickens. It will take around 10 minutes to do so; don't be tempted to turn the heat up. Once the custard is thick, pour into a bowl, press a layer of plastic wrap over it to prevent a skin forming, and leave to cool in the fridge.

8. Finally, assemble the trifle. Sprinkle the kirsch or liqueur over the jam rolls. Scatter the fruit over the cake layer. Once the jelly has almost completely set, give it a stir to break it up a bit, and spoon it over the fruit. Add the custard on top of the jelly. Whisk the double cream, and spoon on top of the custard. Sprinkle edible silver balls and jelly sweets over the top. Refrigerate overnight, if you like, or for a couple of hours at least, to ensure the layers firm up a little, and stay distinct once you spoon the first bit out.

A NOTE: If you're anything like me, you will return regularly to the fridge with a spoon to take a bite until you've scraped the dish clean. This trifle is a dream to serve at Christmas too, as an alternative pudding.

Lane Cake

Maycomb welcomed Aunt Alexandra. Miss Maudie Atkinson baked a
Lane Cake so loaded with shinny it made me tight…
To Kill a Mockingbird, Harper Lee

My dad's old boss Barry bought me my first copy of *To Kill a Mockingbird* when I was ten. He always aimed up with books; buying us things that would sit on our shelves for a year or so before we were ready to tackle them. I must have been about twelve when I first read it. It was a hot summer in Queensland, the kind where you'd sweat through your T-shirt before 11 a.m.

I have never been to the southern states of America, so it is the oppressive heat of Brisbane that I remember when I think about Maycomb County. I think of Jem, Scout and Dill, running in and out of the dusty streets, the sun heavy on their backs. And I think about the women in Maycomb, sweating over Lane Cake in their kitchens, windows open to tempt the non-existent breeze.

It is a truly ridiculous cake to make in the height of summer: four layers of sponge, separated by three layers of boozy, fruity custard. To have any chance of staying between the sponge (rather than oozing down the sides), both custard and cake have to be stone cold when you're assembling it. I'd suggest saving this for a cool weekend; you don't need to re-create the Alabama scene too faithfully. But don't be put off making it. This is a special cake – a true marriage of flavours, textures and booze.

INGREDIENTS

SPONGE
250g/9oz/2¼ sticks
unsalted butter
450g/1lb/2¼ cups caster/
superfine sugar
2tsp vanilla extract
8 egg whites
360g/12⅔oz/2¾ cups
plain/all-purpose flour
2tsp baking powder
1tsp salt
250ml/8½floz/generous
1 cup milk

FILLING
8 egg yolks
225g/8oz/1⅛ cups caster/
superfine sugar
115g/4oz/1 stick butter,
softened
150g/5½oz/1⅓ cups
dried sour cherries
100g/3½oz/1 cup
chopped pecans
1tsp vanilla extract
150ml/5floz/⅔ cup rum,
bourbon or brandy

ICING
340g/12oz/scant 1¾ cups
caster/superfine sugar
¼tsp cream of tartar
Pinch of salt
85ml/6tbsp water
2 egg whites
1½tsp vanilla extract

EQUIPMENT
Four 20cm/8in
sandwich/layer cake
tins (you can do the cake
baking in batches if you
don't have four tins)
Electric hand whisk (you
can use a regular hand
whisk, but it will take
considerable time)

Lane Cake

Serves 16

1. Preheat the oven to 180°C/350°F/Gas 4. Grease the tins and line the base of each with greaseproof paper.

2. To make the cakes, cream the butter and sugar until light and fluffy. Add the vanilla and beat again. Add the egg whites into the mixture two at a time, beating thoroughly each time. Sift the flour, baking powder and salt together, then fold into the mixture one-third at a time, alternating the additions with the milk. The final batter will be smooth but slightly granular.

3. Pour the batter into the sandwich tins and level off the tops. Bake for 20 minutes, until the edges shrink back from the sides and the top springs back when pressed lightly. Cool on a wire rack.

4. While the cakes are cooling, you can get started on the filling. Whisk the egg yolks in a saucepan with the sugar and softened butter. Place the pan over a low heat and cook until the mixture is noticeably thick (it will take 10–15 minutes), ensuring you stir constantly with a wooden spoon or spatula. Remove from the heat, and stir in the cherries, pecans and vanilla. Cover with plastic wrap, pushed right down to the filling so that it doesn't form a skin, and leave to cool in the fridge.

5. Once everything is cool, assemble the cake. Paint each layer with a generous amount of your chosen booze, and then spread a third of the filling between each layer. If it's a warm day, return the cake to the fridge after each layer. Store the cake in the fridge until you're ready to ice it.

6. To make the marshmallow icing, put a saucepan of water on to boil. Place the sugar, cream of tartar, salt, water and egg whites in a heatproof bowl. Beat for one minute with an electric whisk, then place over the saucepan of water and beat on high speed for 7 minutes. Beat in the vanilla.

7. Ice the top and sides of the cake, using the palette knife to ensure a smooth-ish finish. The marshmallow should spread easily, but will set once in place, so resist the temptation to taste or fiddle with it too much.

Blancmange

Carrie prepared a little extemporised supper, consisting of the remainder of the cold joint, a small piece of salmon (which I was to refuse, in case there was not enough to go round), and a blanc-mange and custards.
The Diary of a Nobody, George and Weedon Grossmith

I hadn't eaten a good blancmange until I tried one at my friend Livvy's house. She spends much of her time developing recipes for things that have fallen somewhat out of favour – suet puddings, kidneys and the aforementioned blancmange. Hers was glorious: an enormous, saffron-hued dessert, which I happily dug into with a teaspoon, standing up in her kitchen.

I met Livvy through Twitter first, and then in real life over oysters and cocktails. We were both in the process of leaving careers we had worked hard to establish ourselves in, to run off and spend time in kitchens. Over the next year, we cooked together many times; for events, for this book and for Saturday-night suppers.

We share the same taste in so many things and constantly pass books between us. On my first visit to Livvy's house, I spent a good hour poring over her bookshelves. *The Diary of a Nobody* is one we both love; a year and a bit in the life of Charles Pooter, a lower-middle-class Victorian clerk, and his wife Carrie. It is consistently funny, endlessly charming, and speaks of the mundanity of everyday life in a similar way to Bridget Jones and Adrian Mole nearly a century later.

I've developed this recipe from Livvy's original. In place of her saffron, I have used rose – a little cheaper in Victorian times, and therefore more appropriate for the Pooter household.

Blancmange

Serves 4

1. If you're using gelatine leaves, soak them in a bowl of cold water for 5 minutes.

2. Pour the milk and cream into a saucepan, and stir in the sugar. Place over a low heat and warm gently – don't let it boil. After a couple of minutes, stir the gelatine into the milk.

3. Remove the pan from the heat and stir in the rosewater, tasting to ensure the rose is strong enough. Allow to cool.

4. Pour the liquid into the mould, tapping it on the work surface a couple of times to settle any bubbles. Cover with plastic wrap and transfer to the fridge for at least 4 hours, or overnight.

5. When you are ready to serve, dip the base of the mould into a dish of warm water, being careful not to dribble any on the blancmange. Run a thin bladed knife around the edge, then place a serving plate on top and turn it over. Do this quickly and confidently, so that the blancmange falls straight down onto the plate, rather than sliding about. If it is being stubborn, shake the bowl slightly, or wrap it in a warm, wet tea towel.

6. Serve immediately, topped with rose petals.

INGREDIENTS

4 sheets gelatine (or 10g/3tsp powdered gelatine)

300ml/½ pint/1¼ cups milk

100ml/3⅓floz/generous ⅓ cup double/heavy cream

35g/2½tbsp golden caster/superfine sugar

½tsp rosewater

EQUIPMENT

Small pudding bowl or jelly mould, capable of holding 500ml/17floz liquid

Ice pudding

For the Starkadders and such of the local thorny peasantry as would attend there were syllabubs, ice-pudding, caviar sandwiches, crab patties, trifle, and champagne.
Cold Comfort Farm, Stella Gibbons

Flora Poste is one of my favourite people in literature. She is clever, witty, practical, and able to successfully orchestrate events and people around her. Orphaned, and left without the means to live independently, she thrives under what (in any other novel) would be seen as a rather dire set of circumstances. She quickly moves to the country, is taken in by her relatives the Starkadders, and sets about changing their lives.

The above menu is served as a wedding feast, her greatest triumph. It takes place on Midsummer Eve, the longest day of the year. In researching this dish (I am more familiar with syllabub and trifle), I found various desserts from the 1920s and 1930s labelled as 'ice puddings', but no definitive version. So I created one I would want at the end of a hot summer day – a frozen Eton Mess of sorts.

This is a lovely dessert for a relaxed summer wedding, or a backyard midsummer feast. You can make most of it (the ice cream and the meringues) days in advance, so on the day itself you need do little more than slice fruit and layer the ingredients. Once out of the freezer, you'll need to leave the ice pudding to sit for a good few minutes before turning it out. Give it some time to rest in a shady place, while you get on with pouring the champagne.

Ice Pudding

Serves 10

1. First, make the ice cream. Place the chopped strawberries in a bowl with the vanilla sugar. Stir through and leave to sit. Place the cream and milk in a saucepan with the split vanilla pod, and bring almost to the boil.

2. Whisk the egg yolks with the sugar until pale yellow and thick. Remove the vanilla pod from the milk, then pour it slowly into the yolk mixture, whisking continuously. Rinse the saucepan and pour the mixture back in, then place over a low heat. Stir with a wooden spoon until the custard is thick enough to coat the back of the spoon, then remove from the heat. Pour into a bowl, cover with plastic wrap (push it down so that it touches the skin of the custard to prevent a skin forming) and leave to cool.

3. Use a potato masher to squash the strawberries into a rough purée, then add the lemon juice. Stir through the cooled custard, which will turn the most gorgeous shade of pink.

4. Pour the strawberry custard into an ice-cream maker, and churn until soft set, before transferring to the freezer for a couple of hours. Alternatively, if you don't have an ice-cream maker, place the custard in a container and transfer to the freezer. Remove it every half hour, for around 3 hours, and beat with an electric hand whisk. Finally, freeze for a couple of hours, or overnight.

5. To make the meringues, heat your oven to 200°C/400°F/Gas 6. Spread the sugar out on a lined baking tray and cook in the oven for 8 minutes. Clean a bowl of any fat residue by wiping a cut lemon around the inside of it. Beat the egg whites until foamy, then tip in the hot sugar. Continue to beat for 10 minutes, until very stiff and glossy.

6. Turn your oven down to the lowest setting. Spoon the meringue in big dollops onto a lined baking tray and,

INGREDIENTS

ICE CREAM
300g/10½oz strawberries, hulled and roughly chopped

50g/1¾oz/¼ cup vanilla sugar (or caster/superfine sugar and a vanilla pod)

250ml/8½floz/generous 1 cup double/heavy cream

250ml/8½floz/generous 1 cup milk

1 vanilla pod

5 egg yolks

75g/6tbsp golden caster/superfine sugar

Juice of 1 lemon

MERINGUE
180g/6⅓oz/scant 1 cup caster/superfine sugar

½ lemon

3 egg whites

FRUIT
250g/9oz raspberries

250g/9oz strawberries

EQUIPMENT
Mould or mixing bowl – about 1.5–2L/2½–3½ pints capacity

Mixer or electric hand whisk

Ice-cream maker or freezer-proof container

once the oven has cooled, place the tray inside. Leave for 6 hours. Once they sound hollow inside when tapped, turn the oven off, leaving the meringues inside to cool completely. If you can, wedge your oven door open very slightly with a folded tea towel.

7. A few hours before you wish to serve your ice pudding, remove the ice cream from the freezer and allow to soften for 20 minutes, until you can scoop it easily. Crumble your meringues and combine the raspberries and strawberries, chopping any larger strawberries into pieces.

8. In a pudding mould, or a bowl lined with plastic wrap, alternate layers of ice cream, meringue and fresh fruit, until all ingredients have been used up. Return the pudding to the freezer for at least 2 hours to firm up.

9. When you're ready to serve, turn the mould upside down onto a plate, and allow the pudding to slip out, pulling on the plastic wrap if it is reluctant to do so. Serve immediately with some more fresh fruit.

Queen Ann's Pudding

Her griddlecakes done to a golden-brown hue and queen Ann's
pudding of delightful creaminess had won golden opinions from all...
Ulysses, James Joyce

I first travelled to Dublin a couple of years ago to visit a very dear
friend. This is my favourite way to explore a new city; in the
company of someone who knows where the best cheese toasties are
served, and where to find the coziest bars for a whiskey on a rainy
afternoon. As we walked the streets, she pointed out places that
feature in Joyce's *Ulysses* – from still-standing pubs to street corners.
I returned to London determined to read the book, and to cook
from it. *Ulysses* is so rich in detail, and the minutiae of human life,
that, of course, it is full of food.

We only get a brief glimpse of Gerty MacDowell, whose
griddlecakes and Queen Ann's pudding are mentioned in the quote
above. In fact, until we hear from Molly Bloom at the end of the
novel, Gerty is a rare female voice – a woman on a beach with her
friends, dreaming of the man she is to marry. She imagines the
wife she might one day be – one who takes care of her husband
with comforts like perfect griddlecakes and a delicious Queen of
Puddings. She then flashes her stockings to Leopold Bloom as he
watches her from the edge of the beach.

This Queen of Puddings (perhaps Queen Ann's), though it rates only
a passing mention in the book, is a wonderful dessert. It looks more
glamorous than it really is – it is, for all intents and purposes, a bit
like a bread and butter pudding, with a fancy topping. It is delicious.

INGREDIENTS

CUSTARD

80g/2¾oz/3 slices fresh white bread, crusts cut off and torn into chunks

600ml/1 pint/2½ cups milk

25g/1oz/2tbsp butter

3 egg yolks

40g/1½oz/3¼tbsp caster sugar

JAM

225g/8oz strawberries

225g/8oz/1⅛ cups golden caster/superfine sugar

MERINGUE

3 egg whites

180g/6⅓oz/scant 1 cup caster/superfine sugar

EQUIPMENT

Ovenproof dish – 22cm/8¾in in diameter

Electric hand whisk or mixer

Disposable piping bag

Queen of Puddings

Serves 6

1. Preheat the oven to 160°C/325°F/Gas 3. Grease your baking dish with a little butter. Drop the chunks of bread into the dish and set aside.

2. To make the custard, warm the milk over a low heat. Bring almost to the boil, then turn off the heat and whisk in the butter. In a bowl, whisk the egg yolks and sugar until pale, then pour the warm milk over them, whisking continuously so the yolks don't scramble. Pour the custard over the bread and allow it to sit for 15 minutes.

3. Place the dish in a roasting tin, then pour boiling water around it so that it comes halfway up the sides of the dish. Bake until the custard is set, but still wobbles slightly in the middle – around 25 minutes. Leave to cool.

4. To make the jam, tip the strawberries into an ovenproof dish, and the sugar into another. Put both dishes in the oven (still at 160°C/325°F/Gas 3) for 25 minutes. Carefully pour the hot sugar into the strawberries, and then stir together. Cover, and allow to cool. Spoon the cooled jam over the custard, being careful not to plop it on so heavily that it breaks through – you want to retain the layers.

5. Lastly, prepare the meringue. Beat the egg whites in a clean bowl until foamy, then start slowly adding the caster sugar, beating all the time. Continue on a high speed until the meringue forms stiff peaks. Transfer the meringue to a piping bag, and snip the end off to leave a hole about 1cm/½in across. Pipe peaks of meringue over the top of the jam. If you don't have a piping bag, you can simply spoon the meringue on top.

6. Bake for 15–20 minutes, until the meringue is lightly browned and crisp. Allow to sit for at least 15 minutes before serving – the jam will be molten hot.

Three Kings' Day Bread

*She confessed happiness from those days, she could prepare the Kings'
Day bread with the same enthusiasm she had felt then! If only she
could eat the bread afterward with her sisters, laughing and joking,
just like old times...*
Like Water for Chocolate, Laura Esquivel

When I was twenty, I went to Mexico for two weeks on a terrifically
nerdy Model United Nations Conference. I had no idea what
to expect, but it was so much more fun than I ever could have
anticipated. After a week of parties and simulated debates, we were
left free to explore Mexico, before returning home to university
and real life. We rode horses, climbed down waterfalls, walked up
pyramids, went on a cooking course, and tasted tonnes of tequila. I
fell in love with the country, especially its food.

On my return, I found a copy of *Like Water for Chocolate* in the
second-hand bookshop up the road. Tita, the central character, has
a deep connection to the kitchen. When her mother forbids her
from marrying the man she loves, he marries her sister instead. The
impact this has on all family members plays out over the decades
that follow. Each chapter opens with a recipe that reveals part of
the story – this soft, buttery bread with a tiny ceramic baby hidden
inside comes as a character realizes that she is going to have a child.

This bread, like the other recipes in the book, could feed a small
army. I have reduced Esquivel's original recipe by half, but you
could easily reduce the recipe by half again and still end up with
something very reasonable in size. This recipe takes time, but it's
more than worth it. Be patient, especially if you're making it on
Three Kings' Day (early January) – the cold weather will make each
dough rise take even longer.

{1}　　　　　　　　{2}

{3}　　　　　　　　{4}

{5}　　　　　　　　{6}

{7}

{8}

{9}

{10}

{11}

{12}

STARTER

60ml/2floz/¼ cup milk

15g/1tbsp fresh yeast

125g/4½oz/scant 1 cup plain/all-purpose flour

DOUGH

500g/1lb 2oz/3½ cups strong white bread flour

1tsp coarse sea salt

4 eggs

1tbsp orange blossom water

110ml/3½floz/scant ½ cup milk

150g/5⅓oz/¾ cup caster/superfine sugar

125g/4½oz/1 stick + 1tbsp unsalted butter, at room temperature

250g/9oz mixed dried fruit

GLAZE AND DECORATION

1 egg yolk, beaten

20g/¾oz/5tsp sugar

50g/scant 2oz/heaping ⅓ cup mixed peel/candied fruit

100g/3½oz/¾ cup glacé cherries

EQUIPMENT

Small ceramic baby Jesus (optional)

Three Kings' Day Bread

Makes 1 giant loaf

1. For the starter, warm the milk to body temperature, then stir the yeast through until dissolved. Leave for 10 minutes until it starts to bubble on top. Mix through the flour, then leave to rise for 1 hour until doubled in size.

2. To make the dough, put the strong bread flour and salt in a pile on your work surface and make a well in the centre. Crack the eggs into the centre, and mix around with your hand, bringing some of the flour to mix into them. Add the orange blossom water and the milk a bit at a time, mixing more of the flour into the centre as you do. Add the sugar and continue to mix, gradually starting to knead.

3. Tear your starter into pieces and knead it through the dough until evenly distributed. Continue to knead until the dough is very smooth and elastic. Once it is, add the butter in chunks, kneading to incorporate. Shape into a ball, place in a bowl, cover, and allow to double in size for an hour.

4. Once risen, roll the dough into a long rectangle about 1cm/½in thick. Sprinkle over the dried fruit, leaving a 5cm/2in line at the top of the rectangle. Roll up from the edge closest to you, nestling the baby Jesus inside as you roll. Seal the edge by pinching it closed.

5. Turn the dough over so that the pinched seam is sitting underneath. Transfer to a lined baking sheet, or dish. Curl into a circle, and pinch together the two ends. If the hole in the middle of the circle is small, butter a glass and fit it into the hole, so that the dough rises upwards and outwards, rather than into the centre. Cover, and allow to rise for a final hour.

6. Preheat the oven to 190°C/375°F/Gas 5. When the dough is ready, brush with the beaten egg yolk, sprinkle with sugar and top with the mixed peel and glacé cherries. Make slashes at intervals into the sides of the dough, about 1cm/½in deep, until some of the fruit filling is revealed.

7. Transfer to the oven for 45 minutes, until the bread is golden brown and sounds hollow when tapped underneath. If the bread has expanded and joined up in the middle, give it another 10 minutes or so, as it will need a little longer to bake in the centre. Allow to cool a little before serving – the fruit on top will be incredibly hot.

Raspberry Shrub

*Besides, they didn't call it vinegar-and-water – of course not! Each
child gave his or her swallow a different name, as if the bottle were
like Signor Blitz's and could pour out a dozen things at once. Clover
called her share "Raspberry Shrub"…*
What Katy Did, Susan Coolidge

My sister Lucy and I haven't lived in the same city for nearly
ten years. When we do end up in the same place, it's often for
a wedding, or an engagement party, and so that too brief time
together feels even shorter. We Skype, and WhatsApp, but it's not
the same. We grew up as such a team. Being apart from her often
feels like an important part of me is missing.

She and my brother-in-law moved to Seattle a couple of years ago
and I went out to see them for Lucy's first Thanksgiving. After
celebrating at home, we explored the West Coast together. Through
the whole trip – the sourcing of the Thanksgiving bird, a visit to
the *Mrs Doubtfire* house in San Francisco, a long drive through the
snow, singing at the tops of our lungs – I was thrilled to discover
that we were still the team I remember.

I have rarely eaten better than I did that fortnight; we had a
pages-long list of places to try in each city. On Lucy's birthday,
in Portland, we planned a gastronomic tour, taking in five different
restaurants. Finally, we ended up in Pok Pok where, alongside their
superlative chicken wings, we all ordered shrubs. Lucy and Justin
had been drinking them all year (they're common in Seattle),
and I immediately saw the appeal. They're a better version of
a cordial: sharper, more refreshing and more delicious. They'll
forever remind me of Luce (and of Katy too), so this is my
sister's recipe below.

Raspberry Shrub

Makes around 10 glasses

1. Mash the raspberries, sugar and mint leaves in a bowl. Cover with plastic wrap, and leave in the fridge overnight.

2. The next day, strain the mixture through a sieve (or muslin). Let it sit for a while and then press as much of the fruit through as you can.

3. Add the vinegar, a tablespoon at a time, testing after each addition. It should be a good balance of sweet and sharp, but this is very much down to personal taste. I generally add all the vinegar, but you may not need to.

4. Serve diluted with very cold fizzy water or sparkling wine.

INGREDIENTS

225g/8oz raspberries

60g/5tbsp granulated sugar

4 stalks mint leaves

60ml/2floz/¼ cup good white wine vinegar (or champagne vinegar, if you can get it)

Fizzy water or sparkling wine, to serve

EQUIPMENT

Fine sieve or piece of muslin/cheesecloth

Sterilized bottle

Marmaduke Scarlet's Feast

'There is enough. There is sufficient plum cake, saffron cake, cherry cake, iced fairy cakes, eclairs, gingerbread, meringues, syllabub, almond fingers, rock cakes, chocolate cakes, parkin, cream horns, Devonshire splits, Cornish pasty, jam sandwiches, lemon-curd sandwiches, lettuce sandwiches, cinnamon toast and honey toast to feed twenty or more... when Marmaduke Scarlet is cook there is always enough.'
The Little White Horse, Elizabeth Goudge

I slept in a kitchen for five years. After realising a two-bed in East London was out of our price range, a friend and I found a little one-bedroom flat, and turned the living space into a kitchen/dining room/front room/second bedroom. It wouldn't suit everyone, but it was perfect for me. I've always felt most comfortable in a kitchen and spend much of my time there anyway, waiting for a cake to bake or bread to rise or a stew to bubble away on the stove. Having my bed mere metres from the oven seemed a logical step.

The kitchen is also my favourite place to visit in other people's homes; peeking into cupboards full of spices or flicking through the cookbooks stacked high on a shelf. While parties take place in front rooms and back gardens, I relish time spent in the kitchen, chatting with the host and helping to organize plates of food.

This fascination extends to fictional kitchens too, and there are few I would rather spend time in than Marmaduke Scarlet's at Moonacre Manor. Marmaduke isn't terribly keen on visitors to his kitchen, but I'd happily risk his bad mood in order to see him create this extraordinary spread. I've dreamed about this feast for years; of the cream horns made with the flakiest of flaky pastry, of thick clotted cream spread onto saffron cake, and of the smells that must have travelled through the house that afternoon.

Saffron Cake

Makes 10 slices

1. Warm the milk in a saucepan, but do not boil. Add the saffron and set aside for 15 minutes to infuse.

2. Reheat the milk to body temperature and stir in the yeast until dissolved. Leave for 10 minutes to activate.

3. In a large bowl, combine the flour, sugar, salt and nutmeg. Make a well in the centre and mix in the milk and yeast. Knead for 10 minutes, then form into a ball. Allow to rise in a covered bowl for an hour.

4. Grease your loaf tin with some butter. Knock back the dough and knead the sultanas into it, until they are evenly distributed. Shape into a log, and place into the tin, with the seam at the bottom. Cover and allow to prove for a final hour.

5. Heat the oven to 160°C/325°F/Gas 3. Bake the saffron cake for 25 minutes, until golden. Remove from the oven, cool for 5 minutes in the tin, and then a further 10 minutes on a wire rack. Eat warm, in thick slices spread with clotted cream.

INGREDIENTS

150ml/5floz/⅔ cup milk
20 saffron strands
25g/1oz/5tsp fresh yeast
250g/8¾oz/2 cups strong white bread flour
30g/1oz/2½tbsp golden caster/superfine sugar
Pinch of salt
½tsp grated nutmeg
75g/scant 3oz/heaping ½ cup sultanas/golden raisins

EQUIPMENT
2lb loaf tin

Cream Horns

Makes 12

1. Rub 50g/2oz/½ stick of the butter into the flour, until it resembles breadcrumbs. Mix in the water by hand, bringing the mixture together into a dough. Knead for 10 minutes by hand, until the dough is very smooth and elastic. Rest in the fridge for 30 minutes.

2. Fold a large piece of greaseproof paper into an envelope. Open the envelope up, put the remaining 200g/7oz/ 2 sticks of butter inside. Flatten the butter with a rolling pin; the paper should keep it all contained, and you will end up with a 30 x 20cm/12 x 8in slab of butter. Return to the fridge in its paper to harden.

INGREDIENTS

PASTRY
250g/9oz/2½ sticks unsalted butter
250g/8¾oz/2 cups strong bread flour
125ml/4¼floz/generous ½ cup water
1 egg
30g/1oz/2½tsp caster/superfine sugar
FILLING
300ml/10floz/1¼ cups double/heavy cream
1tsp vanilla extract
2tbsp icing/confectioners' sugar

EQUIPMENT

6 cream horn moulds
(I make my own – see
instructions in step 6)

Disposable piping bag

3. Lightly flour your work surface. Roll the pastry into a large rectangle about 5mm/¼in thick – it's important that it's not too thin, or the butter will leak. Unwrap the slab of butter and place it in the centre of the pastry. Fold each edge of the pastry over the butter to seal it completely. Roll out to a rectangle roughly 60 x 20cm/24 x 8in, fold the top quarter and bottom quarter over to meet in the middle, then fold in half again (to create four layers). Wrap in plastic wrap and rest in the fridge for 30 minutes.

4. Lightly flour your work surface. Remove the pastry from the fridge, and place it in front of you like a book, with the folds on the right-hand side. Roll again into a rectangle roughly 60 x 20cm/24 x 8in. Fold into four layers again and return to the fridge for another 30 minutes.

5. Repeat this process once more, then lightly flour your work surface and roll the pastry out into a 60 x 30cm/ 24 x 12in rectangle. Slice into twelve strips. Return these strips to the fridge for 15 minutes.

6. While the pastry is in the fridge, make (or prepare) some cone moulds. I'm loath to buy moulds that only have one use, so I made mine by rolling cones of cardboard, then covering each with a couple of layers of foil. Grease the moulds, then wind the cold pastry strips around them, starting at the pointed end of the cone, and overlapping each twist of the pastry a little. Place each cone on a lined baking sheet, leaving a little space for them to puff. Brush with beaten egg, brushing from pointed bottom to top to avoid sealing the layers. Sprinkle with a little caster sugar and pop in the fridge for a final 20 minutes chilling time.

7. Preheat your oven to 200°C/400°F/Gas 6. Bake for 12–14 minutes until golden. Cool for 10 minutes, then carefully remove the moulds and cool completely on a wire rack.

8. Whip the cream to soft peaks, adding the vanilla and icing sugar just before it is whipped enough. Transfer to a piping bag, then fill the cooled horns with cream. Eat immediately.

Cornish Pasty
Makes 6

1. Rub the fats into the flour until it resembles fine breadcrumbs. Add the salt and water, combine to make a dough, then knead by hand for 10 minutes until elastic and smooth. You need the dough to hold the filling without splitting, so do knead for a good length of time until you can stretch out the dough without it tearing. Rest in the fridge for an hour.

2. Combine the beef with the diced vegetables. Season with plenty of black pepper.

3. Preheat the oven to 180°C/350°F/Gas 4. Lightly flour your work surface, then roll the pastry out to around 5mm/¼in thick. Using a 15cm/6in plate as a guide, cut circles of pastry out. Re-form the pastry when you need to, ensuring that the thickness is consistent.

4. Place one circle of pastry in front of you. Spoon 4tbsp of the meat and vegetable mix onto one half of it, leaving a 2cm/¾in border. Run a damp finger around the edge of the pastry, and fold the pastry over to create a semicircle. Press closed. Crimp the edges.

5. Repeat with all the discs of pastry. Line a baking tray with greaseproof paper, and place the pasties on the tray, leaving a little space between each. Transfer to the fridge for 30 minutes.

6. Brush each pasty with egg wash and bake for 50 minutes, until they turn a golden, nutty brown. Serve immediately – I like mine with mustard or pickles.

INGREDIENTS

PASTRY
125g/4½oz/⅔ cup lard
125g/4½oz/1⅛ sticks unsalted butter
500g/1lb 2oz/3½ cups strong white bread flour
Generous pinch of salt
170ml/scant 6floz/generous ½ cup water

FILLING
400g/14oz skirt/flank steak, cut into 1cm/⅜in dice
2 medium potatoes, finely diced
2 medium brown onions, finely diced
3 medium carrots, finely diced
Generous grinding of black pepper
1 egg, beaten

christmas

christmas

Christmas is my very favourite time of year. I keep imagining that perhaps I'll grow out of it: tire of the crowds and the commercialization; struggle to manage the plethora of social events; find the enforced jolly family time a strain. But I don't. Every year I overplay the Vince Guaraldi Trio's 'A Charlie Brown Christmas', fill my house with pickles, preserves and mince pies, head to my favourite cinema to watch *It's a Wonderful Life*, and order metres of brown paper and string to wrap gifts. My heart swells when I see Christmas lights and trees all over the city.

My overwhelming affection for the season was considerably heightened by the books I read as a child, and those wintry Christmases I dreamed of. I grew up sweltering on Christmas Day, in and out of the pool, trying to imagine what life might be like in the world Bing Crosby was singing about. I envied the March girls, carolling around the piano and crunching through fresh snow on Christmas morning. I wanted to join Harry and Ron in a game of chess by the roaring fire in Gryffindor Tower. I dreamt of what it would be like to stand alongside the Pevensie children, witnessing Father Christmas make his first trip to snowy Narnia after the long winter.

These fictional Christmases, so different from the wonderful ones I celebrated when I was little, are the ones you'll see in the recipes that follow. Many of these delights benefit from forward planning, and I've included details on how far in advance of the big day you can get them started. Most of them are wonderful to make with children as well, so do keep little hands busy through December whisking buckwheats, stirring fruitcake and filling mince pies.

A Merry Christmas to you all.

Christmas Cake

Their father cut the cake.
'Delicious fruitcake,' he said, brushing crumbs from his fur. 'And just
the right amount of icing.'
The young wombats agreed.
Wombats Don't Have Christmas, Jane Burrell and Michael Dugan

Throughout my childhood, my parents read my sister and me
to sleep. When Mum and Dad divorced, his voice disappeared
from our nightly storytime ritual. So he sat, with a tape deck and
a microphone, and recorded himself reading six of our favourite
stories. He gave this tape to us for Christmas, with a picture of the
three of us on the cover. Lucy and I played it regularly. It became so
familiar, I now associate those stories with his unmistakable timbre.

As an adult, suffering for the first time with insomnia, I would read
late into the night, but was never quite sure whether the act of
reading was keeping me up, as well as keeping me calm. So Dad
copied the original tape onto a CD (he even printed the same photo
on the cover) and popped it in the post, so I could play those six
stories over and over as I was going to sleep.

One of them, *Wombats Don't Have Christmas*, is about a family of
wombats whose father doesn't think that wombats should celebrate
Christmas. The little wombats and their mother secretly plan a
wonderful day, including carols, stockings, holly and cake, and trick
their father into celebrating after all. He loves all of it, of course,
especially the fruitcake.

I adore Christmas cake. I like that it sits around for days after the
pudding has disappeared, quietly inviting everyone to take a little
slice to enjoy with a mid-afternoon cup of tea. This cake isn't boozy,
unlike most of the Christmas cakes I have eaten. The lack of brandy
means you can make it and eat it immediately, rather than feeling
like you should get started on it months in advance. I always forget
to start my Christmas cake early enough, so this one is an ideal last-
minute solution.

Christmas Cake

Provides 12 generous slices

1. Preheat the oven to 150°C/300°F/Gas 2 and grease and line the cake tin. Put the flour, dried fruit, ginger, salt and bicarbonate of soda in a mixing bowl and stir to combine.

2. Add the cream, treacle and sugar to the melted butter, and whisk well. Add the wet ingredients to the dry flour mixture and stir through.

3. Whisk the eggs until light and frothy and then fold through the batter. The batter should be dark, rich and heavy. Spoon into the cake tin and bake for 90 minutes, checking the top after an hour. If it is browning too quickly (mine often do), cover with a sheet of foil. When a skewer inserted into the cake comes out clean, remove it from the oven.

4. Cool on a wire rack in the tin for 10 minutes, then remove from the tin and cool completely.

5. To make the marzipan, sift the sugars into a bowl, and add the ground almonds.* Mix together with your hands, then add the egg. Again, mix and squelch the marzipan together with your hands: you need to feel when it is ready. The marzipan should come together into a ball, without sticking too much to the bowl or your hands. If it is too dry, add a little egg white. If it is too sticky, add a little more icing sugar. Shape into a ball, wrap in plastic wrap and store in the fridge for at least an hour, or until you need it.

6. When the cake is stone cold (if it is even slightly warm, the marzipan won't stick well to it), you can prepare it for icing. If your cake has domed on top, start by trimming the top so it is flat. Keep the trimmings as sustenance to nibble on; cake decorating is hard work. Flip the cake over and put it bottom-side up on a serving plate.

7. Warm the apricot jam in a small saucepan, then sieve to eliminate any lumps. Brush it over the top and sides of the cake. Dust your work surface with a little icing sugar

INGREDIENTS

SPONGE
500g/1lb 2oz/3¾ cups plain/all-purpose flour

150g/5½oz/heaping 1 cup sultanas/golden raisins (you can use regular raisins, but I prefer plump sultanas)

75g/2½oz/½ cup chopped dried dates

50g/2oz/½ cup chopped dried cherries (plain dried, rather than glacé, are better here)

2tsp ground ginger

Pinch of salt

½tsp bicarbonate of soda/baking soda

200g/7oz/1¾ sticks unsalted butter, melted and cooled

200ml/7oz/scant 1 cup double/heavy cream

100g/4½tbsp treacle/molasses

180g/6½oz/scant 1 cup soft brown sugar

2 eggs

150g/5½oz/½ cup apricot jam

MARZIPAN*
100g/3½oz/½ cup golden caster sugar

150g/5½oz/1 cup icing/confectioners' sugar

250g/8¾oz/2 cups ground almonds

1 egg (and an extra white, if you need it)

ICING
2 egg whites

350g/12⅓oz/2½ cups icing/confectioners' sugar

1tsp glycerine

EQUIPMENT
20cm/8in loose-based cake tin

String

* Most Christmas cakes are covered with marzipan and royal icing from a packet, and you can definitely do that. But if you want to go the whole hog, it is lovely to make your own. You will need to allow a couple of days for each layer to dry properly.

and roll the marzipan into a circle wide enough to go over the top and down the sides of your cake (measure this by running a piece of string from the base on one side, over the top and down the other side). As you roll, keep lifting the marzipan up and re-dusting your work surface with icing sugar. If it's warm in your house, you can roll the marzipan between two pieces of greaseproof paper, if you prefer.

8. When your marzipan is large enough, lift it up (using your rolling pin for support, if needed) and lay it over the cake. Smooth it over the top and down the sides. Trim the excess at the base of the cake, and leave to dry out for a day.

9. To make the royal icing, beat the egg whites with an electric whisk until they are frothy. Add two-thirds of the icing sugar, a tablespoon at a time, beating on a high speed until stiff peaks form. Add the rest of the icing sugar, along with the glycerine, and beat until very stiff.

10. Spoon the icing onto the cake, and smooth it over the top, and then around the sides using a palette knife. If you're worried about getting a smooth finish, little snowy peaks look lovely too. Allow the cake to dry for a day before you cut into it. This icing will also preserve it for a few weeks (or longer) if you want to get ahead of yourself; just store it in an airtight box until Christmas.

Turkish Delight

*'It is dull, Son of Adam, to drink without eating,' said the Queen
presently. 'What would you like best to eat?'*
'Turkish Delight, please, your Majesty,' said Edmund.
The Lion, the Witch and the Wardrobe, C. S. Lewis

I was obsessed by Turkish delight long before I ever tried a piece.
I decided that for Edmund to choose it as the thing he'd most like
to eat in the world, it had to be pretty special. By the time he'd
abandoned his siblings for the promise of kingship and Turkish
delight, I was hooked. I had to try it. In Australia, you can buy bars
of chocolate-covered Turkish delight, and they quickly became
my favourite – more for Edmund Pevensie than for their heavily
floral taste.

I encountered real Turkish delight for the first time on a trip to
Istanbul, and finally understood what the fuss was about. My friend
Liz and I stood in the Spice Market, surrounded by rainbow-hued
spices, dried fruit and nuts, and buckets of Turkish delight. The
pistachio and pomegranate varieties were both delicious, but it's
the light pink cubes I really fell for – the kind that were served with
tea after our meals.

The recipe below is for this classic, pink, rose-scented sweet. Do
feel free to add your own flavourings or nuts once you get the basic
recipe down. These should be eaten within a week of making them.
Try to do the final step – rolling them in icing sugar and cornflour –
as close as possible to gifting them; do it too long beforehand and
the sweets will have absorbed your decoration by the time the box
is opened.

Turkish Delight

Makes around 30 squares

1. Place the sugar and lemon juice in a small saucepan with 175ml/6floz/¾ cup of the water. Put the pan over a low-medium heat and stir until the sugar is dissolved. Once the liquid is clear, stop stirring and heat until the sugar syrup reaches 118°C/245°F (around 15 minutes).

2. Line a baking tray with plastic wrap, smoothing the base and sides as much as possible. Sift the cornflour into a medium saucepan, along with the cream of tartar and 300ml/½ pint/1¼ cups water. Place over a low heat and stir continuously. The mixture will start to thicken. Keep cooking it until it resembles hair gel – thick and gloopy.

3. Once the sugar syrup is ready, put the cornflour mixture back over a low heat. While stirring, slowly pour the syrup in. Continue to stir over a low heat for around an hour. The mixture will look strange (and separated) at first, but it will come together. When it's done, it will have taken on a golden tinge and be very thick and difficult to stir. I know this is a long time to keep stirring, but I find it soothing – it's something you can do with a Christmas film playing.

4. Remove from the heat and beat in the rosewater and food colouring.

5. Scoop the Turkish delight into the lined tin – this will be messy. Smooth the top of the mixture with a wet spatula and push the top down. Cover with a tea towel and allow it to set overnight in a cool room.

6. The next day, take the Turkish delight out of the tin and peel the plastic wrap off. Wet a knife with hot water and slice into squares. Sift the cornflour and icing sugar into a shallow bowl (along with the edible glitter if you're using it). Drop the squares into the bowl and toss to coat each piece. Store in a cool, dry place, with greaseproof paper between the layers.

INGREDIENTS
450g/1lb/2¼ cups granulated sugar
1tbsp lemon juice
475ml/16floz/2 cups water
90g/3¼oz/scant 1 cup cornflour/cornstarch
½tsp cream of tartar
1tbsp rosewater
Pink food colouring (ideally paste)

TO DECORATE
40g/1½oz/4½tbsp cornflour/cornstarch
40g/1½oz/4½tbsp icing/confectioners' sugar
Edible glitter (optional)

EQUIPMENT
Small, straight-sided baking tray (mine is 12 x 20cm/4¾ x 8in)

The Lion, the Witch and the Wardrobe, C. S. Lewis { } TURKISH DELIGHT

Mince Pies

When my stepdad Geoff moved in with us, he brought a new level of Christmas into our house. The decorations went up earlier (on 4 December each year, the day after the birthday he and my sister share), and 1950s crooners sang to us about White Christmas and snow as we ate our breakfast every morning. He is oft to be seen in a Santa hat during the month of December. Watching Christmas films became a yearly ritual too; we would curl up on the couch and cry with Jimmy Stewart and Donna Reed, laugh with Bill Murray and sing with Bing Crosby.

And then I moved to London. The mince pies on the couch in front of films, the toasted panettone after Midnight Mass, my great-grandmother's Christmas puddings; they are all still happening in my old home, but I am impossibly far away from it now.

That first winter, as days became shorter and the leaves fell from the trees (all at once, it seemed, on the first day of November), I started to plan for my first Christmas without my family. My flatmates and I bought an enormous tree, and walked it home through East London. I attended a screening of *It's a Wonderful Life* at the Prince Charles Cinema. And I bought a copy of *Nigella Christmas*, and started to cook from it. In the absence of the old rituals, I decided to make the best of it. It was time to make my own.

These mince pies were the first things I made from the book, and I have reproduced them, with annual variations, every year since. They are delicious; a bit fruitier and fresher than I was used to – still rich and full of flavour, but lighter without the usual suet. Nigella makes her mincemeat with plenty of fresh cranberries, but I replace these with more dried fruit and a couple of grated apples, to make them similar to the ones I ate at home. Ten thousand miles away, I always want to capture my family in any way I can.

This Christmas in *Behind the Scenes at the Museum* is pivotal. It's the moment when everything changes for the Lennox family. The rituals they have had in previous years fall apart, and Patricia and Ruby spend the days after Christmas in front of the television, with only mince pies and tinned food to sustain them. These sisters, on the couch together, make me feel homesick, and I long for a Boxing Day with my sister and a Christmas film. In her absence, I return to my new rituals, and make a batch of mince pies.

INGREDIENTS

MINCEMEAT

75ml/5tbsp/⅓ cup port wine

75g/6tbsp dark brown sugar

1tsp ground ginger

½tsp ground cloves

1tsp ground cinnamon

2 small apples, unpeeled, grated

150g/5½oz/heaping 1 cup sultanas/golden raisins

150g/5½oz/heaping 1 cup raisins

50g/2oz/scant ½ cup dried cranberries

Zest and juice of 2 clementines (about 60ml/2floz/¼ cup)

1tsp vanilla extract

½tsp almond extract

2tbsp honey

PASTRY

90g/3¼oz/generous ¾ stick butter, cubed

90g/6½tbsp vegetable shortening, cubed (or the same amount of butter again, if you prefer)

360g/12⅔oz/2¾ cups plain/all-purpose flour

Zest and juice of 2 clementines

Pinch of salt

Icing/confectioners' sugar, to decorate

EQUIPMENT

Sterilized jars or tin for mincemeat storage

Shallow-cup muffin tins

A fluted biscuit cutter (about 1cm/½in larger in diameter than the top of your muffin cups)

A star-shaped biscuit cutter (the width of your muffin cups)

Food processor

Mince Pies

Makes 24

1. Make the mincemeat. Warm the port and brown sugar in a saucepan over a low heat. Swirl the pan until the sugar dissolves. Add the spices, grated apple and dried fruit, along with the zest and juice of the clementines. Cook for around 20 minutes on a medium heat, stirring every so often to ensure the mixture isn't sticking. Once the liquid has reduced, turn off the heat and add the vanilla and almond extracts and the honey. Beat well. Transfer the mixture to jars (which make a lovely gift) or an airtight container. This will keep for a good few months, but can also be used the same day (once cool).

2. To make the pastry, toss the fats through the flour and put the whole lot in the freezer for 20 minutes. Place the clementine zest and juice into a glass with a pinch of salt, and chill in the fridge. Remove the flour mix from the freezer and blitz in a food processor until it resembles breadcrumbs (this can be done by hand if you like). Slowly dribble in the clementine juice and zest, stopping when the pastry comes together. If you need more liquid, add some chilled water. Tip the pastry out, squidge together into a ball, cover in plastic wrap and chill for at least 1 hour.

3. Preheat the oven to 190°C/375°F/Gas 5. Cut the pastry into quarters, storing it in the fridge until needed. Roll each piece of pastry out to the thickness of a pound coin (about ⅛in) between two sheets of greaseproof paper. Cut fluted circles and stars out of the pastry, bringing it back together and rolling out again to use it all. Push each pastry circle into a greased muffin tin, fill with a tablespoon of the mincemeat and top with a pastry star. Don't fill them right to the brim, as they'll bubble up and spill over.

4. Bake for 15 minutes, or until golden brown. Allow the tarts to cool in the tin, then push one edge (lightly – you don't want to break the pastry) and the tart should pop out. Place on a wire rack and, once cool, dust with icing sugar.

Buckwheats

Meg was already covering the buckwheats, and piling the bread into
one big plate.
'I thought you'd do it,' said Mrs. March, smiling as if satisfied. 'You shall
all go and help me, and when we come back we will have bread and
milk for breakfast, and make it up at dinnertime.'
Little Women, Louisa May Alcott

My Christmases are now spent with my surrogate family in the
Cotswolds. On Christmas morning each year, we whisk together
the ingredients for blinis. We top them with gravlax, soured cream
and dill, and serve them with champagne. They're what we eat
as we open our stockings – hand-sewn sacks or wellington boots,
filled with useful toiletries, beautiful Christmas decorations, an
item of stationery or two, chocolate coins and a satsuma in the toe.
The process for making our blinis isn't terribly different to these
traditional Civil War-era buckwheats – a yeasted batter, left to rise
for an hour, then cooked in small rounds on a heavy cast-iron pan.

Though the book spans seasons, and indeed years, *Little Women*
will always be a Christmas story for me. It's hardly surprising;
the opening chapters see the March sisters enjoy Christmas Eve,
prepare Christmas breakfast, rehearse a play and then enjoy Old
Mr Laurence's gastronomic gifts as the day draws to a close. From
the very first line, our attention is drawn to the season, and to this
being a Christmas different from ones before: *"'Christmas won't be*
Christmas without any presents," grumbled Jo, lying on the rug.'

To be honest, I'd happily leave the presents, so long as I can keep
the buckwheat pancakes.

350ml/scant 12floz/1½
cups lukewarm milk
(at body temperature,
around 35ºC/95ºF)
10g/1tbsp fast-action
yeast/easy-bake yeast
250g/8¾oz/2 cups
buckwheat flour
2 eggs
Pinch of salt
40g/1½oz/3tbsp butter

Buckwheat Pancakes
Makes 25

1. Combine 250ml/8½floz of the milk with the yeast and flour. It will be thick and gluggy, but leave for an hour until it is noticeably risen and full of bubbles.

2. After an hour, whisk in the 2 eggs, a pinch of salt and the remainder of the milk.

3. Melt some of the butter in a heavy-based frying pan (cast iron is great here if you have it), and dollop circles of the batter into the pan. Cook until bubbly on top and then flip over for another minute.

3. Eat immediately with gravlax and soured cream, butter and cheese, or some golden syrup.

Christmas Dinner

There never was such a goose. Bob said he didn't believe there ever was such a goose cooked. Its tenderness and flavour, size and cheapness, were the themes of universal admiration. Eked out by apple sauce and mashed potatoes, it was a sufficient dinner for the whole family; indeed, as Mrs. Cratchit said with great delight (surveying one small atom of a bone upon the dish), they hadn't ate it all at last!
A *Christmas Carol*, Charles Dickens

Something about cooking Christmas dinner always makes me anxious. I place pressure on myself for everything to be perfect, which is impossibly unrealistic; I've always had a couple of glasses of fizz by the time it comes to cooking dinner, and more often than not there are so many oven trays to coordinate that nothing ends up being ready at the right time.

Then, in 2015, I cooked Christmas dinner with only two of us in the kitchen. There are normally many more; each person in charge of an element or two, jostling for space. But it was a quiet year and my Cotswolds 'brother' Tom and I decided to give the rest of the family Christmas dinner as a gift. We bought the cockerel and the sides, and then he peeled, chopped and washed up, while I cooked. We watched *The Empire Strikes Back* as we worked. It was a dream. I have never been more relaxed on Christmas Day.

This menu is perfect for that sort of Christmas cooking. Even with a relatively small oven, the Cratchit's Christmas dinner is achievable; much of it is done on the stove while the bird roasts, and the stuffing goes into the oven just as the bird comes out to rest. It is a rich, delicious and decadent meal – goose is much more expensive now than it was in Victorian England – but it is well worth trying at least once.

I am not at all ashamed to admit that my first introduction to Ebenezer Scrooge's tale was through the Muppets. More than twenty years on, *The Muppet Christmas Carol* remains, for me, the definitive on-screen version of the story. However, I also love the book itself: Dickens's compassion for his characters, his belief in the potential for people to change, and his masterful depiction of a Victorian Christmas (which has shaped so much of what we see as 'Christmas' today) have given the story a lasting magic.

The moment here, observed by Ebenezer Scrooge as he stands beside the Ghost of Christmas Present, is a turning point. Surrounded by merriment, generosity and family, he finally sees his faithful employee as the man he is to his children, and the potential joy of celebrating Christmas Day.

INGREDIENTS

GRAVY

30g/1oz/2tbsp butter

Goose giblets (not the liver) and wing tips

2 brown onions, roughly chopped

1 carrot, roughly chopped

2 celery sticks, roughly chopped

6 peppercorns

250ml/8½floz/generous 1 cup white wine

20g/2⅓tbsp plain/all-purpose flour

GOOSE

4–5kg/8¾–11lb goose

Salt and pepper

STUFFING

3 brown onions, diced

200g/7oz streaky bacon, sliced

200g/7oz pork mince/ground pork

30g/1oz/2½ cups sage, finely chopped

30g/1oz/1 cup parsley, finely chopped

150g/5½oz/3 cups fresh white breadcrumbs

Freshly ground black pepper

75g/2½oz/⅓ cup goose fat

APPLE SAUCE

50g/2oz/½ stick butter

1kg/2¼lb Bramley/cooking apples, peeled and diced

3tbsp light brown sugar

MASH

2kg/4½lb potatoes, peeled and diced

60ml/2floz/¼ cup whole milk

50g/2oz/½ stick butter

Generous pinch of salt

Christmas Dinner

Serves 8

1. Start the gravy in advance: melt the butter in a large saucepan and cook the giblets and wing tips until browned. Add the roughly chopped vegetables, peppercorns and 2L/3½ pints/8½ cups of water. Simmer over a low heat for 2 hours to reduce. Strain the liquid and store until Christmas Day.

2. If your bird is frozen, leave it on a low shelf in your refrigerator to defrost overnight. An hour before it needs to go in the oven, remove it from the fridge and any packaging to bring it to room temperature. Preheat the oven to 200°C/400°F/Gas 6.

3. Dry the skin of the goose with kitchen paper. Prick the skin, but not the flesh, with a sharp knife, then rub with salt and pepper. Set up a roasting tray with a rack at the base, so that the fat from the goose has somewhere to drain away from the bird. Place the bird on the rack, breast side up and legs as wide apart as possible. Roast for 30 minutes per kg/65 minutes per lb, plus an additional 30 minutes (my 4.3kg/9½lb one took just over two and a half hours).

4. After an hour, remove the goose from the oven and tip the fat from the tray into a bowl. Set this aside for the stuffing, and return the bird to the oven.

5. To prepare the stuffing, fry the diced onion in some goose fat until translucent, and tip into a bowl. Fry the bacon and pork mince, and add these to the bowl. Add the chopped herbs, along with the breadcrumbs and a very generous grinding of pepper. Warm the goose fat until liquid in a small saucepan and pour over the stuffing. Stir through, then transfer to a greased ovenproof dish.

6. For the apple sauce: melt the butter, add the diced apples and the sugar, and cook for 15 minutes over a medium heat. Stir them around to prevent them browning.

7. Remove the goose from the oven, transfer to a serving dish and cover with a sheet of foil. Leave to rest for 30 minutes while you finish the gravy and prepare the mash. Transfer the stuffing to the oven and bake for 30 minutes.

8. To finish the gravy, pour the goose fat from the roasting tin and add to the bowl of fat from earlier. Place the roasting tin on the heat, and add the white wine. Reduce the liquid by half, stirring any scraps of goose left over in the pan into the wine. Tip the liquid into a saucepan. Put the flour into a small bowl and ladle a little of the juices into the bowl. Whisk until smooth, then tip the floury liquid back into the saucepan and whisk well.

9. Pour 600ml/1 pint/2½ cups of the goose stock into the saucepan, and reduce until the gravy is the consistency you like. Strain the gravy into a serving jug.

10. To make the mash, boil the potatoes until tender. Drain, then mash until smooth. Add the milk and butter and stir though, then flavour with salt.

11. Carve the goose at the table, and serve it alongside the mash, warm apple sauce, gravy and piping hot stuffing.

Smoking Bishop

'A merry Christmas, Bob!' said Scrooge with an earnestness that could not be mistaken, as he clapped him on the back. 'A merrier Christmas, Bob, my good fellow, than I have given you for many a year! I'll raise your salary, and endeavour to assist your struggling family, and we will discuss your affairs this very afternoon, over a Christmas bowl of smoking bishop, Bob! Make up the fires and buy another coal-scuttle before you dot another i, Bob Cratchit!'
A *Christmas Carol*, Charles Dickens

I discovered mulled wine during my first December in England. In Australia, drinks around Christmas are usually served ice cold – I am partial to sangria, rosé and sparkling wine. Here, in cozy pubs, or strolling through outdoor Christmas markets in Europe, mulled wine is the perfect drink.

This one takes a little longer than most recipes, but the flavour of the spices and the clementine is well worth your time. You can easily scale up the recipe for a party, but this is a lovely amount for two to share late on Christmas Day, once the washing up has been done. You could 'discuss your affairs' over it, as Scrooge and Cratchit do, but it's also great in front of a fire with a good book.

Smoking Bishop

Makes 2 generous drinks

1. Preheat the oven to 190°C/375°F/Gas 5. Stick 6 of the cloves into the orange and place it in the oven for around 30 minutes, or until it is lightly browned and filling your kitchen with a strong scent of Christmas.

2. Place the remaining cloves along with the other spices in a small saucepan with 285ml/9½floz of water. Bring to the boil and allow to reduce by about half. Leave to steep for 10 minutes, then sieve into a jar. Tie a muslin square over the top of the jar to act as a very fine strainer.

3. Pour the wine and port into a saucepan and place over a low heat. Once hot, light a match and, very carefully, place it on the top of the liquid. The wine should ignite with a blue flame. Allow it to burn for a few seconds and then blow it out. Pour the spiced water into the wine, and add the orange from the oven. Keep over a low heat for around 10 minutes.

4. To serve, place the sugar in a bowl and roll one of the clementines in it. Squash it around until the sugar turns a light shade of orange, then divide the sugar between two glasses. Squeeze the juice from the clementine and divide it between the glasses as well. Cut the second clementine into thick slices and place one in each glass. Ladle the hot wine into the glasses, stir, then grate a little nutmeg over the top. Serve while still piping hot.

INGREDIENTS
10 cloves
1 orange
1 stick of cinnamon
3cm/1¼in chunk of ginger
½tsp ground mace
1tsp allspice (or 5 crushed allspice berries)
325ml/11floz red wine
175ml/6floz port
2tsp granulated sugar
2 clementines, peeled
Fresh nutmeg, to serve

EQUIPMENT
Small piece of muslin
Matches

Christmas Pudding

That was the pudding! In half a minute Mrs. Cratchit entered – flushed, but smiling proudly – with the pudding, like a speckled cannon-ball, so hard and firm, blazing in half of half-a-quarter of ignited brandy, and bedight with Christmas holly stuck into the top.
A Christmas Carol, Charles Dickens

The pudding here is one I have been eating since childhood. My great-grandmother, who was alive for the first decade of my life, would have a house full of them from August each year. I remember puddings hanging from broom handles and wooden spoons; big calico knots stiffening as they slowly dried out. My mother still speaks of the year that twenty-four were made to give as gifts.

This recipe is my great-grandmother's, written out by my mum before she left home to live in England in her twenties (exactly thirty years before I would do precisely the same thing). It contains Bundaberg rum – a very Australian rum, made from Queensland sugar cane. You could substitute brandy instead if this is more to your taste, but the rum here is how my family make it.

I'd suggest making your puddings at least a couple of months before Christmas – not only do you need time for the flavours to develop, but the maturation time also stops them crumbling when you finally pull back the calico. In my experience, puddings last for at least a year, but do keep them away from damp; you don't want the calico to become a hospitable place for mould.

INGREDIENTS

1kg/2¼lb mixed dried fruit

1 apple, grated

1 carrot, grated

1tsp grated nutmeg

1tsp ground cinnamon

4tsp mixed spice/ pumpkin pie spice

1tbsp marmalade

1tbsp golden syrup

75g/scant 3oz/heaping ½ cup flaked/slivered almonds

125ml/4floz/½ cup Bundaberg rum (another golden rum can be substituted, or brandy, if you prefer)

250g/9oz/2¼ sticks butter

220g/about 8oz/1⅛ cups light brown sugar

4 eggs

130g/4½oz/1 cup self-raising flour

130g/4½oz/1 cup plain/ all-purpose flour

115g/4oz/1¼ cups dry breadcrumbs

½tsp salt

50ml/2oz/¼ cup brandy (if you want a flaming pudding)

EQUIPMENT

2 squares calico/ unbleached cotton – 50cm/20in squared

String

Christmas Pudding

Makes 2 puddings that each serve 8 – one for your family, one to give away

1. Soak the dried fruit, apple, carrot, spices, marmalade, syrup and almonds in rum overnight.

2. Soak the calico in water. Cream the butter and sugar. Add the eggs, one at a time, beating well after each addition. Sift the flours together and fold into the batter with the breadcrumbs and salt. Stir in the soaked fruit.

3. Wring out the calico and sprinkle lightly with flour. Divide the mixture into two and spoon half into each sheet of calico. Pull up the corners and the edges. Tie with string, leaving a very small hole in the top. This step is easier with two people, as you need to hold around the top of the pudding while pulling the fabric firmly to make a well-shaped pudding. Fill the hole left at the middle of the tie with flour. Knot the corners together to aid lifting out of the water (a wooden spoon provides a good handle here).

4. Bring a large saucepan of water to the boil. Ease the puddings into the pan and bring back to the boil. Reduce the heat and simmer for 7 hours, topping up the water when you need to. Hang over a bowl/sink to drip overnight. Do not allow the puddings to rest on their bottoms, as this will affect their shape as they dry.

5. Once they have dripped dry, hang the puddings in an airy place to dry out completely. Once bone dry, including in the folds of the fabric, store in a cool, dark place until Christmas.

6. On Christmas Day, boil the pudding in the calico for an hour. Unwrap and place on a plate. If you want a flaming pudding, gently warm the brandy in a small saucepan. Remove from the heat and, being very careful not to burn yourself, hold a lighted match to the brandy. It should ignite with a blue flame. Pour over the pudding. Serve with custard, rum butter, ice cream or thick cream.

{1}

{2}

{3}

{4}

{5}

{6}

Crystallized Ginger

But all the old desserts, the Elvas plums and Carlsbad plums and almonds and raisins, and crystallised fruit and ginger. Dear me, I sound like a catalogue from Fortnum and Mason!
The Adventure of the Christmas Pudding, Agatha Christie

Though there are videos of us together as toddlers, photos taken on trips when we were children, and a couple of pen pal letters, I didn't really get to know my Cotswolds 'sister' Anna until we were in our twenties. She and I moved to London at the same time, and our parents were keen that we should meet. We felt the pressure of their expectations on our friendship; they had been friends for so long and we knew that they wanted us to be too. Thankfully, as soon as I met her, I was desperate for us to be friends. She made me laugh, she was open and warm, and she liked the same books that I did. On my first trip to stay with Anna's family, I pored over her bookshelves, and found them lined with Christie's novels. I was delighted.

I vividly remember telling a teacher I loved Agatha Christie, and getting a patronizing smile and nod in return. I hadn't realized there was a 'correct' answer to her querying my favourite writers, but apparently Christie wasn't it. I wasn't confident enough in my convictions to ignore her reaction and loudly vocalize my love for the Queen of Crime. Instead, she was pushed in my mind to a place labelled 'guilty pleasures', and stayed there for years. Now, every Christmas, I pop upstairs to Anna's room and borrow another Christie. We've both long since made our way through the canon, but I keep returning to my favourites.

This crystallized ginger, a favourite of my grandad's when I was growing up and now one of mine too, is a breeze to make. It fills the house with the sweet, heady scent of ginger syrup; just the sort of thing I long for on a cold December day. It is a welcome gift, but this recipe makes enough for you to keep some for yourself.

Crystallized Ginger

Makes around 100 pieces – plenty to go under the tree

1. Slice the ginger into very thin discs and place in a small saucepan. Cover with water, then bring to a simmer over a medium heat and let it bubble away for 12 minutes. Strain off the cooking liquid, setting it aside for later, then cover the ginger with more water and simmer for a further 12 minutes. Strain the liquid, again retaining it for later.

2. Put the sugar, salt and cooked ginger in a large saucepan along with 300g/10½oz/3 cups of the sugar and 375ml/12½ floz of the cooking liquid. Bring to the boil, then simmer until the syrup resembles runny honey.

4. While the syrup is bubbling away, put out a cooling rack with a lined baking tray underneath to catch the drips. Rub the cooling rack with a tiny amount of flavourless oil so the ginger doesn't stick. Place the remaining 100g/3½oz/1 cup of sugar in a shallow bowl.

5. Remove the saucepan from the heat and set aside to cool slightly. Scoop the ginger out with a slotted spoon, drop the pieces into the sugar and toss to coat. Transfer to the cooling rack and allow to dry for a couple of hours, or overnight. Store in a jar or airtight container; the ginger will keep for a few weeks at room temperature. You can eat the pieces as they are, or chop them up and add them to biscuits, cakes, or puddings.

A NOTE: The leftover ginger syrup can be poured over ice cream or pancakes, or added to cakes. Any excess sugar is perfect for lending a gingery flavour to your bakes.

INGREDIENTS

200g/7oz/2 cups ginger (peeled weight)

2tbsp honey

Pinch salt

400g/14oz/4 cups golden caster sugar

Flavourless oil

New Year's Day Turkey Curry

Noon. London: my flat. Ugh. The last thing on earth I feel physically, emotionally or mentally equipped to do is drive to Una and Geoffrey Alconbury's New Year's Day Turkey Curry Buffet in Grafton Underwood.
Bridget Jones's Diary, Helen Fielding

In the days following Christmas, when the decorations are still up but the time off work is drawing to a close, I'm always faced with the dilemma of leftovers. No matter how carefully I cater, or how much we eat on Christmas Day, the fridge is stocked high with varying sizes of Tupperware containers filled with roast vegetables, and foil parcels packed with slices of roast meat.

My Cotswold mum's solution to this is a kind of tournament-style Ready, Steady, Cook, where an increasingly unappealing combination of ingredients is used to make dinner, or a hotch-potch lunch. Everything from the fridge is placed on the table, the one rule being that five fewer containers go back in than came out.

In Bridget's family, it's the Turkey Curry Buffet that clears the fridge. Despite Una and Geoffrey's questionable skill as hosts, it's a brilliant use of whatever leftover bird you have, and will provide a suitable vehicle for leftover veg too. If you're suffering slightly after seeing in the New Year the night before, you'll be pleased to know that it is a wonderfully lazy dish to make – requiring nothing more than some chopping and stirring.

Leftover Turkey Curry

Serves 4 or more – depending on how plentiful the leftovers are

1. Warm the fat in a large saucepan over a medium heat. Add the onion and stir for a couple of minutes until softened and translucent, but not browned. Add the garlic and cook for another couple of minutes, until fragrant. Add the spices and cook, stirring frequently, for at least 5 minutes. By this stage, the onion should be completely coated with the spices and the saucepan should be wonderfully fragrant.

2. Add the potatoes and carrots. If they are raw, stir them for 5 minutes or so, to soften them. If they are leftover roast veg, just give them a minute as they'll already be soft.

3. Add the stock and stir well. Bring to the boil and simmer away for 10 minutes or so, until the vegetables are tender and the sauce slightly reduced. Stir through the yoghurt and then add the shredded meat. Cook for a final couple of minutes to ensure the turkey is hot, then remove from the heat and stir the coriander leaves through. Serve with rice, mango chutney and poppadoms. And a beer.

INGREDIENTS

2tbsp fat (leftover from the bird, vegetable oil or clarified butter)

1 large brown onion, thinly sliced

2 cloves garlic, finely chopped

2tsp ground cumin

2tsp ground coriander

1tsp ground ginger

1tsp ground turmeric

4 cardamom pods, crushed lightly

2 large potatoes, roughly chopped (you can use leftover roast potatoes, if you like)

2 large carrots, roughly chopped (again, leftover roasted ones are fine here too)

400ml/14floz/1¾ cups chicken or turkey stock*

3tbsp natural/plain yoghurt

300g/10½oz leftover turkey, stripped from the carcass and shredded

Large handful of chopped coriander/cilantro

*You can make the stock with the turkey carcass, once you have stripped it. Roughly chop 2 sticks of celery, 2 carrots, and 2 brown onions and add them to a saucepan with some parsley stalks, 10 peppercorns and the turkey carcass. Cover with water and bring to a simmer over a medium heat. After 1 hour, strain and reserve the stock.

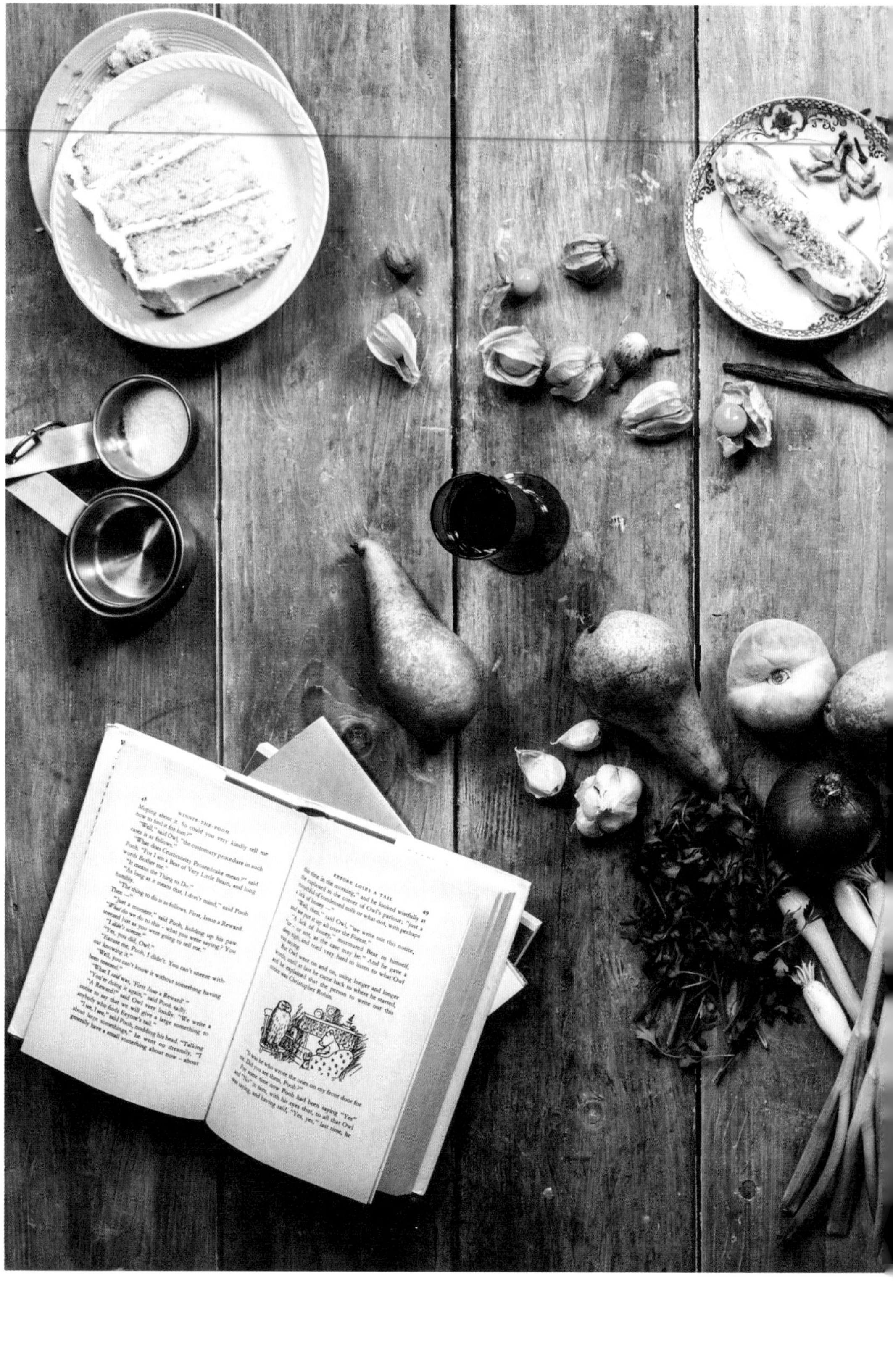

recipe index

author index

extended copyright

thank you

To my family, for everything. I wish more than anything that the world was a little smaller, and that you were all a little closer. This book is for you.

To Ingela, Chris, Anna, Tom and Mia, for inviting me into your home, for allowing me to spend days cooking every time I visit, and for being the best support network and surrogate family I could imagine.

To Francesca, Lois and Eli, for giving me a place in your home, for tasting the first (awful) batch of black sesame ice cream, for helping me to roll cream horns, for licking bowls, for all the hand modelling. And for your beautiful house, which is such a big part of what lies in these pages.

To Zoe and to Madeleine, who both 'got' this book immediately, and have championed it from those very first meetings. You are a true dream team; I feel incredibly lucky to be working with you.

To the incomparable Lean, who happily sat and took notes while I explained the plot and mood of over fifty books. Your photographs are completely beautiful and absolutely perfect – I can't imagine the book without them. I can't wait to work with you again. You are an absolute wonder.

To the best shoot team imaginable: Livvy, Jess, Liz, Bry, Tom and Anna, who made custard, threw chocolate cake in my general direction, blew bubbles, wrapped all my possessions in brown paper and string, ran to the supermarket for butter, ironed fabric, and indulged my desire to play the soundrack from *Hamilton* at least once a day.

To my dear friends, who made sure that none of the food, during testing or photographing, went to waste. And who all let me rabbit on about the book every time we spoke over the past few years.

To Jack, to Evie, to Jess, to Nic, to Liv, to Max, to Tom and to Anna, for your lovely, patient hands.

To the aunts, for being my virtual office full of colleagues and cheerleaders.

To Ellie and the Props Team at the National Theatre for the loan of all the crockery, and for generously allowing us hours in the props store to trawl through plates, cups and pots for the perfect pieces.

To Natalia, Terry and the whole team at the LRB, for assuring me the blog would be a book one day, and for talking confidently about the launch before I'd even found an agent.

To the books team at the *Guardian*, especially Marta and Sian, for championing the blog in so public a forum.

To the whole team at Head of Zeus, who have worked so hard and so tirelessly to get this book into your hands, and especially Jessie, for the glorious book design.

To everyone who suggested a favourite book. To those who tested recipes, making sure they work in ovens and on stovetops across the world.

And to @markymarket, who somehow found us a goose in July.

Thank you, all of you. This book wouldn't be what it is without you.

300

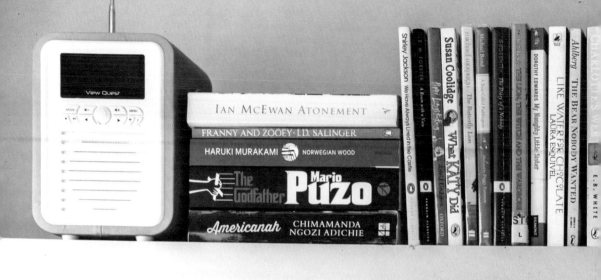

View Quest

Ian McEwan · Atonement

FRANNY AND ZOOEY · J.D. SALINGER

HARUKI MURAKAMI · NORWEGIAN WOOD

The Godfather · Mario Puzo

Americanah · CHIMAMANDA NGOZI ADICHIE

Shirley Jackson · We Have Always Lived in the Castle

E.M. FORSTER · A Room with a View

Susan Coolidge · What Katy Did

Michael Bond · The Butterfly Lion

P.G. Wodehouse

Patricia Highsmith · The Diary of a Nobody

DOROTHY EDWARDS · My Naughty Little Sister

LIKE WATER FOR CHOCOLATE · LAURA ESQUIVEL

Ahlberg

THE BEAR NOBODY WANTED

E.B. WHITE · CHARLOTTE'S WEB

SHERLOCK HOLMES

MOBY DICK

Anna Karenina

ULYSSES · JAMES JOYCE

FOLIO

THE ESSEX SERPENT · SARAH PERRY

HOW I LIVE NOW · MEG ROSOFF

MARCEL PROUST · Remembrance of Things Past

A LITTLE PRINCESS · FRANCES HODGSON BURNETT

Sue Townsend · The Secret Diary of Adrian Mole Aged 13¾

Gabriel Garcia Marquez · Love in the Time of Cholera

banana yoshimoto · kitchen

The Little White Horse · Elizabeth Goudge

HELEN FIELDING · Bridget Jones's Diary

BRIAN JACQUES · REDWALL

John Marsden · Tomorrow, When the War Began

The Hundred and One Dalmatians

Life of Pi · Yann Martel

THE RAILWAY CHILDREN · E. NESBIT

THE FAMOUS FIVE · Five Go to the Valley Together

Sylvia Plath · The Bell Jar

TO KILL A MOCKINGBIRD · HARPER LEE

THE HOBBIT · J.R.R. TOLKIEN

DAPHNE DU MAURIER · Rebecca

Mary Wesley

MEG ROSOFF · HOW I LIVE NOW

Graham Greene · The End of the Affair

HARRY

Dr. Seuss

MATILDA · Roald Dahl